I0137356

The European Union, Antisemitism,

and the Politics of Denial

STUDIES IN ANTISEMITISM

Vadim Rossman, *Russian Intellectual Antisemitism in the Post-Communist Era* (2002)

Anthony D. Kauders, *Democratization and the Jews: Munich, 1945–1965* (2004)

Cesare D. De Michelis, *The Non-Existent Manuscript: A Study of the Protocols of the Sages of Zion* (2004)

Robert S. Wistrich, *Laboratory for World Destruction: Germans and Jews in Central Europe* (2007)

Graciela Ben-Dror, *The Catholic Church and the Jews: Argentina, 1933–1945* (2008)

Andrei Oişteanu, *Inventing the Jew: Antisemitic Stereotypes in Romanian and Other Central-East European Cultures* (2009)

Olaf Blaschke, *Offenders or Victims? German Jews and the Causes of Modern Catholic Antisemitism* (2009)

Robert S. Wistrich, *From Ambivalence to Betrayal: The Left, the Jews, and Israel* (2012)

Efraim Sicher and Linda Weinhouse, *Under Postcolonial Eyes: Figuring the "jew" in Contemporary British Writing* (2012)

The European Union, Antisemitism, and the Politics of Denial

R. Amy Elman

Published by the University of Nebraska Press, Lincoln and London, for the
Vidal Sassoon International Center for the Study of Antisemitism (SICSA)
The Hebrew University of Jerusalem

© 2014 by the Vidal Sassoon International Center for the Study of Antisemitism
All rights reserved
Manufactured in the United States of America ∞

Manufactured and distributed for the Vidal Sassoon International Center for the Study of Antisemitism (SICSA), The Hebrew University of Jerusalem, by the University of Nebraska Press

The Studies in Antisemitism series brings together major new research on the complex phenomenon of worldwide antisemitism, ancient and modern, from a broad range of perspectives: religious, economic, social, pyschological, cultural, and political.

Robert S. Wistrich, chairman of the Vidal Sassoon International Center for the Study of Antisemitism, The Hebrew University of Jerusalem,
Series Editor

Library of Congress Cataloguing-in-Publication Data

Elman, R. Amy, 1961–, author.
The European Union, antisemitism, and the politics of denial / R. Amy Elman.
pages   cm — (Studies in antisemitism)

Includes bibliographical references and index.
ISBN 978-0-8032-5541-8 (hardback: alk. paper)
ISBN 978-0-8032-6693-3 (pdf).
1. Antisemitism—European Union countries. 2. European Union countries—Politics and government—21st century. 3. Antisemitism—European Union countries—Public opinion. 4. Public opinion—European Union countries. 5. European Union countries—Ethnic relations. I. Title.
DS146.E85E46 2015
305.892'404—dc23
2014015271

SICSA Production Editor: Alifa Saadya

This book is dedicated to Dr. Edward Alexander
and is in memory of his wife, Lois.
Together they taught me the importance of Jewish living.

Table of Contents

TABLES

Acknowledgments

This work began as a lecture during my stay as a National Endowment for the Humanities fellow at the State University of New York (Potsdam). My gratitude extends especially to my hosts, Mylene Catel, Geoffrey Clark, and Celine Philibert. I was fortunate thereafter to receive generous and ongoing support from Andrei Markovits at the University of Michigan (Ann Arbor) and Robert S. Wistrich at the Vidal Sassoon International Center for the Study of Antisemitsim (SICSA) at the Hebrew University of Jerusalem. The staff at SICSA is unparalleled in the support they offered me during my stays in Israel and I am especially grateful to Alifa Saadya for her careful attention to the final stages of this manuscript. Without a sabbatical from Kalamazoo College and my stay at the Center for European Studies at Harvard University, I would have been unable to complete this manuscript. During my research travels, several people provided me with incredible support. I thank Jennifer Cohen Katz and her entire family, Diane Henin, Malka Marcovich, and Agneta Sandell. A number of prominent political actors, scholars, and activists gave me the gift of their time. Several invited me to their conferences, offices, and even into their homes. For that I thank Henrik Bachner, Lena Einhorn, Stefano Gatti, Manfred Gerstenfeld, Betti Guetta, Lena Jersenius, Elisabeth Keubler, Zvi Mazel, Celeste Montoya, Mark Pollack, Alexander Pollak, Alvin H. Rosenfeld, and Mikael Tossavainen. My gratitude extends as well to Ronald Eissens and Suzette Bronkhorst for providing the invaluable networking and news resource, ICARE/Magenta Foundation. This work relied, too, on the the indomitable intellect of my friend Lisa D. Brush, whose support (and criticism) means more to me than perhaps she knows. While there are many more friends and colleagues who helped make the completion of this work possible, I am especially indebted to Peter L. Corrigan, Bernice Dubois, Jonathan L. Laurans, Lesa L. Lockford, Jane Petitjean, Laurie Pruitt, Martin Schain, Barry Shanley, Alexandra Silets, the Rush family, and Susan Weinger.

List of Abbreviations

AENM	Alliance of European National Movements
AJC	American Jewish Committee
BZÖ	Alliance for the Future of Austria
CEC	Commission for the European Communities (European Commission)
CERD	Committee on the Elimination of Discrimination (UN)
CIA	Central Intelligence Agency (US)
COE	Council of Europe
CRA	Centre for Research on Antisemitism (Berlin)
EC	European Community
ECFR	European Council for Fatwa and Research
ECJ	European Court of Justice
ECHR	European Convention on Human Rights
ECtHR	European Court of Human Rights
EEC	European Economic Community
EJC	European Jewish Congress
EMU	European Monetary Union
ENAR	European Network against Racism
EP	European Parliament
EU	European Union
EUMC	European Union Monitoring Centre on Racism and Xenophobia
EUJS	European Union of Jewish Students
FPÖ	Freedom Party (Austria)
FRA	European Union Fundamental Rights Agency
ICARE	Internet Centre Anti-Racism Europe
ICERD	International Convention on the Elimination of Discrimination (UN)
IHRA	International Holocaust Remembrance Alliance (formerly ITF)
IKG	Israelitische Kultusgemeinde (Austria)
ITF	International Task Force for International Cooperation on Holocaust Education, Remembrance and Research
LHF	Living History Forum (Sweden)
LHP	Living History Project (Sweden)

MEP	Member of the European Parliament
NGO	Non-governmental organization
NSDAP	Nazi Party (National-Socialist German Workers Party)
OHPI	Online Hate Prevention Institute (Australia)
OJ	*Official Journal of the European Communities*
OSCE	Organization for Security and Cooperation in Europe
ÖVP	People's Party (Austria)
RAXEN	European Information Network on Racism and Xenophobia
SKMA	Swedish Committee against Antisemitism
SPÖ	Social Democrats (Austria)
SWC	Simon Wiesenthal Center
TEU	Treaty on European Union (commonly referred to as "Maastricht Treaty")
TFEU	Treaty on the Functioning of the European Union
UN	United Nations
WCAR	World Conference against Racism (UN)
WJC	World Jewish Congress

Introduction

In the aftermath of the Second World War, Europe's politicians constructed a "common market" on the supposition that a cohesive economic union would diminish the rabid nationalism that, in part, led to genocide. Indeed, the Preamble of the European Community's founding treaty requires Member States "to substitute. . .age-old rivalries [through] the merging of their essential interests and create, by establishing an economic community, the basis for a broader and deeper community among peoples long divided by bloody conflicts."[1]

Decades later, in accepting the Nobel Peace Prize on behalf of the European Union (EU), the President of the European Commission explained, "The genius of the founding fathers was precisely in understanding that to guarantee peace in the 20th century, nations needed to think beyond the nation-state."[2]

As nationalism's primary losers, Europe's Jews were perhaps the major beneficiaries of this transnational emphasis insofar as any tamping down of nationalism would extinguish the potential for future antisemitic coalescence. Though, as I argue here, this hope might prove "unwarrantedly optimistic."[3] Indeed, some maintain that the repressed and sullied patriotic pride resulting from Europe's post-nationalism may ignite the very conflicts the creation of the EU attempted to avert.[4] This position implies therefore that Europe's integration is unlikely to reduce, much less resolve, antisemitism. So, which is it—or as my Nana would ask, is Europe's integration "good for Jews"? While the question defies a clear-cut verdict, it invites an analysis of the utopian ambitions of Europe's political architects from the perspective both of those responsible for implementing Europe's lofty goals, as well as of others (i.e., Jews) whose presence in Europe has long been and continues to be precarious.

Recent Incidents of Antisemitism

The European Union now operates as the world's largest single market as well as its largest trader of goods and services. As such, however, the integrated market has not translated into a unified social voice against antisemitism. Taunting references to Auschwitz and other examples of the verbal arsenal of antisemitism recur in social discourse. For example, at soccer matches rival fans taunt Jewish players and others with chants such as "The train is leaving for Auschwitz" and "Gas the Jews."[5] In addition, arsonist attacks on synagogues, desecrated Jewish graves, anti-Jewish boycotts, and violence directed against Jews because they are Jews, raise considerable concerns.

In 2009, a barrage of threatening and abusive emails and telephone calls to Jewish organizations in Britain and an arsonist attack on a London synagogue led that country's All Parliamentary Group against Antisemitism to condemn efforts to use the mounting conflict in Gaza as a pretext for anti-Jewish violence. France's former President, Nicolas Sarkozy, issued a similar statement after antisemites there set French Jewish synagogues ablaze.[6] Three years earlier, in 2006, a gang brutally murdered a young Frenchman, Ilan Halimi, because he was Jewish. Following the Madrid bombing of 2004, Spanish police officers uncovered a plot by Islamic militants to bomb a Jewish retreat center outside the country's capital. In 2012, French authorities were unable to subvert a similar plot when a man murdered four Jews outside a Jewish day school in France's south. What's more, those openly denouncing antisemitism are also at risk of losing their lives. Consider the case of Mehmet Sahin, a Dutch-Turkish doctoral student. In 2013, the Mayor of Arnhem advised Mr. Sahin and his family to go into hiding after he received death threats for reproaching teens from his community for their support of Hitler and the *Shoah* on Dutch television. These events underscore the deadly dimensions of antisemitism and the fact that Europe's economic and political integration has not been an effective antidote to antisemitism.

As Europe's Jews of the twenty-first century defensively adopt stringent security measures for themselves and their religious and cultural organizations, the question arises whether or not Europe's political institutions and Member States have come to tolerate or even dismiss the circumstances that necessitate such vigilance? In many respects, the EU has increased emphasis on combating a generalized concept of discrimination. However, general rhetoric about discrimination, especially in a broader context of controversies about whether Europe's integration entails the erosion of state sovereignty, the ascent of supranational institutions, and the salience of postnational identity produces a climate in which specific inequities and hostilities (e.g., against Jews) are elided and even effaced. It is thus rare that explicit denunciations of antisemitism extend beyond Holocaust commemorations where public officials promise moral clarity and political courage in the future. At present, the ritual posturing pertaining to prior antisemitism can serve as a diversion from confronting its current manifestations.[7] Understanding this dynamic of denial might lessen the incredulity of those shocked by the above-noted episodes. After all, the Dutch had just chaired the International Holocaust Remembrance Alliance (IHRA) in 2011, an initiative begun by Sweden over a decade earlier when it was known as the Task Force for International Cooperation on Holocaust Education, Remembrance and Research (ITF).

SCHOLARLY ACCOUNTS

Scholarly considerations of the EU's efforts to address discrimination give scant attention to antismitism.[8] At the same time, scholarship on contemporary antisemitism in Europe rarely engages the political context of European integration.[9] There are exceptions to be sure. The work of Erik Bleich, Steven Beller, Lars Rensmann, and Julius Schoeps notably defy this dichotomy. Bleich, whose primary focus is on the politics of racism (in Germany, France, Great Britain, and the United States), offers a chapter on Holocaust denial yet he extends only cursory attention to the EU.[10] Beller's historical emphasis, by contrast, focuses on the "pluralizing" influence of the Jews on the EU but gives short shrift to the actual policy responses of EU institutions to contemporary antisemitism.[11] Thus, Beller characterizes "the emerging institutions of the European Union [as] very good for the Jews," and argues that concerns about European antisemitism are alarmist and misplaced. Further, he considers that "the main threat to Jews in Europe lies in the reassertion of atavistic nationalist ideologies and the rise in the persecution of minorities, not the growth in transnational institutions of the European Union."[12] Like Beller, Rensmann and Schoeps similarly suggest "antisemitic mobilizations. . .face serious restrictions in the transnational publics of the European Union."[13] Yet, they, like Beller, offer scarce evidence to support these claims. Unlike these scholars, who neither attend to EU policy nor the political dynamics of European integration, my work—with its attention to Member States *and* the EU's key policy-making institutions—encourages consideration of whether Europe's integration has unintentionally prompted the reassertion of atavistic nationalism or the "counter-cosmopolitanism" that may result in a concomitant resurgence of antisemitism.

To bridge scholarly considerations of European integration and antisemitism, I rely in part on Europe's leading politicians. Their statements, however symbolic, underscore the relevance of Jews and antisemitism for scholarly debates concerning what substantive role, if any, the EU has in providing potential remedies for prejudice. As Göran Adamson reminds us, official political statements from these authorities are often more revealing than those put forward by less tactically restrained commentators.[14] Determining which level of governance (if any) is best suited to provide redress is essential to discovering how best to mitigate antisemitism in the EU. To do so, I explore the deliberations over state sovereignty and European supranationalism with an eye toward generating beneficial insights for Jews and other claimants of discrimination.

THE EUROPE UNION'S RESPONSE TO ANTISEMITISM

Antisemitism and the position of Jews in Europe has, on occasion, been center-stage in the political discourse of Europe's politicians. Following his investiture as EU Commission President (1999–2004), Romano Prodi traveled to Auschwitz and there discussed the inextricable links between European integration and antisemitism. Insisting that we assess civilizations by their treatment of minorities, Prodi focused on Europe's Jews because, he reasoned, they are Europe's first and oldest Europeans.[15] That is, while Europe's (Gentile) citizens are "just starting to learn the complex art of living with multiple allegiances, Jews have been forced to master this art since antiquity."[16] He continued, "They were Jewish and Italian, or Jewish and French, Jewish and Spanish, Jewish and Polish, Jewish and German. Proud of their ties with Jewish communities throughout the continent, and equally proud of their bonds with their own country."[17] Emphasizing the Jewish community's internal plurality and its trend-setting civic engagement, Diana Pinto[18] and Steven Beller[19] similarly imply that Jews are among the most European of EU citizens.

If European Jews are, as Prodi and others imply, the quintessential embodiment of a transnational European identity, antisemitism strikes at the heart of the European project—one meant to tame, not eliminate, the nation-state.[20] The question for those interested in Europe's integration in general and Jews (and other minorities) more specifically is this: how might "Europe" best respond to and implement efforts against this virulent prejudice? The fact that Prodi and other EU officials have publicly repudiated antisemitism testifies to the success of Jews and their allies in politicizing it. Exploring the consequences of the EU's response to contemporary antisemitism generates insights into both European governance and the potential relief offered to claimants of discrimination.

If, as supranationalists argue, the power of states to act independently has declined, Jews and other minorities interested in organizing to end violence and discrimination would do best to invest their energies elsewhere, in transnational arenas. If, however, state-centered intergovernmentalists are correct in asserting that the nation-state remains the primary unit for dispensing and protecting rights and privileges, it would be premature at best (or perhaps even illogical) for activists to pursue their aspirations within supranational contexts.

Still, as Prodi's comments suggest, there is another possibility: state sovereignty and transnational unification need not be a zero-sum game. As the political analyst Glyn Morgan explains, the EU is "conceived as a supranational community that coexists with national governments" and thus "encourages citizens to see themselves as both nationals and Europeans."[21] The increased interdependence and harmonization among Europe's Member States that potentially inspires European identity is not only compatible with national influence, it might enhance it. Indeed, I have elsewhere argued (concerning gender inequality) that the augmented cooperation and competition between these levels of governance make the boundaries between Member States and transnational actors (such as the EU) more difficult to delineate.[22]

While blurred boundaries can pose a problem for those seeking optimal access points for positive social change, they can also enhance the permeability of states and transnational actors to varied claims for social justice. Which is it for those Europeans seeking actions against and remedy for antisemitism? Over the last decade, several investigations into European antisemitism have helped foster a more sophisticated understanding of its present (some argue "new") manifestations, but none has sought a satisfactory explanation for what role (if any) European institutions might play in efforts to help end it.

This work establishes new territory by providing an overview of the specific circumstances that obliged the Community's institutional triangle— its Council, Commission, and Parliament—to take action against antisemitism. Recognizing that supranational efforts are superfluous unless the Member States inform and implement them, this work then offers a fine-grained conceptually rigorous account of this social problem by reference to Sweden and Austria. By asking whether, how, and to what end these states have implemented efforts to end antisemitism, we are able to analyze how Europe's integration recasts state power.

Because the EU's initial laws and related policies pertaining to antisemitism began well before Sweden or Austria entered into European Union (in 1995), we commence with a brief description of the three key EU institutions that initiated these efforts. All Member State governments, not least the two that are our focus, have their appropriate ministers negotiate legislation and countless policies in private meetings under the auspices of Europe's primary decision-making body, the Council of the European Union (formerly the Council of Ministers).[23] Prior to the adoption of the Lisbon Treaty in 2009, this largely intergovernmental Council responded to policy proposals from the European Commission and the European Parliament. The Commission, often referred to as the EU's policy engine, served as an independent political body that advocates the Community's *collective* interests while the Parliament influenced budgetary decisions and policy directions through detailed reports, amendments, non-binding resolutions, and vetoes on select bills. Although the Members of the European Parliament (MEPs) labored within the only directly elected international assembly in the world, most critics recognized the institution as the EU's most democratic and least powerful because its primary role was as an influential observer. In fact, until 2009, MEPs were actually unable to legislate. The Treaty of Lisbon then granted parliamentarians considerably more power because, rather than pressuring the Commission to forward legislation to the Council as it did in the past, MEPs now work with both bodies to adopt EU-wide legislation. Although the European Court of Justice (ECJ) interprets and upholds this legislation, it has yet to issue a direct ruling pertaining specifically to antisemitism. Our focus thus remains on the EU's three other institutions and the two Member States that have been prominent interlocutors in the development and implementation of EU policy pertaining to antisemitism.

By observing the behavior of two seemingly dissimilar Member States through juxtaposition, we are able to glean general insights into state sovereignty, transnational prowess, and the reciprocal relationship between these levels of governance. The similarities between Austria and Sweden include the fact that, in 1995, both social democracies of then approximately 8 million residents entered into the EU as affluent neutral latecomers in the aftermath of the Cold War. Thus, one cannot attribute their differing responses to antisemitism to the size and strength of their democracies, the timing of their membership or the relative strength or weakness of their economies. Instead, the relevant dissimilarities between these two Member States reside in their history and standing in the Community.

Although the EU holds Sweden in high regard for its educational efforts against antisemitism,[24] Sweden has only recently begun to confront its historical complicity with Nazism.[25] By contrast, Austria was (until 2012) the first and only Member State to receive the EU's formal condemnation following the triumph of the far right in its 1999 national elections.[26] Yet, prior to its entrance into Europe, Austria was among the first Member States to acknowledge its willing collaboration with the Nazis,[27] a past that persists in haunting it.

By considering the EU's varied responses to and subsequent effects (however slight) on the distinctive conditions within Sweden and Austria as each confronts antisemitism, we come closer to answering the primary riddle that motivates this work: what role, if any, does Europe have in mitigating discrimination in general and antisemitism more specifically? After reaching a tentative answer to this question through a historical comparative analysis of the EU's response and those of two of its comparable Member States, this work concludes with a general overview of this transnational polity's more recent efforts to combat antisemitism, particularly in the decade since 9/11.[28] There is no better time to understand and expect stepped up transnational efforts against this discrimination than amidst its global resurgence in the twenty-first century.

I suggest that while efforts to combat antisemitism (and racism more generally) may appear to have inspired some of the EU's foundational rhetoric, political actors throughout the EU rarely regard Jews as sufficiently oppressed to warrant either state or Union interventions. Thus, Jews receive "virtual redress"—sporadic rhetoric that condemns the continent's past crimes while proving insufficient in countering current antisemitism. In sum, as the conflicting forces of intergovernmentalism and supranationalism pull activists in different directions, elected leaders and public officials at both the Member State and transnational levels often ignore, downplay, or deny current injustices against Jews. This point is evident, not least, through the EU's efforts to counter racism and xenophobia.

When, for instance, the European Commission—the EU's executive arm—established a European Union Monitoring Centre on Racism and Xenophobia (EUMC) in Vienna in 1997, it included antisemitism in the portfolio of this watchdog agency. The regulation that established the Centre obliges it to "provide the Community and the Member States. . .with objective, reliable and comparative data at the European level on the phenomenon of racism, xenophobia *and anti-Semitism* in order to help them *when* they take measures or formulate courses of action within their respective areas of competence."[29] That is, the regulation does not oblige Member States to counter antisemitism, racism, and xenophobia, but contends that the Centre must assist them when they do.

Unsurprisingly, while some states assume responsibility for monitoring antisemitism, many do not. Records are often unreliable; statistics are relatively new or non-existent and crimes against Jews have been notoriously underreported. In fact, according to its 2011 overview of antisemitism in the EU, the Fundamental Rights Agency (FRA, formerly the EUMC) found only Austria, France, Germany, and Sweden had "collect[ed] sufficient criminal justice data allowing for a trend analysis of recorded anti-Semitic crimes."[30] Upon scrutiny, this conclusion seems too generous. For instance, in Sweden, the data collection methodology changed so that the results before and after 2005 were no longer comparable.[31] Moreover, in both Germany and Austria, official statistical data are highly circumscribed because those authorities collecting it focus almost exclusively on incidents involving right wing criminality.[32] Thus, far fewer reported incidents likely result from this approach. For this reason, among many, one must interpret such statistics with care.

Because there is still no genuinely comparative basis for the evaluation of antisemitic incidents throughout all Member States by the FRA or any other European institution, I do not offer a comparative analysis of antisemitic incidents. Rather, I consider, in general terms, the capacities of the EU and its Member States to recognize and respond to antisemitism when it comes to their attention.

As the absence of antisemitism from the Centre's title suggests, the EUMC extended relatively limited attention to antisemitism, a position in keeping with the Community's often inconsistent commitment to countering prejudice against a people who are neither "White" nor "Black" and are often, though not always, EU nationals. Although Jews long ago negotiated their presence in a complex racial world in which Europe's Gentiles regarded them as non-white,[33] the price of admission into a white privileged mainstream can be steep. It can represent a collective amnesia among Jews of their roots and/or a denial of Jewish oppression and history.[34] The latter problem has emerged, paradoxically, within the very settings that claim to counter racism.

In its preparatory text for the 2001 United Nations (UN) World Conference against Racism, Xenophobia and Related Intolerance in Durban, South Africa, the Commission detailed its own anti-discrimination efforts and those of the EUMC without a single reference to antisemitism.[35] Yet, a year after the conference ended, the EU Presidency issued a statement to the UN that reads, "The European Union attaches great importance to the fight against anti-Semitism and welcomes the call of the Durban Conference to take concrete action to combat this manifestation of racism."[36] Ironically, Durban's final action program excluded virtually all references to antisemitism.[37] Had the EU extended greater prominence to the above stated sentiment against antisemitism *prior to* or during Durban, it may have been better able to stem the tide of antisemitism that enveloped the conference.

Still, as we will note, this was not the only time that the EU was slow to side with social justice.

The next chapter details the Community's initial reservations for confronting racism more generally. It thus provides a historical foundation from which to better understand the EUMC's policies and the early actions of the two Member States that are our focus, Sweden and Austria.

ORGANIZATION OF THE BOOK

The EU's policies and administrative structures to counter discrimination may be distinctive and relatively new, but they did not arise from a coherent and deliberate plan. Ongoing struggles and bargaining among the Member States and EU institutions about discrimination leave their mark in the form of improvisational policies and explicit settlements that specify (or even waffle on) the rights and expectations of affected parties. The next section's historical investigation into the establishment of the European Union Monitoring Centre underscores this point. The agency's goal was to provide the Community and the Member States with "objective, reliable and comparable data" on racism, xenophobia and antisemitism in an effort to end these discriminations as if they are commensurable. Yet, I suggest that while the EUMC is an important political actor, it is not a primary architect of non-discrimination. I make similar claims about the European Commissioners, heads of state, and Members of the European Parliament who helped establish the agency. Although one should recognize the initial importance of all these players, I suggest that there is a more tenuous relationship between them, their plans, policies, and outcomes than we may realize. In recognizing this, one can better discern the difference between rhetoric and reality, national sovereignty and transnational power, as activists and others adjust their strategies and expectations accordingly.

The meaning(s) of policies and their consequences are not determined entirely by the intentions of those who create them. There are, in fact, two key factors in the formation of policy to consider. First, those who use, analyze, abandon, or deny others access to policies can affect the policies themselves. Second, the global context of multi-level governance can influence the way that various actors view policies. For instance, activists engaged on behalf of Jews (particularly survivors of the *Shoah* and their families) must consider international factors (e.g., international law) while mobilizing within a Community whose national histories and state provisions for Holocaust denial vary despite the EU's attempts to harmonize these policies. Thus, the pursuit of social justice is often serendipitous and complicated, with unintended and often confusing and capricious consequences. Nonetheless, this entire nexus of complex influences informs all subsequent policy debates, interventions, and inertia.

An analysis and accurate assessment of the significance of the EU's most recent investigations and initiatives to counter antisemitism require an historical exploration of their context. This work's next section, thus, offers a consideration of the Community's earliest condemnations of racism and identifies the key institutions (e.g., the Parliament) within which policies emerged and explores the reasons for the EU's stated interest in advancing them. Chapter 2 then details the consequences of the Community's first policies (through 2000) by exploring the Member States within which such efforts were implemented and informed. Subsequent to this discussion, Chapter 3 moves into a synopsis of the success and shortcomings of these efforts before considering the reforms taken to improve upon them, while Chapter 4 again considers their consequences by reference to the Member States after 9/11. The book thus pursues an essentially chronological structure.

In moving from the EU's first measures against racism to current considerations of their impact for Jews, one confronts several ironies but perhaps none more compelling than the Community's reliance on non-EU actors to shore up its own efforts against discrimination. The last section (Chapter 5) thus suggests that the seemingly byzantine and often blurry dimensions of the EU's anti-discrimination efforts become clear when one notes how each level of "integrated Europe" off-loads responsibility onto another level for the promise of fulfilling it. The reader is urged in the following chapters to watch closely as the language and politics of integration increase expectations through equitable rhetoric, while the responsibility for antisemitism and the implementation of measures to end it are scattered and so elusive that the promise of substantive redress is easily deferred and even denied.

NOTES

1. Treaty of Paris (Formally the Treaty establishing the European Economic and Steel Community [ECSC]), Treaty, 18 April 1951. This initial treaty was repeatedly amended by other Treaties (e.g., the Treaty of Amsterdam and the Treaty of Lisbon), including accession treaties. The accession treaties extended the European Community from six Member States (i.e., France, Germany, Italy, Belgium, the Netherlands, and Luxembourg) to the twenty-eight that now comprise the European Union (see Table 2, p. 23). Only after the Treaty on European Union (i.e., the "Maastricht Treaty") had come into force, in 1993, did commentators begin to refer to

the European Community (EC) as the "European Union" (EU). Though I often use the term "Community" when referring to matters prior to 1993, others whom I quote may use the terms interchangeably.

2. José Manuel Durão Barroso, "From War to Peace: A European Tale" (paper read at Acceptance of the Nobel Peace Prize Award to the European Union, Oslo, 10 Dec. 2012).

3. Hannah Arendt and Jerome Kohn, *Essays in Understanding, 1930–1954* (New York, 1994), 416.

4. See, e.g., Bruce S. Thornton, *Decline and Fall: Europe's Slow-Motion Suicide* (New York, 2007), 132–33.

5. Carlo Balestri, *Racism, Football and the Internet* (Vienna, 2002); European Union Agency for Fundamental Rights (FRA), *Anti-Semitism: Summary overview of the situation in the European Union 2001–2010* (Vienna, 2011); John Mann and Johnny Cohen, *Antisemitism in European Football: A Scar on the Beautiful Game* (London, 2008).

6. Johnny Paul, "Gaza-linked attacks on Jews sweep Europe," *Jerusalem Post*, 7 Jan. 2009.

7. Daniel Schammenthal, "End the Holocaust Memorials," *Wall Street Journal*, 28 Jan. 2009.

8. See, e.g., Mark Bell, *Racism and Equality in the European Union* (Oxford, 2008); Robert Maier, "Does a Supranational Europe Stimulate and/or Combat Racism," in *Europe's New Racism: Causes, Manifestations, and Solutions*, edited by the Evens Foundation (New York, 2002).

9. See, e.g., Pierre-André Taguieff, *Rising from the Muck: The New Anti-Semitism in Europe* (Chicago, 2004); also Emanuele Ottolenghi, "Making Sense of European Anti-Semitism," *Human Rights Review* 8, no. 2 (2007): 104–26; and John Rosenthal, "Anti-semitism and Ethnicity in Europe," *Policy Review* (Oct.–Nov. 2003):17–38.

10. Erik Bleich, *The Freedom to Be Racist?: How the United States and Europe Struggle to Preserve Freedom and Combat Racism* (New York, 2011), 23, 123–24, 135.

11. Steven Beller, "Is Europe good for the Jews? Jews and the pluralist tradition in historical perspective," *European Judaism* 42, no. 1 (2009):134–55.

12. Ibid., 134.

13. Lars Rensmann and Julius H. Schoeps, *Politics and Resentment: Antisemitism and Counter-Cosmopolitanism in the European Union, Jewish Identities in a Changing World* (Leiden; Boston, 2010), 59.

14. Göran Adamson, S"elective Perceptions: The Stockholm International Forum on the Holocaust," *Patterns of Prejudice* 34, no. 3 (2000): 66.

15. Romano Prodi, "A Union of minorities" (Paper read at Against anti-Semitism, For a Union of Diversity, Brussels, 19 Feb. 2004). While Prodi's comments and Auschwitz visit may border on philosemitism and a desire to overcome the continent's fascist past, his credentials as the consumate EU leader cannot be discounted. He took office as Commission President after a disgraced Commission resigned. He then enhanced the body's power and legitimacy through numerous projects including, but not limited to, the adoption of the Euro, the Treaties of Amsterdam and Nice and, not least, the polity's eastward expansion following the Cold War.

16. Ibid., 2–3.

17. Ibid.

18. Diana Pinto, "Are There Jewish Answers to Europe's Questions?," *European*

Judaism 39, no. 2 (2006): 47–57.

19. Steven Beller, "Is Europe good for the Jews? Jews and the pluralist tradition in historical perspective," *European Judaism* 42, no. 1 (2009):134–55.

20. Joseph Weiler, *The Constitution of Europe: "Do the New Clothes Have an Emperor?" And Other Essays on European Integration* (Cambridge, U.K., 1999), 342.

21. Glyn Morgan, *The Idea of a European Superstate: Public Justification and European Integration* (Princeton, N.J., 2005), 115.

22. R. Amy Elman, "Testing the Limits of European Citizenship: Ethnic Hatred and Male Violence," *National Women's Studies Association Journal* 13 no. 3 (2001): 49–69; Elman, *Sexual Equality in an Integrated Europe: Virtual Equality* (New York, 2007).

23. This "Council" is not to be confused with the European Council, conceivably the EU's most visible body because it meets semiannually, usually in Brussels, for highly publicized "summits." While these meetings typically promote the EU's most visible decisions and appear to provide key guidelines for the Council, Commission, and Parliament, we are more concerned with the political intricacies of policy making that transpire in advance of these summits. For this reason, we turn first to the institution previously known as the Council of Ministers. For a cursory overview of the EU's main institutions and how they operate, visit the European Union's official website, "How the EU works," http://europa.eu/abc/12lessons/lesson_4/index_en.htm.

24. See, for instance, Werner Bergman and Juliane Wetzel, *Manifestations of anti-Semitism in the European Union: First Synthesis Report* (Vienna, 2003), 65.

25. See, e.g., "Sweden followed Nazi marriage laws," *The Local*, 4 Apr. 2006, http://www.thelocal.se/3464 /20060404/. See also Chapter 2 for additional examples.

26. The unique character of that rebuke is considered in greater detail in Chapter 2. Poland marks the second state to be reprimanded. In June 2006, the European Parliament passed a Resolution on the increase in racist and homophobic violence in Europe (P6 TA (2006) 0273). It expressly condemned Poland's government for a general rise in racism, xenophobia, antisemitism, and homophobia. The Parliament then called on the Member States and EU institutions to take action. For instance, it requested the withdrawal of funding for parties failing to abide by the Charter of Fundamental Rights. Years later, in January 2012, MEPs called for the suspension of Hungary's voting rights because, they reasoned, its right-wing government breached the Union's fundamental democratic values when, among other things, it passed a censorious media law and rescinded the Constitution, replacing it with an ominous Basic Law that centralized power. Still, as we will soon note, these reprimands generated nowhere near the level of debate that confronted the actions taken against Austria.

27. Avi Beker, "Restitution Issues Destroy National Myths" in *Europe's Crumbling Myths: The Post-Holocaust Origins of Today's Anti-Semitism*, edited by Manfred Gerstenfeld (Jerusalem, 2003), 167.

28. Though the connection between these terrorist attacks on the United States with legislative developments in the EU may impress some as awkward, 9/11 galvanized the EU to adopt some of the measures against discrimination that are our focus. For clarity on this matter, see the legal scholar Laurent Pech, "The Law of Holocaust Denial in Europe: Towards a (qualified) EU-wide Criminal Prohibition" in *Genocide Denials and the Law*, edited by Ludovic Hennebel and Thomas Hochmann (Oxford; New York, 2011), 185–234.

29. Council Regulation (EC) 1035/97 establishing a European Monitoring Centre

on Racism and Xenophobia. OJ L 151/1, 10.06.1997.

30. European Union Agency for Fundamental Rights (FRA), *Anti-Semitism: Summary overview of the situation in the European Union 2001–2010*, 31.

31. Ibid., 18.

32. Ibid., 5, 14.

33. Sander Gilman, *The Jew's Body* (London, 1991).

34. Michael Lerner, *The Socialism of Fools: Anti-Semitism on the Left* (Oakland, Calif., 1992). See also Robert S. Wistrich, *A Lethal Obsession. Anti-Semitism from Antiquity to the Global Jihad* (New York, 2010), Chapter 15.

35. European Commission, *European Union action to combat racism: European Commission contribution to the world conference against racism, racial discrimination, xenophobia and related intolerance: Durban, South Africa, 31 August–7 September 2001* (Luxembourg, 2001).

36. "European Union Presidency, EU Presidency Statement—Racism" (paper read at the United Nations General Assembly, New York, 23 Oct. 2002).

37. According to the final platform of the World Conference against Racism, Racial Discrimination, Xenophobia and Related Intolerance, only two references to antisemitism remained. Paragraph 61 reads, "We recognize with deep concern the increase in anti-Semitism and Islamophobia in various parts of the world, as well as the emergence of racial and violent movements based on racism and discriminatory ideas against Jewish, Muslim and Arab communities." The other, Paragraph 150, "Calls upon States, in opposing all forms of racism, to recognize the need to counter anti-Semitism, anti-Arabism and Islamophobia world-wide, and urges all States to take effective measures to prevent the emergence of movements based on racism and discriminatory ideas concerning these communities." http://www.un.org/WCAR/durban.pdf.

CHAPTER ONE

Early Paths to EU Action

Lest it be assumed that the EU was keen to address racism in general, consider again the Commission's 1996 explanatory memorandum regarding the EUMC's establishment. It explained: "The point is *not* to take specific measures to combat racism or xenophobia. . . ." Indeed, the Commission insisted it would not "modify the system for protecting human rights in the Community or. . .[in] any of its Member States."[1] Rather, the EUMC conformed to the Commission's earlier 1986 Joint Declaration (signed with the Council and Parliament), which emphasized "adequate and objective information" for "making all *citizens* aware of the dangers of racism and xenophobia."[2] If for some Members of the European Parliament, the new Centre's founding served as a starting point for concrete action, for both the Commission and Council it was a culmination.[3] This section explains the reasons for the Community's reluctance to enact further reform and considers why, within a few years, the EU appears to have overcome its initial hesitance.

To begin, the Commission understood racism as an essentially national problem, one it had no explicit legal basis to address.[4] Moreover, neither the Commission nor the Council had an interest in quarreling with Member States over non-EU nationals whose legal fate frequently involved intense (local) debates about xenophobia and racism. For their part, Member States "were anxious to make migrant workers *less welcome* in order to reserve jobs for their own nationals, who had the inestimable bargaining advantage of possessing votes. . . ."[5] As for human rights (especially for non-EU nationals), the EU had long emphasized the ability of others, like the Council of Europe (COE) and the UN, to intervene in those issues it wished to side-step.[6]

When, in the 1970s, most Member States brought their national laws in line with the UN's International Convention on the Elimination of Racial Discrimination (ICERD), the level of protection against racial and ethnic discrimination varied considerably across the European Community. Adopted in 1965, in the aftermath of an alarming rise of antisemitism, the Convention came into force in 1969.[7] Because Article 2 of ICERD allows states significant discretion to interpret and implement their obligations, several ignored the Convention (e.g., Ireland). Still other states avoid adopting further policies by pointing to the provisions against discrimination already provided by their constitutions (e.g., Germany) or other social policies (e.g., France). More controversially, Article 4 of ICERD calls on states to condemn propaganda and organizations "which attempt to justify or promote racial hatred and discrimination in any form. . . ."[8] The UK strenuously objected to this expectation, insisting it had neither the intention nor the power to ban individuals or groups for their extreme or racist views. By contrast, Belgium and France prohibited only those racist acts found intentionally discriminatory while the Netherlands took a more expansive position to counter actions discriminatory in effect. Ireland distinguished itself as the sole EU Member State that refused to ratify any aspect of the ICERD, until December of 2000.

In the 1980s, the European Parliament maintained that differences among the Member States in how they dealt with racism obliged the adoption of minimum community-wide standards. Without sufficient protection it was argued that European nationals would be less inclined to exercise their freedom of (occupational) movement across the single market, a freedom needed to shore up the Community's prosperity. Although it was common for most MEPs to forge social justice claims in such economic terms, these politicians' initial interest in countering racism may have derived as much from the increased presence in their chamber of elected extreme right representatives in 1984 (from 0 to 16) as from market-oriented concerns. Those hoping for and committed to racial justice were no doubt disappointed to find that the very institution that had (in 1979) elected Simone Veil (a woman survivor of Auschwitz) as its first president now also housed its first far right Group of the European Right. In response to that group gaining an institutional foothold, 109 left-leaning MEPs (25 percent of the 434 representatives) called for the immediate creation of a parliamentary Committee of Inquiry to address the rise of pan-European fascism and racism. That Committee produced and then named its detailed account after its prominent rapporteur, Dimitrios Evrigenis.

The 1985 *Evrigenis Report* warned that although there had been a sharp decline in the number of militant right-wing organizations throughout the Member States in the 1970s, there was "no question of an increase in organized fascism."[9] According to the MEP Glyn Ford, Chair of the Committee of Inquiry, this complex finding is explained, in part, by "the tacit acceptance of the authorities that there is an 'acceptable' level of racism."[10] Yet, unable to fully grasp racism's broad appeal, Ford attributes the rise of fascism in Western Europe solely to the "impotence amongst the politicians of the traditional conservative Right who are afraid of losing voters."[11] Though compelling, this explanation overlooks his ideological peers, many of whom also proved unwilling to confront the creep of racism.

Yet, despite concerns over fascism's rising appeal, for Europe's Jews the *Evrigenis Report* may have been mildly reassuring. After acknowledging that fascists had "historically" chosen Jews and others as "particular" targets,[12] the investigation reflected briefly on current conditions for Jews and found: "Anti-Semitism in Europe is a limited phenomenon confined to a small minority."[13] Thus, the authors consigned anti-Jewish hatred to decades past and/or a contemporary occasional outburst.

Having concluded that antisemitism was a prejudice that necessitated no specific remedy, the MEPs focused instead on the adoption of the above-noted 1986 Joint Declaration against Racism and Xenophobia. That Declaration was the Community's first high-level acknowledgment that the problem of racism and xenophobia was one it should address. However, as I will detail below, the EU's first explicit formal condemnation of antisemitism came years later, in 1995, through the Parliament's Resolution on Racism, Xenophobia and Anti-Semitism.[14]

Two days after the Community's first Declaration Against Racism and Xenophobia, 53 percent of Austrian voters elected the former UN Secretary General and (former) Nazi intelligence officer Kurt Waldheim as their president. His ascent "perfectly encapsulated the postwar Austrian inability to confront the moral implications and meaning of the Nazi Holocaust."[15] Additionally, the election of a prominent Austrian who had previously denied his Nazi affiliation unleashed antisemitism and effectively ended any qualms that Austrians with antisemitic convictions may have had in expressing themselves.[16]

During his election campaign for this largely ceremonial though prestigious post, Waldheim linked his fate with that of his generation and country by claiming he had merely "done his duty" under Germany. This rationalization suggests that following orders makes one conscientious and beyond reproach—not least from "the foreign press" and "the Jews" who refused to forget his history as he claimed he had. Waldheim's past included, among other "duties," service to a unit charged with savagery against Yugoslav partisans and the deportation of Jews from Greece. When his political rivals disclosed these aspects of his life, he characterized these opponents as "conspiratorial" and "defamatory," yet when recounting the events himself, he insisted he was duty bound. Waldheim claimed that he had simply failed to mention what were, to him, minor incidents of his life.[17] For some of his supporters, the atrocities associated with Waldheim were treated as "Jewish inspired" libel.[18] Antisemitism could also be said to undergird the defiant campaign posters that proclaimed, "We Austrians decide whom *we* will vote for."[19]

The European Community was in no meaningful position to challenge this election in tone or outcome. Not only was Austria not a Member State, the newly adopted Joint Declaration lacked teeth for the Community to take action if it were. According to the chair of the Parliament's Legal Affairs and Citizens' Rights Committee, the Declaration was a "simple insipid document" that was neither forceful nor inspiring.[20] Tasked with the general supervision of "human rights problems in the Community," the Legal Committee was acutely aware that, without coordinated action at the European level, the Joint Declaration was fruitless.

Three years later, the largely symbolic character of the 1986 Joint Declaration became clearer; little had been done to implement it and yet Europe was entering a new political era that evidently demanded urgent action. The Community was getting far larger (see Table 2, p. 23); Spain and Portugal had recently joined the Community; the Cold War had reached its end. Political uncertainty and the rapid spread of racist violence and fascist organizing in the former Communist bloc and in the West was manifest in, among other developments, the extreme right's electoral success in Germany and France. An apprehensive and dissatisfied European Parliament thus called for the establishment of a new Committee of Inquiry and report.[21]

Given the Parliament's (earlier) institutional limitations (before the 2009 Lisbon Treaty), it could do nothing but monitor and present well-documented evidence of discrimination, including data on how few steps were taken to counter it. Yet, this circumscribed purview may explain the tenacity of some MEPs to do just that. Additionally, their high-minded principles may have derived from their limited capacity to implement them. Concomitantly, the body's high absenteeism rate also enabled a core group of anti-racist MEP activists to gain influence.[22] These activist MEPs, in turn, helped constitute the institution as a progressive light in efforts to end race discrimination. Clearly Glyn Ford was one such voice and, again, he emerged as chair the second Committee of Inquiry.

According to Ford, the second Committee of Inquiry "adopted virtually the same approach in gathering information as its predecessor."[23] It was, thus, able to "build up a fairly complete picture of the implementation (or non-implementation) of the Joint Declaration of 1986."[24] The Committee invited all ministers and civil servants responsible for combating racism to Brussels for hearings. It also solicited written submissions from and held public hearings with various local organizations including, but not limited to, immigrants and Jewish groups. The Committee's first recommendation (and there were dozens) concerned the Legal Affairs and Citizens' Rights Committee and called for the extension of its remit to include "all questions pertaining to racism, antisemitism and xenophobia."[25] Within five years, the EUMC was established and it assumed this responsibility.

Although Ford acknowledged that antisemitism had become (by 1989) "more overt than at any time since the Second World War,"[26] the problem received scant attention in the final report. The notable exception was the section on Austria, which, like Sweden at the time, was not yet a Member State. Noting Waldheim's electoral victory and the meteoric rise of the far right (FPÖ) party,[27] Ford's Committee of Inquiry worried about the potential danger of racism in Austria, especially in the form of antisemitism.[28] In addition, its report documented the desecration of Jewish gravestones across Europe, including in Sweden.[29] Last, this second investigation emphasized the Parliament's disappointment with the Council, Commission and Member States—as none had taken up the matter of racism more generally. However, whether the frustrations expressed by this core group of dedicated MEPs represent the Parliament and its stated commitment to countering racism is impossible to determine, especially given the above noted rate of absenteeism among parliamentarians.

With the possible exception of the 1986 Declaration, the Parliament's 1991 follow-up investigation found that none of the first report's forty recommendations had been fully implemented and that there was "no action at the community level to confront and tackle the root causes of racism and xenophobia."[30] Worse, the Council's antipathy toward the Parliament's efforts to engage it on this matter became clear when both the French and then the Irish President of the Council of Ministers refused to meet with the investigative Committee. This obstructionism proved consistent with Ireland's persistent refusal to adopt ICERD. While the obstructionism abated somewhat when the Italians took up the European presidency in 1990, for still more years the Parliament was largely on its own.

This climate buttressed the Commission's reluctance to pursue anti-racist initiatives and Member States (as noted above) proved unreliable as well, a point further evidenced by their general indifference to Europe's most recent genocide. Europe's leaders may have seemed certain of their strength and authority to manage Yugoslavia's disintegration in 1991, when the representative of the Council of Ministers proclaimed, "If anyone can do anything here, it is the EC," but such confidence was unwarranted and soon diminished.[31] As the Pulitzer prize-winning journalist Samantha Power notes, "whatever the long-term promise of the European Union (EU), it was not long into the Balkan wars before European weaknesses were exposed."[32] The EU's exclusive reliance on diplomacy to resolve the conflict doomed it to failure. By April of 1992, leaders from the United States asked, as Henry Kissinger before them, "What's Europe's phone number?"[33] In the absence of robust EU leadership and mounting concern over massive refugees flows, Member States pursued "concerted efforts" to stop refugees from leaving the former Yugoslavia, a response that exacerbated the carnage as Serbian forces called for a "Greater Serbia" and "ethnically cleansed" the country.[34] In particular, Serbian nationalists cast the region's Muslims in the despised role that Nazi ideology had assigned Jews decades earlier.

By the mid 1990s, the Balkan crisis revealed the relative impotence of the EU on the world stage and resulted in EU citizens making connections between their memories of Hitler's death camps and their glimpses of Serb-run concentration camps. Clearly, action was necessary. In 1995, just months before the Dayton Peace accord signing in Paris, the European Parliament adopted its Resolution on Racism, Xenophobia and Anti-Semitism. It notes, because "racism, xenophobia, anti-semitism and ethnic cleansing. . .have caused great conflicts and suffering to various regions and nations of Europe throughout history" with "deep and lasting wounds. . .[that are] still rampant as the 20th century draws to a close,"[35] it is "necessary for the Commission to study ways in which the Community, whilst respecting the principle of subsidiarity, can act against racism, xenophobia, anti-semitism and Holocaust denial at the European level."[36]

The following year, in 1996, the Parliament issued a resolution designating 1997 the European Year against Racism and the Council along with representatives from all the Member States agreed. The Commission followed with a Community-wide survey on racism and over 3 million euro in funding, mainly for consciousness raising projects throughout the Member States. There were 177 such projects. Of these, the legal scholar Mark Bell found an "overwhelming emphasis on immigrant-related racism" and that "aside from discrimination against migrants, the other main target group of policy in this period was the Jewish community."[37] More precisely, just five of 177 projects concerned Jews and only two of these considered antisemitism after World War II.[38] This stress was in keeping with the Parliament's first reports (in 1986 and 1991) on racism, which suggested that antisemitism (however important to consider) was a prejudice of the past. Nonetheless, these more recent efforts marked the first time that the EU took tangible steps with the Member Sates to combat racism.

THE TURNING POINT: 1997

The 1997 European Year against Racism may have offered "an opportunity" for "all the Community Institutions to engage jointly in raising awareness of the dangers of racism, xenophobia *and anti-Semitism* for Europe,"[39] but the robust scope of this objective went largely unnoticed. The Commission's own European-wide survey on racism epitomizes the oversight.

Not only did the survey offer no definition of racism; it contained no questions specific to antisemitism. The ironic dimensions of this evasion are evident when one understands that the codification of "race" throughout Europe provided for the destruction of European Jewry. The EU's experts insisted that they wanted to present the term "racism" as it is "commonly used to describe a process of prejudice which leads to groups [*sic*] being stigmatized, discriminated against and *considered as inferior* because of the particular characteristics of their group."[40]

TABLE 1: DEGREE OF EXPRESSED RACISM

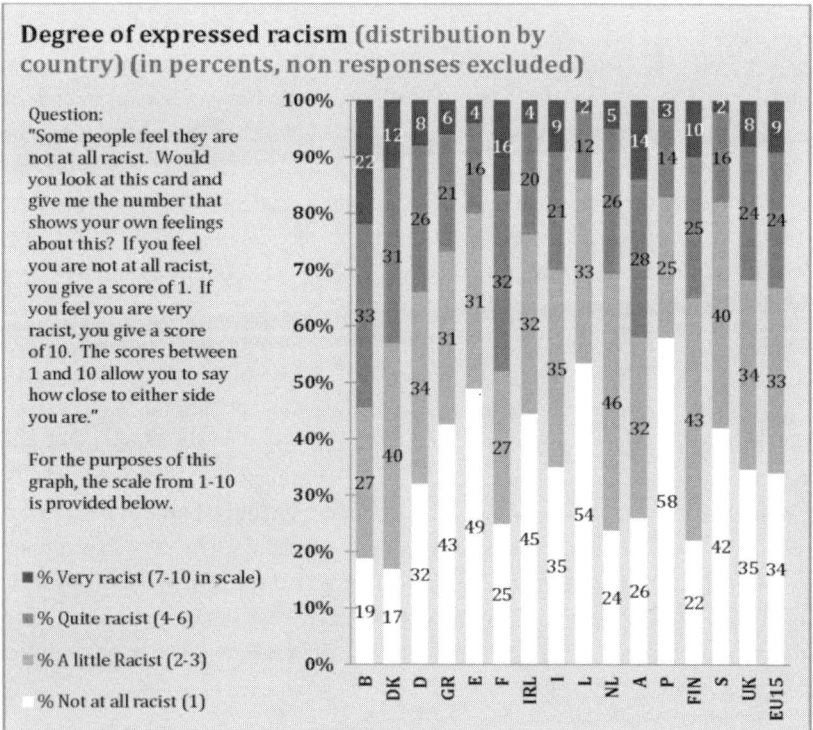

Degree of expressed racism (distribution by country) (in percents, non responses excluded)

Question: "Some people feel they are not at all racist. Would you look at this card and give me the number that shows your own feelings about this? If you feel you are not at all racist, you give a score of 1. If you feel you are very racist, you give a score of 10. The scores between 1 and 10 allow you to say how close to either side you are."

For the purposes of this graph, the scale from 1-10 is provided below.

■ % Very racist (7-10 in scale)

■ % Quite racist (4-6)

■ % A little Racist (2-3)

% Not at all racist (1)

Source: *Racism and Xenophobia in Europe: Eurobarometer Opinion Poll*, 47.

This seemingly broad approach to racism holds limited utility for gauging antisemitism because "while racism usually makes people 'small' in order to enslave, exploit or expel them, anti-Semitism makes the Jews delusionally 'big.'" Matthias Küntzel explains, "The most important characteristic of anti-Semitism is a conspiracy theory that holds the Jews responsible for both capitalism and communism, AIDS, revolutions and financial crises—in short, for every 'inexplicable' catastrophe of modernity."[41] A century earlier, Leon Pinsker emphasized this protean character of antisemitism. He wrote: "For the living, the Jew is a dead man; for the natives, an alien and a vagrant; for property holders, a beggar; for the poor, an exploiter and a millionaire; for the patriots, a man without a country; for all classes, a hated rival."[42]

For Walter Laqueur, the current contempt for Jews, increasingly referred to as the "new anti-Semitism," is "aimed not at the physical elimination of the Jews as prewar racialist anti-Semitism, but merely at the reduction of the Jewish influence, real or perceived."[43] For Robert S. Wistrich, the novelty of this bigotry stems not from what Laqueur suggests are its relatively more moderate aspirations, but from the way that it targets Israel as the "collective Jew" among nations. He writes that antisemitism is

> no longer expressed primarily in the form of a direct assault upon the rights of Jews to live as equal members of the non-Jewish societies which they inhabit. Rather, the 'new' antisemitism involves the denial of the rights of the Jewish people to live as an equal member within the family of nations.[44]

Wistrich also finds that "the 'new' anti-Semitism in western Europe has tended to come from the traditional victims of the Far Right—the alienated, the uprooted, the marginalized, relatively poor immigrants (Arab, Turk, and African) who have settled in Europe over the last thirty years."[45] Because the real and imagined social, economic, and cultural success of Europe's Jews is less admired than envied, Jews have once again become a people against whom a violent and visceral discrimination is not only acceptable—it is justified. Antisemitism is thus a moniker that, like racism, may sometimes be worn with pride.

When the Eurobarometer survey was released in 1997, it revealed that 33 percent of the 16,241 people questioned across the then-fifteen Member States openly described themselves as "quite racist" or "very racist."[46] In Sweden, by contrast, only 18 percent identified as "quite racist" or "very racist" while 42 percent of Austrians described themselves in this way. Allan Pred's analysis of racism in Sweden helps explain the difference: For Swedes, "the national identity-based taboo on publicly admitting to any form of racism" may result in a preference for identifying as only "slightly racist."[47] In this case, 40 percent of Swedes admitted to being "a little racist" as opposed to 32 percent of Austrians.[48] Moreover, of those insisting that they were "not at all racist," 42 percent of Swedes identified in this way while only 26 percent of Austrians did. For a comparison of these two Member States with the then-other thirteen, see Table 1, page 20.

EU officials were swift to express their concern though hesitant to act. Jacques Santer, then President of the Commission, remarked that the findings were "worrying" but neither he nor his colleagues pursued a follow-up survey to help determine what actions, if any, are needed and which, if any EU initiatives, have been effective in countering racism, however ambiguously defined.[49] To date, the EU has conducted no similar study, complicating efforts to measure the success of subsequent surveys and measures, including the anti-discrimination clause of the Treaty of Amsterdam and the Race Directive.[50] While treaties like Amsterdam function as "primary legislation," directives—though binding—introduce broad objectives without dictating the means by which each state achieves them. The Race Directive is no exception.

If prior to 1997, the EU had chosen to leave most matters of discrimination to its Member States to resolve, the Treaty of Amsterdam signaled a shift from this position. Through the incorporation of a general non-discrimination clause (Article 13), the legal community's capacity to intervene against unlawful discrimination expanded. Article 13 states, "The Council, acting unanimously on a proposal from the Commission and after consulting the European Parliament may take appropriate action to combat discrimination based on sex, racial or ethnic origin, religion or belief, disability, age or sexual orientation."[51]

While the Treaty's ostensible reach is impressive, its requirement that the Council must reach a unanimous vote on a Commission proposal before it "may take appropriate action" dilutes its strength. By declining to assert that the Council "shall" endeavor to take action, Member States did not establish a directly effective provision but, instead, left it to the Community institutions to adopt "appropriate" measures. In turn, these same institutions continue to emphasize the powers of the (now twenty-eight) Member States to provide redress. The dizzying dimensions of these progressive postures become clearer when one notes the way that each level of "integrated Europe" off-loads responsibility for stemming discrimination onto another institution and/or level of governance.

TABLE 2: EUROPEAN UNION ENLARGEMENTS OVER TIME

1958	1973	1981	1986	1995	2004	2007	2013
Belgium	Denmark	Greece	Portugal	Austria	Cyprus	Bulgaria	Croatia
France	Ireland		Spain	Finland	Czech R.	Romania	
Germany	U.K.			Sweden	Estonia		
Italy					Hungary		
Luxembourg					Latvia		
Netherlands					Lithuania		
					Malta		
					Poland		
					Slovakia		
					Slovenia		

Still, the Amsterdam Treaty proved a significant political development because its expectation of "appropriate action" against discrimination, though vague, obliges the strengthening of and improvement in EU institutions. This was done with an eye to accommodating the ten accession states that joined in 2004 (see Table 2, above).[52] With the exception of sex discrimination narrowly conceived, the EU had long denied itself the capacity to interfere in other arenas of injustice.[53]

Then, a month after the Amsterdam Treaty took effect in the spring of 1999, the Council called for the drafting of a Union Charter of Fundamental Rights, at the urging of the then German presidency of the Union. The Commission's homepage explains, "a debate on human rights and the European Union was launched in 1998, sparked off by the 50th anniversary of the Universal Declaration of Human Rights."[54] According to Gráinne de Búrca, the German presidency seized this initiative to "launch something which would constitute a high profile move as far as human rights and the European Union was concerned, but simultaneously which would not, in its view, introduce any concrete policy changes nor alter anything significant within the existing legal, political and constitutional framework."[55] From this angle, it seems that the EU remained no less cautious about its commitments to stem discrimination than it had prior to the Charter and the Treaty of Amsterdam.

For its part, as the chief arbiter of EU law, the European Court of Justice (ECJ) had earlier established that the Community's founding treaties did not explicitly empower it to accede to the European Convention on Human Rights. Despite all Member States already being signatories, fundamental rights were clearly subordinate to the demands of economic integration.[56] As such, fundamental rights (including rights to non-discrimination) would emerge in response to other concerns.

The Council's request for a rights-oriented initiative came amid a legitimacy crisis involving allegations of corruption and incompetence against the Commission that resulted in that body's collective resignation on March 15, 1999. The Council formally announced its intention to propose a European Charter in April. "The securing of a greater degree of popular legitimacy, then, was quite expressly the primary aim of the political proposal to draft a Charter."[57] The Charter was adopted a year later,[58] together with two separate directives to counter discrimination, one concerned race[59] and the other religion (or belief, disability, age or sexual orientation).[60] After looking further into the Charter, we will consider both directives—but only after offering some background on the two Member States central to our study as each (in its own way) facilitated the adoption of this legislation.

While the Amsterdam Treaty delineates explicitly the discrimination it is willing to prohibit, the 2000 Charter of Fundamental Rights offers a list of basic values it declares the Community will uphold when implementing Union law. According to the Charter's Preamble, "social progress and scientific and technological developments" combined to change society in ways that made "it necessary to strengthen the protection of fundamental rights" by making them more visible.[61]

The Charter details the rights of EU citizens in 54 articles and six chapters entitled dignity, freedoms, equality, solidarity, citizens' rights, and justice. The following clauses relate closely to this study:

> Article 10. Everyone has the right to freedom of thought, conscience and religion. This right includes freedom to change religion or belief and freedom, either alone or in community with others and in public or in private, to manifest religion or belief, in worship, teaching, practice and observance.
>
> Article 11. Everyone has the right to freedom of expression. This right shall include freedom to hold opinions and to receive and impart information and ideas without interference by public authority and regardless of frontiers.
>
> Article 21. Any discrimination based on any ground such as sex, race, colour, ethnic or social origin, genetic features, language, religion or belief, political or any other opinion, membership of a national minority, property, birth, disability, age or sexual orientation shall be prohibited.

Article 22. The Union shall respect cultural, religious and linguistic diversity.

Although these articles restate already agreed to positions in varied legislation, sufficient opposition from some Member States to the Charter prevented its complete inclusion into the 2001 Nice Treaty,[62] which would have rendered it legally binding. Nonetheless, years later, the Lisbon Treaty[63] introduced the Charter into Europe's primary law, a matter we will address below.

CONCLUSION

Whether one regards the Charter as a rhetorical flourish or a renewed and increased commitment to a catalogue of fundamental rights, many critics and supporters alike consider its adoption by the EU a significant move toward enhancing its legitimacy, particularly following the Commission's crisis of 1999. That the then newly-reconstituted Commission relinquished its earlier position that it had "no power" to stem various manifestations of discrimination within the Member States serves as a telling reminder of just how far this body has drifted from its more conservative moorings.

To determine the substantive character of this shift as well as the consequences of the EU's earlier reluctance to confront antisemitism, we turn our attention to Sweden and Austria and consider their response to the early Europeanization of this policy area.

NOTES

1. European Commission, "Proposal for a Council Regulation (EC) establishing a European Monitoring Centre for Racism and Xenophobia" COM (96) 615, 27.11.1996, 3, emphasis added.

2. Joint Declaration by the European Parliament, the Council and the Commission against racism and xenophobia, 11 June 1986, OJ C 158, 25.6.1986, 1, emphasis added.

3. Mark Bell, *Anti-Discrimination Law and the European Union* (Oxford, 2004), 61.

4. European Commission, "Communication from the Commission on racism, xenophobia and anti-semitism. Proposal for a Council decision designating 1997 as European Year against Racism" COM (95) 653 final, 13.12.1995, 3.

5. Stephen George, *Politics and Policy in the European Community* (Oxford, 1991), 208, emphasis added.

6. R. Amy Elman, *Sexual Equality in an Integrated Europe: Virtual Equality* (New York, 2007); See also Andrew Williams, *EU Human Rights Policies: A Study in Irony* (Oxford, 2004).

7. The Sub-Commission on the Prevention of Discrimination and Protection of

Minorities—a forerunner to the Committee for the Elimination of Racism (CERD)—issued an earlier resolution that condemned racism in 1960. In it, the group stated it was "deeply concerned by the manifestations of anti-Semitism and other forms of racial and national hatred and religious and racial prejudices of a similar nature, which have occurred in various countries reminiscent of the crimes and outrages committed by the Nazis prior to and during the Second World War." In Michael Banton, *International Action Against Racial Discrimination* (Oxford, 1996), 53. However, by 1965 any reference to antisemitism was excluded from the final Convention after Arab delegates to the UN argued that the Jewish homeland was itself tantamount to Nazism. Ibid., 58–9.

8. United Nations General Assembly, *International Convention on the Elimination of All Forms of Racial Discrimination*, 21 Dec. 1965, United Nations, Treaty Series, vol. 660, 218.

9. European Parliament, *Committee of Inquiry into the Rise of Fascism and Racism in Europe: Report on the findings of inquiry* (Luxembourg, 1985), 71.

10. Glyn Ford, *Fascist Europe: The Rise of Racism and Xenophobia* (London, 1992), xviii.

11. Ibid.

12. European Parliament, *Committee of Inquiry into the Rise of Fascism and Racism in Europe*, 19, 24.

13. Ibid., 52, see also note 171.

14. Resolution on racism, xenophobia and anti-semitism, OJ C 308, 20.11.1995.

15. Robert S. Wistrich, *A Lethal Obsession. Anti-Semitism from Antiquity to the Global Jihad* (New York, 2010), 227.

16. Ruth Wodak, "The Waldheim Affair and Anti-semitic Prejudice in Austrian Public Discourse," *Patterns of Prejudice* 24, no. 2–4 (1990): 18–33.

17. Ruth Wodak and Anton Pelinka, *The Haider Phenomenon in Austria* (New Brunswick, 2002), xi–xii.

18. Wistrich, *A Lethal Obsession,* 227.

19. Andrei S. Markovits and Anson Rabinbach, "Why Waldheim Won in Austria," *Dissent* 33 (Fall 1986), 410.

20. Debates of the European Parliament, No. 2-340/108, 11.6.1986.

21. Ford, *Fascist Europe*, 106.

22. Carlo Ruzza, "Anti-racism and EU institutions," *Journal of European Integration* 22, no. 2 (2000):156.

23. Ford, *Fascist Europe*, 4.

24. Ibid., 7.

25. Ibid., 144.

26. Ibid., xi.

27. Ibid., 37-9.

28. Ibid., 81.

29. Ibid., 84.

30. Ibid., 87.

31. Samantha Power, *A Problem from Hell: America and the Age of Genocide* (New York, 2003), 259.

32. Ibid. Yet, it seems this weakness has been forgotten. When the EU received the 2012 Nobel Peace Prize, the awarding Committee claimed the EU had "for over six decades contributed to the advancement of peace and reconciliation, democracy and human rights in Europe" (http://www.nobelprize.org/nobel_prizes/peace/laureates/2012/eu.html). While it is true that none of the Balkan countries were

Member States of "Europe" at the time of the genocide, they were (and still are) in the heart of Europe. We will return to the EU's more recent position on the Balkan crisis and this prize later in the manuscript.

33. Quoted in Power, *A problem from Hell*, 259.

34. Saskia Sassen, *Guests and Aliens* (New York, 1999), 125.

35. Resolution of the European Parliament on racism, xenophobia and anti-semitism, OJ C 126, 22.05.1995, Para. A.

36. Ibid., Para. 5. The principle of subsidiarity was introduced in the Maastricht Treaty and is now in Article 5 of the TEU. It holds that the EU "shall act only if and in so far as the objectives of the proposed action cannot be sufficiently achieved by the Member States. . .but can rather, by reason of the scale or effects of the proposed action, be better achieved at Union level."

37. Mark Bell, *Racism and Equality in the European Union* (Oxford, 2008), 72.

38. European Commission, European Year Against Racism: the Commission announces grant support to European anti-racism projects (Brussels, 1997).

39. European Commission, *The European Institutions in the Fight against Racism: Selected Texts* (Luxembourg, 1997), 5, emphasis added.

40. European Commission, *Racism and Xenophobia in Europe Eurobarometer Opinion Poll No 47.1: Draft final report presented at the Closing Conference of the European Year Against Racism* (Brussels 1997), 6, emphasis added.

41. Matthias Küntzel, "'Islamophobia' or 'Truthophobia,'" *Wall Street Journal*, 8 Dec. 2008.

42. Quoted in Arthur Hertzberg, *The Zionist Idea: A Historical Analysis and Reader* (Philadelphia, 1997), 188.

43. Walter Laqueur, *The Changing Face of Antisemitism: From Ancient Times to the Present Day* (New York, 2006), 16.

44. Robert S. Wistrich, *From Ambivalence to Betrayal: The Left, the Jews, and Israel* (Lincoln, Neb., 2012), 1.

45. Wistrich, *A Lethal Obsession,* 42.

46. European Commission, *Eurobarometer 47: Racism and Xenophobia in Europe* (Brussels, 1997).

47. Allan Pred, *Even in Sweden: Racisms, Racialized Spaces and the Popular Geographical Imagination* (Berkeley, 2000), Chapter 2, note 45.

48. European Commission, *Eurobarometer 47*, 2.

49. European Commission, *1997 European Year Against Racism: Closing Conference Report* (Luxembourg, 1998), 5.

50. However, three years after the EU's special Eurobarometer opinion poll on racism, the EUMC conducted its own survey that found that 20 percent of EU respondents believed that the EU should return all legally established immigrants from outside of the EU to their country of origin. Even those children born inside the EU to immigrant parents fell into this category. See Eva Thalhammer et al., *Attitudes towards minority groups in the European Union: A special analysis of the Euro-barometer 2000 survey on behalf of the European Union Monitoring Centre on Racism and Xenophobia* (Vienna, 2001), 45.

51. Treaty of Amsterdam amending the Treaty on European Union, the Treaties Establishing the European Communities and Certain Related Acts, OJ C 340, 10.11.1997.

52. These are Cyprus, the Czech Republic, Estonia, Hungary, Latvia, Lithuania, Malta, Poland, the Slovak Republic, and Slovenia. All ten joined on 1 May 2004 and Bulgaria and Romania joined in 2007 (See Table 2, p. 23). The treaty's conclusion

reached at the December 1997 Luxembourg summit by the European Council's President reads, "As a prerequisite for enlargement of the Union, the operation of the institutions must be strengthened and improved in keeping with the institutional provisions of the Amsterdam Treaty." (DOC/97/24, 14.12.1997).

53. R. Amy Elman, "The EU and Women: Virtual Equality" in *The State of the European Union: Deepening and Widening*, edited by Pierre-Henri Laurent and Marc Maresceau (Boulder, Colo., 2008); Elman, *Sexual Equality*.

54. European Commission, *The Charter of Fundamental Rights of the EU—all personal, civil, political, economic and social rights in one simple text* (Brussels, 2009), http://ec.europa.eu/justice_home/fsj/rights/charter /fsj_rights_charter_en.htm.

55. Gráinne de Búrca, "The Drafting of the European Union Charter of Fundamental Rights," *European Law Review* 26 (April 2001): 129.

56. Jason Coppel and Aidan O'Neill, "The ECJ: Taking Rights Seriously," *Legal Studies* 12 (1992): 227–45.

57. Gráinne de Búrca, "The drafting": 131; See also Koen Lenaerts, "Fundamental Rights in the European Union," *European Law Review* 25 (Dec. 2000): 576.

58. Charter of Fundamental Rights of the European Union. OJ C 83, 30.03.2010.

59. Council Directive 2000/43/EC of 29 June 2000 implementing the principle of equal treatment between persons irrespective of racial or ethnic origin. OJ L 180, 19.07.2000.

60. Council Directive 2000/78/EC of 27 Nov. 2000 establishing a general framework for equal treatment in employment and occupation. OJ L 303, 02.12.2000.

61. Charter of Fundamental Rights of the European Union, Para 4.

62. Treaty of Nice Treaty. OJ C 80, 10.03.2001.

63. Treaty of Lisbon. OJ C 306, 17.12.2007.

CHAPTER TWO

Member States before 9/11

In Europe's more expansive context of stepped up anti-discrimination efforts, it seems Member States themselves could also no longer ignore the challenges of antisemitism. Austria and Sweden, late entrants into the EU (both in 1995, along with Finland), proved no exception. As both moved onto a world stage that foregrounds Europe's integration, each state invariably confronts the persistent prejudice of antisemitism through its own history and present political system. Thus, while Sweden distinguishes itself as a vibrant example of the modern European "welfare state" (with an ostensibly neutral past and a social democratic consensus which undermines the electoral appeal of extremist parties), Austria (which was annexed by Nazi Germany in March of 1938) is often remembered as Hitler's homeland and most devoted disciple. In short, "Austria has the dubious distinction of being the birthplace of modern anti-Semitism."[1]

Few Member States have garnered more dissimilar public attention regarding their recent struggles with antisemitism than Sweden and Austria. As Austria continues to snag headlines for wrongdoing, Sweden generally remains a Teflon state where even the most insidious incriminations rarely stick. Both countries thus offer an exciting opportunity to explore the consequences of integration on their Member States and, in turn, the influence of these states on the EU.

Despite their differences, both Member States are among the EU's most affluent and stable social democracies. When they entered into the EU, Austria ranked eighth among all nations regarding its gross national product per capita and Sweden ranked tenth.[2] Only three Member States ranked higher—Luxembourg, Denmark, and Germany. Moreover, Social Democrats in Austria and Sweden have long been nearly synonymous with governance. These relatively small-sized states have significant reputations and small Jewish communities (both under .5 percent), weary of drawing attention to themselves.

We begin with Sweden, a country whose reputation as a "moral superpower" made it an especially attractive candidate for EU accession. "Having reappeared in a number of related discursive forms over centuries,"

Sweden's vision of itself as outstanding is "deeply sedimented" and inextricably connected to a belief in the moral and political superiority of Nordic civilization more generally.[3] According to a comparative study of four EU referenda campaigns (in Austria, Finland, Norway, and Sweden), this view has rendered Sweden's politicians particularly intent on exporting their model to the rest of Europe.[4] In turn, Europe appears to hold itself in as high regard as Sweden does itself. That country's former deputy Prime Minister, Per Ahlmark, explains somewhat cheekily: "As a Swede I have heard this boasting all my life. And, as we have not been at war for two centuries, it proves that Sweden is sort of a moral superpower. This type of bragging has now become part of EU ideology. We are the moral continent."[5]

SWEDEN

As the EU ceremoniously endorsed Amsterdam's progressive ambitions in June of 1997, the mood in Sweden was hardly festive; a national study had just revealed that 30 percent of that country's teenage students doubted that the Holocaust happened.[6] That same month, international press reports also linked Swedish iron exports to the strength of Hitler's military machine and exposed the country's postwar hoarding of German gold, much of it looted from Nazi victims.

By summer's end, the benevolence that previously cloaked Swedish neutrality further unravelled. The country's largest newspaper, *Dagens Nyheter*, disclosed that approximately 60,000 women had been forcibly sterilized under Social Democratic governance from 1935 and into the 1960s, with unanimous support from the other parties. Moreover, the laws governing sterilization quietly persisted and were put into occasional practice until 1976. Labelled genetically or racially "inferior," the victims were typically poor and disabled women; often from non-Nordic backgrounds.[7] The program's advocates included prominent Swedish reformers Gunnar and Alva Myrdal, outspoken critics of U.S. racism. While supporting Sweden's sterilization policies for the developmentally disabled and others "unfit for life," the Myrdals insisted that they were "not out to protect the 'race,'" but were interested in "freeing society of social problems."[8] According to Pred, such logic explains the long-standing resistance among most Swedes to draw parallels between their state's sterilization programs and Nazi racial policy.[9]

Once renowned for its humanitarianism, the country's vision of itself as the world's conscience tumbled as a torrent of unflattering news fuelled Sweden's diminishing sense of exceptionalism and its place in Europe. The progressive credentials that Sweden brought to the EU only two years prior, as a new entrant, were at stake. The *New York Times* chronicled Sweden's fall from grace in several articles.[10] In an article entitled "Sweden, Once the World's Conscience, Now Drifts," readers discover that "the country that. . . preached racial tolerance has now developed segregated communities in Stockholm's suburbs for many of the 800,000 immigrants."[11] It concludes: "Once a nation that spoke out on conditions around the world, Sweden has become inward-looking and self-absorbed."[12] While this assessment may ring true generally, the opposite might characterize Sweden's understanding of the Holocaust. That is, Swedes remain outspoken concerning Nazis and their sympathizers in other countries while often denying the persistence of Swedish antisemitism and their own state's complicity with Nazism.[13]

With Sweden's ethical esteem on the wane and his own popularity diminishing, then Social Democratic Prime Minister, Göran Persson, focused on the Holocaust scepticism of his country's pupils and mobilized unanimous parliamentary support for educational programs to off-set the historical amnesia suggested by the findings of the above-noted study. By January 1998, his government launched the "Living History Project"; the purpose of which was to "spread knowledge about the Holocaust and to encourage discussion of issues relating to humanity, democracy, and equality, *using the Holocaust as a point of departure.*"[14]

The Living History Project (LHP) was multifaceted and comprised nearly two-dozen initiatives. These fell into each of four spheres to service memory: public commemorations, general information campaigns, lesson plans for primary and secondary schools and, finally, the establishment of a national research center on genocide at Uppsala University. Eventually, an International Task Force for International Cooperation on Holocaust Education, Remembrance and Research (ITF) emerged. No less crucial to the LHP's success was the vigorous public relations campaign undertaken on its behalf. This included slick multilingual brochures, a website (in both Swedish and English), and four high profile international conferences. The first of these was on Holocaust education.[15]

When the government convened the Stockholm International Forum on Education, Remembrance and Research in 2000, the conference lasted three days (January 26–28) and commemorated the fifty-fifth anniversary of the liberation of Auschwitz. As the Nazi's largest concentration camp and killing center, Auschwitz casts its shadow over an integrated Europe keen to distance itself from the values of that past.[16] The conference brought scholars and government leaders together from over forty countries. Among them were nearly two-dozen heads of state, the largest gathering of top-level leaders in Sweden since the 1986 funeral of the former assassinated Prime Minister, Olof Palme.

The conference helped establish an international day of Holocaust remembrance (on January 27) and concluded with a "commitment to plant the seeds of a better future amidst the soil of the past." This "Stockholm Declaration" continues, "We empathize with the victims' suffering and draw inspiration from their struggle. Our commitment must be to remember the victims who perished, respect the survivors still with us, and reaffirm humanity's common aspiration for mutual understanding and justice."[17] In retrospect, this and similar statements may be chilling for their conspicuous avoidance in expressly confronting contemporary antisemitism—a point to which we will return.

Prime Minister Persson inaugurated his Living History educational initiative two years prior to the Stockholm conference, again with a brief speech commemorating the liberation of Auschwitz. Calling upon Swedes to "remember the appalling crimes of the past," Persson argued, "To deny the crimes committed in the name of Nazism is to be party to them."[18] With memory serving as a crucial act that permits and encourages resistance to evil, what, then, are Swedes specifically encouraged to remember about Nazism?

Throughout this speech, Persson portrayed Nazism as an anti-democratic ideology whose numerous victims also included Jews. In fact, he twice mentioned Jews; first among a long list of victims and second as children, all of whom he reminds us had "a name and a face."[19] Such was the tone and circumscribed focus on Jews. In the context of Holocaust remembrance, this approach is especially misleading because, as Elie Wiesel has wisely remarked, while not all victims were Jews, all Jews were victims.

As if the project's legitimacy rested on the muted recognition that the overwhelming majority of Holocaust victims were Jews, one notes their striking absence from the government's information packet designed to promote the Living History Project. Instead, one finds occasional references throughout to "11 million who *died* in the Holocaust."[20] It would appear that "murder" is too strong and unpleasant a term. Reference to it, like that to Jews, emerges only within the Prime Minister's remarks. Interestingly, years later, Persson's (2004) speech memorializing the Holocaust remained essentially the same as his first in 1998. Both contained only a passing mention of Jews—by reference to culture. "We grieve the enormous loss that the Holocaust has meant—for close relatives and friends, for Jewish culture, for our culture and for the world, for you and me and our children."[21]

According to the government's promotional flyer, "the aim" of Holocaust education within schools "is to create an opportunity for active meetings, where parents and staff have a chance to discuss compassion, tolerance, xenophobia and human rights."[22] Absent antisemitism and subsumed under a discussion of intolerance today, these lesson plans satisfied the EU's equally ambiguous call for action through its "1997 European Year against Racism." Mona Sahlin, Persson's protégé, oversaw Sweden's compliance with this EU program.

The Living History Project's first and most visible initiative is a Holocaust primer (*Tell ye your children*) that departs from the above-noted script by foregrounding Jewish existence, persecution, and extermination.[23] However, its selective depictions of Swedish history mirror the favorable images often invoked by the state's governing elite. For example, rather than acknowledge Sweden's profitable trading policies with Nazi Germany, the primer places Sweden solely within a context of "bureaucratic resistance" where civil servants become (neutral) critics whose subsequent privileges enabled efficient opposition to the Final Solution.[24] Translated into seven languages, the government-sponsored booklet was widely available and mailed to every Swedish household with school-age children.

Tell ye your children opens as the Holocaust is about to close, in 1945; Sweden's "white buses" were evacuating Scandinavian prisoners from the Neuengamme concentration camp outside Hamburg, Germany. This historical snapshot is a Swedish staple. In welcoming delegates to the international conference in 2000, Persson immediately mentioned these buses sent under the auspices of the Swedish Red Cross. A Swedish documentary on the children and grandchildren of Holocaust survivors, released two years earlier, also opens with this portrait.[25] Yet, while the film concludes with the son of one survivor insisting the Holocaust was "not just about the Jews," the booklet strikes a less evasive and thus more haunting and sobering note: those evacuating the camp left behind twenty *Jewish* children between the ages of five and twelve. Interestingly, neither the primer's co-authors, Stéphen Bruchfeld and Paul Levine, nor the Prime Minister proffer explanations for why these children were abandoned, though the now iconic character of this event seems to demand it.[26]

The concentration camp evacuation is the first of only seven specific references to Sweden in the booklet's 84 pages. Nearly all are positive and pertain to Jews (from Germany, Hungary, Norway, and Denmark) who find refuge in Sweden. Ignored are the thousands denied exile and still others, like Carl Adam Nycop, who lived in Sweden under intimidation.[27] A former editor of one of the leading evening newspapers *Expressen*, Nycop was a young Stockholmer when he noticed a chalk mark on his apartment door. He later learned Swedish Nazis marked Jewish households to identify and later dispose of Jews—as was done elsewhere in Europe.[28] As the Holocaust scholar Raul Hilberg notes, identifying Jews was the first step in the "destructive process." It may have seemed relatively harmless, but it set a foundation for administrative continuity.[29] Recall, as well, the J-stamped passports. The Nazis adopted these after the *Anschluss*, at the urging of Sweden and Switzerland. Both countries were intent on restricting German and Austrian Jews access and warned Nazis that if they would not distinguish Jews in German-issued passports, their governments would establish new visa regulations for all Germans. The Nazis responded by stamping a large J into German Jewish passports. Conspicuously identified and unable to escape Nazi occupied Europe, this administrative stigmatization at the urging of two "neutral" nation-states rendered Jews especially vulnerable to annihilation.

While most scholars suggest Sweden was even-handed in its "neutrality," the research of Steven Koblik, David Mel Paul, and Margareta Paul on Swedish policies toward Jews during the war offers a much-needed corrective, one that the booklet's authors chose to ignore.[30] Koblik and his co-authors were struck by "the *sensitivity* shown Germany throughout the *conflict*"[31] and they attribute the country's reluctance to aid Jewish victims of Nazism to mounting antisemitism and the limited financial resources of Sweden's small Jewish community.[32]

When, in 1943, Sweden offered a temporary haven to Jewish children, it did so only after insisting that Western powers provide for their maintenance and then their immediate removal. Sweden was willing to help (young) Jews, but it did not want to be a permanent refuge for them.[33] In their historical study of the country's immigration policies, Ingvar Svanberg and Mattias Tydén found that Swedish politicians (in the 1930s) repeatedly referred to Jews as "unwanted refugees."[34]

Following the introduction of the 1935 Nuremberg laws in Germany, Sweden's government responded with an investigative report that refused to designate as political refugees "those who have left their country because belonging to their race has resulted in a diminished ability to support themselves or has caused them feelings of discomfort." Nevertheless, such people (i.e., German Jews) *could* be accepted on humanitarian grounds, as long as they "did not entail any risks or cause any trouble" for Sweden.[35] In 1937, the Parliament increased immigration restrictions. Sweden's authorities clearly regarded most Jews as too much trouble and thus turned away those without relatives already in the country.

In contrast to Koblik, Tydén and Svanberg, the authors of Sweden's Holocaust primer, ignore the government's restrictive refugee and passport policies, its transit agreements with the Nazis (e.g., two million German soldiers travelled through Sweden on special trains to and from Norway), its heavy trade with Axis-controlled Europe, and its energetic suppression of anti-Nazi views. Instead, the primer's authors sanitize the antisemitism that found expression among the country's elite.

In their synopsis of the Swedish press, Bruchfeld and Levine provide limited evidence of the pervasive antisemitism that characterized it. Readers are informed, "Swedish newspapers frequently published German anti-Jewish actions."[36] Yet, without descriptions to illustrate the insidious analysis that permeated much of that reporting, one could assume the press was simply delivering the news. This was not the case. In a small inset, the co-authors introduce the Swedish journalist Fritz Lönnegren who, with special permission from the Nazis, covered the formation of a Lithuanian ghetto for the "pro-German" Stockholm evening paper, *Aftonbladet*. "Lönnegren," they write, "expresses *understanding* for the cruelties of Lithuanian mobs against the Jews after the German entry, as well as *sympathy* for the creation of the ghetto."[37] This "sympathy" for antisemites cuts deep. For example, one Swedish newspaper's explanation for *Kristallnacht* reads: "Experiences with history have shown that Jews have difficulties living with other peoples. . .[and] have a big responsibility for the development of anti-Semitism in many countries."[38] More recently, this position finds expression among Swedes insisting that Israeli policies are to blame for attacks against Jews in Sweden, a point to which we will return.

Although anti-Jewish sentiment was common during the Second World War, the primer focuses instead on Torgny Segerstedt, a prominent newspaper editor from Gothenburg who was one of "Sweden's leading critics of his country's policy of *accommodation* with Nazi Germany."[39] Segerstedt certainly deserves our attention, but suggesting he (like Raoul Wallenberg) represented Sweden's mainstream during the war is misleading. Sweden's former Prime Minister (1946–1968) and prominent wartime politician, Tage Erlander, disdained Segerstedt and he insisted that many others in Sweden shared his view.[40] Considering that, in 1940, Sweden's King Gustaf V appealed directly to Segerstedt and asked that he desist from criticizing Hitler, we have little reason to doubt Erlander's account.

Years before the Living History Project began, the renowned Swedish journalist Maria Pia Boëthius observed "it is a paradox that the newspapers that went against the government's politics and censorship are today remembered while the newspapers that followed the government's decrees and were regarded as sensible are forgotten."[41] In consequence, exactly how Sweden "accommodated" the Nazis remains every bit as mysterious for the booklet's readers as why the white buses at Neuengamme left Jewish children to languish. Sadly, the buses are remembered while the children they left behind are often forgotten.

Tell ye your children would remain indistinguishable from other Holocaust primers were it not for Sweden's promotion of it as a panacea to the country's collective amnesia and yet it fails to recognize Sweden's own connections, however indirect, to this tragic past. Nowhere is this paradox in greater evidence than in the pamphlet's concise overview of Social Darwinism and its connections to eugenics. The authors credit the French diplomat Arthur de Gobineau for his racist typology and the "German-Englishman," H. S. Chamberlain, for his influential antisemitism.[42] Yet, Sweden's own antisemitism and its contributions to the popularization of Social Darwinism are conspicuously absent.

In 1922 Sweden was the first European state to sponsor an institute for "racial science" at Uppsala University. Herman Lundberg was the institute's founder and Hermann Göring's mentor. Göring lived in Swedish exile from 1925 to 1927, following the failed Munich beer hall *Putsch* in 1923. After the German government granted a general amnesty for political refugees in 1927, Göring left for Hitler's inner circle and Lundberg continued his work. Lundberg legitimized Hitler's Aryan doctrines and, in confirming "racial superiority," this Swede bolstered the national superiority complex of his compatriots.[43] The pervasiveness of this ideology became evident when, on May 22, 1933, the *New York Times* reported on a march of 50,000 Swedish fascists on Stockholm in opposition to the left. The event marked the country's largest conservative demonstration and throngs of spectators lined the streets to support the fascists, arms outstretched in Nazi salutes.

By 1937, Sweden's Church pursued pro-Nazi policies when, for instance, its clergy insisted that Swedes marrying German Gentiles sign a statement affirming that none of the grandparents of these Germans were Jewish. In those cases that did not conform to this expectation, Swedish courts annulled suspect marriages and declared the children born within them as "illegitimate."[44]

Rather than acknowledge Sweden's troubling past, Bruchfeld and Levine explain: "The ideas of the 'eugenics movement' were realized during the first half of the twentieth century in Europe and the United States with the sterilization of hundreds of thousands of people, mostly women."[45] Composed during the clamor of front page revelations concerning Sweden's own forced sterilization programs, the booklet's omission proves startling, particularly as

Sweden's own efforts preceded that of the Nazis and continued for nearly two decades after their defeat.

Although the authors understandably focused their greatest attention on the Nazis and their persecution of European Jews, failing to mention Swedish sterilization programs while noting the racism and "eugenics movements" of other Europeans and the United States is curious. It is, however, consistent with the general disinclination of Swedes to confront their own demons.

When, in 1992, the prominent journalist Maria Pia Boëthius published *Heder och Samvete: Sverige och andra världskriget* (Honor and conscience: Sweden and World War II), she received little praise and considerable controversy for emphasizing Sweden's complicity with Nazism. In retrospect, it might have been foolish to expect a different reception. So few writers addressed this subject that decades after the war, only one book touched on Sweden's treatment of the Jews and its principle consideration was Swedish immigration policy (1936–1942) more generally.[46] The earlier mentioned exploration of Swedish policy toward Jews during the war by Koblik and his colleagues followed in 1988 and while that work remains exceptional, Boëthius's book first generated fierce debate. Other writers followed, but her accessible journalist style was especially effective in countering contemporary schoolbook portraits of the state's benevolent neutrality.[47]

More importantly, perhaps, Boëthius revealed the reluctance of prominent figures, including the former Social Democratic Prime Minister, Ingvar Carlsson, to discuss this past—a position seemingly at odds with the government's later educational initiatives.

By June 2003, the EU singled out Sweden for praise at a special meeting in Vienna to combat antisemitism. It was hosted by the Organization for Security and Cooperation in Europe (OSCE), the first international organization to treat antisemitism as a "distinct human rights issue." The European Commission asserted: "There have been many excellent initiatives by individual Member States to address the issues of anti-Semitism, Holocaust education and intercultural understanding, but special mention must be given to the Government of Sweden. . . ."[48] The empirical grounds for this praise are shaky at best, and not least for reasons stated above.

Well over a decade has passed since Sweden first held its international conference on the Holocaust and unveiled its educational projects, but despite their favourable press, the measurable consequences of these efforts are spectacularly unimpressive. Police statistics show the number of antisemitic crimes essentially unchanged or somewhat increased (in Malmö).[49] Furthermore, in a follow-up survey that asked today's teens about the Holocaust, researchers determined a slight decrease since 1997 in the percentage certain that the Holocaust occurred.[50] In the latter survey, 62 percent reported that they were "completely certain" that the Holocaust took place, as opposed to 71 percent in the 1997 study. The 8 percent increase of doubters raises substantive concern about the effectiveness of the state's program, one that was to have countered the appalling doubt rate of nearly 30 percent.[51] In Austria, a similar study from 1995 revealed that only 7 percent believed it "possible that the Nazi extermination of the Jews never happened."[52] Crucially, researchers in Sweden also found an increase in the proportion of students who "believe there is too much talk about Nazism and the extermination of the Jews."[53] This view is not limited to Sweden's youth.

Consider Sweden's first and (to date) only quantitative national survey of antisemitism, conducted in 2004 by Henrik Bachner and Jonas Ring.[54] Of 3,000 Swedes surveyed, 14 percent of those aged between 16 and 75 believe that Jews use the Holocaust for political or economic ends.[55] Moreover, 26 percent believe that there is a "Jewish influence" over the world's economy, and 15 percent regard that influence too great—this might explain why 25 percent of Swedes oppose electing a Jewish head of state.[56] Similar Austrian studies conducted years earlier reached comparable conclusions. There 19 percent believe Jews "had too much influence" in Austrian society and 28 percent agreed that Jews were "exploiting the Nazi Holocaust for their own purposes."[57] While these data may be less shocking coming from the birthplace of modern antisemitism, the fact that Sweden was no better than Austria—and perhaps even worse—gave pause.

Characterizing the results of this survey as "shameful," Göran Persson stated that while he was "not surprised that anti-Semitism exists in Sweden" he was "surprised" that it was so prevalent.[58] Heléne Lööw, former Director of the Living History Forum (previously the Living History Project), was similarly stunned by the pervasiveness of antisemitic beliefs throughout the political spectrum—a point to which we will return.[59]

One wonders whether the EU (and others) will continue to refer to the educational materials of Sweden as benchmarking "best practice" in the midst of limited evidence to support the claim. Having already received extensive praise, the Living History Forum is unlikely to receive much criticism for its apparent reverse pedagogical effects. Instead, as we will later note, one finds a greater receptiveness to the Forum's claims for additional revenues to remedy the prejudice that its follow-up study revealed.

If, despite its questionable success in confronting antisemitism, Sweden is still praised as a country to which other Member States might aspire, what confidence can we have in the EU and its other assessments and efforts? In answering this query, we turn to the dissimilar case of Austria, the first Member State to have received the EU's condemnation. Perhaps not co-incidentally, Austria's censure came in early 2000, on the heels of Sweden's first international Holocaust conference.

AUSTRIA

Jörg Haider's rise to prominence in the elections of 1999 (with 27 percent of the national vote) epitomized Austria's troubled relationship with its Nazi past and exposed the EU's limited grasp of the dilemmas posed by the appeal of his far right Freedom Party (*Freiheitliche Partei Österreichs*, FPÖ). Founded in 1956 by Anton Reinthaller, an early member of the Nazi Party (NSDAP), the FPÖ may be understood as an indirect successor to the Austrian NSDAP. Indeed, the party was later chaired by other Nazi notables like Hermann Neubacher, former mayor of Vienna during the Nazi era, and Lothar Rendulic, a former general in the *Wehrmacht* (Germany's armed services). Haider and his FPÖ colleagues so prided themselves on this ideological inheritance that their party's parliamentarian, Reinhard Gaugg, explained: NAZI stands for "new, attractive, single-minded and ingenuous."[60]

While several commentators have attributed the success of this anti-EU, anti-immigrant and nationalist party less to antisemitism than to the widespread disillusionment of Austrians with a corrupt political establish-ment,[61] most agree that the FPÖ had been marginal until Haider assumed leadership within it. Prior to his lead, the FPÖ posed little threat to Austria's "Grand Coalition" of Social Democrats and Conservatives from the People's Party, ÖVP. It garnered just 5 percent of the national vote in 1983. Then, in 1986, Haider brought it to 9.7 percent. In 1990 the party received 16.6 percent and, in 1994, 22.5 percent. Five years later, the FPÖ entered a governing coalition. According to the noted political scientist Andrei S. Mar-kovits, "the party's rapidly improving electoral fate under Haider. . .can only be described as meteorically successful."[62] This historical snapshot is evoked not to suggest that the FPÖ had no influence prior to Haider. Rather, whether in governing alone or in the grand coalition, the Social Democrats (SPÖ) had been Austria's perpetual power holders.

The SPÖ was Austria's catchall party, one that included former card-carrying Nazis—as when Chancellor Kreisky broke with the traditional coalition in 1970 and appointed four to ministerial posts immediately following his election. As an assimilated Jew who had spent the war years in Sweden, Bruno Kreisky appears to have been as captivated by the hegemony of Sweden's Social Democrats as he was openly disdainful of (other) Jews, whom he publicly vilified as "a repulsive people."[63] Interestingly, Kreisky referred to Sweden as his "second fatherland"[64] and after returning to Austria, he was determined to secure his own power and thus that of his Social Democratic party. That he enjoyed unprecedented and uninterrupted electoral triumphs as Austria's Chancellor from 1970 until his retirement, in 1983, is a testament to his shrewd political pragmatism.

According to the political scientist Walter Manoschek, Kreisky's early controversial cabinet appointments signalled to the FPÖ and others that the SPÖ was willing to conduct business with former Nazis as a purchase price for power.[65] "Since 1945, nothing like this had occurred in Austria or anywhere else in Europe."[66]

For those Jews who may have wondered whether Austria's election of a Jewish-born Social Democratic Federal Chancellor meant that the cradle of political antisemitism had truly changed—the answer was clear and disappointing. Kreisky's adamant defence of the youthful "political mistakes" of his (former) Nazi colleagues contrasted sharply with his efforts to destroy the human rights advocate Simon Wiesenthal, a man whose dedicated search for Nazi war criminals Kreisky took as a challenge to Austria's (and thus his own) image.[67] Moreover, it is likely that Kreisky calibrated his continued harassment of Wiesenthal to enhance his own standing as an Austrian patriot. Robert Wistrich explains that Kreisky acted as if his "prime duty was to exculpate Austrians from the burdens of their recent past. The fact that a Jewish chancellor was providing them with absolution from terrible sins, and with an alibi for ignoring the Nazi legacy, was doubtless reassuring to many of his fellow citizens and ultimately increased Kreisky's popularity."[68] Then, after Kreisky's retirement, the SPÖ partnered with the FPÖ (from 1983 through 1986), thus granting the far right party its first access to state power.

Austria's postwar political stability rested, in large measure, on the special knack of its political elites to avoid, rather than confront, Austria's Nazi past. This helps explain Kreisky's appeal, the catchall character of his Social Democratic party, and the FPÖ's earlier inability to garner more than 5 or 6 percent of the national vote. As Manoschek argues, all of Austria's political parties "were assiduous in integrating former Nazis into the mainstream," but the SPÖ later distinguished itself from its counterparts by being the first to admit that it "had made grave errors in this regard."[69] Thus the party acknowledged its partial responsibility for Haider's success.

As it has for other of Austria's popular politicians, antisemitism played no small part in Haider's appeal. Like Kreisky, Haider proved an adamant defender of Kurt Waldheim. Pandering to antisemitic prejudices worked. In one of its most notorious expressions, Haider was cheered by delegates in

Nazi regalia when, in 1986, he assumed his party's chair at the Innsbruck Convention.[70] One year later, he asked if it was necessary to have 140,000 unemployed and 180,000 immigrant workers in Austria, a query purposefully reminiscent of Nazi posters which read, "500,000 Unemployed—400,000 Jews: The solution is easy." Haider often repeated this remark. Yet, even when his rhetoric was not as antisemitic, his xenophobic and nationalist positions served as a constant reminder to Jews that their own position within Austria's symbolic political order was, at best, tenuous.[71]

Inflammatory to the core, one of Haider's most infamous statements came in 1991 during a local parliamentary debate in Carinthia, where he was then governor. He declared, "An orderly employment policy was carried out in the Third Reich, which the government in Vienna cannot manage."[72] The editorial staff of Austria's largest newspaper, *Kronen Zeitung,* defended this remark, stating that the Nazis had indeed created jobs and reduced unemployment. In addition, they printed a barrage of letters insisting that Haider was a victim of vindictive elites. While the uproar over Haider's comment led to his eventual resignation, it also propelled him into the political spotlight. In that glare, an infuriated and impenitent Haider called his critics "vermin" over whom "blue acid" should be thrown. The reference was unmistakable. The Nazis used Zyklon B (also known as "blue acid") to exterminate those whom they referred to as "vermin."[73]

Haider's notoriety emboldened his bigotry at home and facilitated his public relations stunts abroad, in an apparent effort to redeem his (international) image. Consider his choreographed visit to the United States Holocaust Museum in 1994. Emerging seemingly rehabilitated, Haider exclaimed, "We must do everything to enforce tolerance,"[74] a seemingly anodyne statement that is nonetheless concerning to critics of moral relativism. After all, for whom was Haider pleading tolerance? Less than two years later, he referred to the members of the *Waffen SS* as honourable men, deserving of respect. When asked if he was aware that the *Waffen SS* had been branded a criminal organization at Nuremberg, he replied that this did not interest him in the least.[75] Apparently no less disinterested in the existence of concentration camps, Haider characterized them as "penal camps," a term that implies that those who suffered within them were guilty and serving some kind of sentence.[76] Constrained by Austrian legislation outlawing Holocaust denial (see below), Haider often relied on a "soft form of Holocaust denial" within which the Nazis' crimes against the Jews are "questioned, trivialized, or whitewashed."[77]

Haider's views were clearly shared by those of his party as a whole. The FPÖ's ideological attachment to elements of the NSDP was evidenced, not least, by other prominent members. Consider, too, John Gudenus, a retired legislator who served in Austria's upper house. In 1995, he famously questioned the existence of gas chambers, a query that forced his resignation.[78] A decade later, an unrepentant Gudenus received a one-year suspended sentence when he called for the existence of gas chambers to be "seriously debated." In a country where the promotion of Nazi propaganda and Holocaust denial is a crime that is punishable by jail up to ten years, such queries are rarely gaffes. This was especially the case because his earlier comments followed the adoption of a 1992 amendment to the National Socialism Prohibition Law of 1945. Austria distinguished itself as the first country to have such a law. It is a distinction that the FPÖ (and not just Gudenus) has been loath to honor and one that took the EU until 2008 to emulate in the form of an all carrot, no stick, (non-binding) decision.[79]

By 1997, the FPÖ had already achieved more than any other far right European party by capturing 28 percent of the vote in Europe's parliamentary elections. Yet, despite this showing, no political umbrella group within this EU institution accepted the party as a member. The European Parliament's ostracism of the FPÖ that year foreshadowed the larger community's actions in response to the party's ascendance into Austria's governing coalition in 2000.[80]

When the FPÖ finished second (behind the SPÖ) in Austria's general elections in 1999, it established itself as the party of choice for those under 30. Haider, the "boutique fascist," was charismatic, young, deeply tanned, and fashionably androgynous.[81] While the FPÖ had always attracted more men than women, Haider's leadership increased this gender gap and the party's popularity soared among Austria's least educated. For the first time in the country's history, the FPÖ garnered greater support from working class voters than the SPÖ. This situation led Markovits to conclude that, "sociologically speaking," under Haider the FPÖ had assumed an Old Left party profile.[82]

With this influence and after months of negotiations, the FPÖ coalesced with the ÖVP to establish a new government on January 25, 2000—just as delegates were gathering in Stockholm for the international conference on the Holocaust. The Stockholm event was, in large measure, a political showcase of strategic opposition to parties like the FPÖ. Two days later, conference attendees marked the 55th anniversary of Auschwitz's liberation.

While Swedish political identity (and the country's international reputation) is forged in a virtually unquestioned faith in that state's unyielding commitment to social equality and humanitarian neutrality, Austrian identity is fastened to the belief that Austria was "the first victim" of Hitler's aggression. As Markovits and his colleague Anson Rabinbach explain: "The myth surrounding German occupation quickly yielded two results: first, it made the painful process of facing the past irrelevant, since Austria, like Czechoslovakia, Poland, and the rest of Europe, was victimized by German aggression. Second, it served to crystallize Austrian pride as a neutral, autonomous, and respected member of the family of nations."[83] The Allies first legitimized this standpoint in 1943 with their Moscow Declaration to ensure "a rapid and orderly transition from war to peace," the United States, United Kingdom, China and the Soviet Union obtained several commitments.[84] These included, but were not limited to, the prosecution of war criminals, the regulation of arms, and the recognition of Italian and Austrian sovereignty. For the Allies, insisting on Austria's autonomy was an indispensable means of ensuring Germany's weakness in a postwar world.[85]

Defining Austria as "the first free country to fall a victim to Hitlerite aggression," the Allies rendered Germany's annexation of Austria in 1938 "null and void." Embracing their "victim" status, Austrians typically overlooked the Declaration's later part: "Austria is reminded, however that she has a responsibility, which she cannot evade, for participation in the war at the side of Hitlerite Germany. . . ."[86]

This selective reading of the Declaration offered "Austrian politicians and journalists a useful handle on which to hang their attempt at collective exculpation from the Third Reich."[87] Three years after this Declaration, the government issued a collection of documents entitled, *Red-White-Red-Book: Justice for Austria*.[88] The publication would further distance Austria from responsibility for the Second World War and the Holocaust by promoting a national narrative that placed fascism and Nazism as aberrations to an otherwise positive past.[89]

By marked contrast, Austria's few surviving Jews functioned as embodied reminders of the country's shared responsibility for the Holocaust.[90] As such—"in the popular imagination"—they "remained a foreign entity that was persistently constructed as inherently antagonistic to the Austrian state."[91]

Whatever Austria's success in establishing itself as a victim of Nazism and denying its role as Hitler's enthusiastic accomplice, its political elite has been loath to contradict this goal to triumph at the ballot box. Austria's politicians have thus been rhetorically anti-Nazi for international purposes while paying domestic tributes to those who felt defeated by the war's outcome.[92] The reluctance to alienate Gentile voters helps explain why neither of Austria's two major parties publicly repudiated the FPÖ's propaganda (e.g., widely circulated posters calling for the election of "pure Austrians")—until one week prior to the 1999 election. By then, it was too late.

Shortly after the Freedom Party entered into Austria's coalition government with the ÖVP in early 2000, the EU's other fourteen Member States took the unprecedented step of working together to suspend links with Austria. Because Austria had not yet done anything in explicit violation of the Amsterdam Treaty, "the fourteen" took on Austria through "bilateral" sanctions, each claiming it acted independently to protect the common values of the EU. Pretence was abundant. Michael Gehler explains, "On the one hand, the attempt was made to feign that the measures had come from 'the Union'; on the other hand, in case of legal objections, only the bilateral level of the procedures was emphasized without making reference to the full EU."[93] The resulting sanctions entailed each of the fourteen discouraging cultural exchanges, limiting ambassadorial contact, and withdrawing support to Austrian candidates in international posts.

The European Parliament followed with a resolution that contained no explicit recognition of the FPÖ's antisemitism but condemned the "insulting xenophobic and racist statements issued by the leader of the Austrian Free-dom Party, Jörg Haider, over many years."[94] The Parliament's failure to overtly address the antisemitic dimensions of Haider and his party may be in keeping with this body's general reserve in combating antisemitism but it is nonetheless curious considering that it is antisemitism that rendered the FPÖ's populism distinctive.[95] The Parliament's resolution thus suggests that its objections to the party derived less from a concern with Austria's meager attempts to come to terms with its Nazi past than some suggest.[96]

In addition to not mentioning antisemitism, the resolution essentially confers to the Parliament the same task that the Commission had already bestowed to the Viennese-based EU Monitoring Centre in the 1997 regula-tion that established the watchdog agency. That is, the Parliament called on itself, together with the Commission and the Council, "to monitor develop-ments especially regarding racism and xenophobia in Austria and throughout Europe."[97] The resolution also stresses that the Commission will suspend any state that poses "a *serious and persistent* breach" of Article 6(1) of the Amsterdam Treaty.[98] That Article establishes the Community's commitment to "the principles of liberty, democracy, respect for human rights and fundamental freedoms, and the rule of law, principles which are common to the Member States."[99]

In turn, the European Commission also warned Austria that any violation of the Amsterdam Treaty by the new government could result in the coun-try's eventual expulsion from the EU, a possibility for any Member State that

violates its commitments. For the prominent European historian and com-
mentator Tony Judt, such actions did not imply "a strong and united European front against renascent fascism but rather a collective lack of confidence
in the EU's own mechanisms and rules of governance."[100] Perhaps, though
few Europeans even possess a sufficient awareness of the protections the EU
does offer. In 2004, nearly 20 percent of those Europeans surveyed claimed
they had never even heard of the European Commission[101] and the year prior
nearly two-thirds of Europeans were unaware that they even possessed rights
against discrimination, [102] a statistic that remains essentially unchanged.[103]
Worse yet, the apparent ignorance of these Europeans does not distinguish
them from those political elites charged with implementing the EU's anti-
discrimination policies. Few of these fully understand how the institutions
function and how the laws are executed[104]—a point to which we will return.

The EU's rebuke of Austria generated much criticism, not least from
Haider's most outspoken critics. Many of the country's leading intellectuals
came forward. They penned letters to opinion journals throughout Europe and
North America. They explained that they found it understandable that the
then fourteen EU Member States needed to emphasize their opposition to a
governing coalition that included Haider's party. Nonetheless, they also
feared that the isolation resulting from the EU's sanctions would "weaken
precisely those forces in Austrian politics and society which are in the
position to counter the possible dangers."[105] The concern that sanctions were
premature and even counterproductive was best expressed by Judt who
suggested they might strengthen the Austrian and European extreme right.[106]
Others disagreed. Markovits, for example, believed that a stern message
would have the intended effect of discouraging this outcome.[107]

The insistence of commentators that "Austria is a stable and democratic
country, entirely belonging to the European family" was impossible to
deny.[108] Ironically, even Haider's route to power proved consistent with
Austria's constitution and the spirit of Europe's as well.[109] Not only was
Haider democratically elected, in joining Austria's governing coalition he
signed a declaration with the leader of the ÖVP, Wolfgang Schuessel. The
declaration, entitled "Responsibility According to Austria—A Future in the
Heart of Europe," was released one day prior to their government's swearing
in—the same day the European Parliament issued its resolution.[110]

The above-mentioned declaration of "responsibility" appears to have
affirmed a commitment to "an Austria in which xenophobia, anti-Semitism
and racism have no place." It continues, "The Federal Government supports
the Charter of European Political Parties for a Non-Racist Society and
commits itself to work for the exemplary realisation of its fundamental

principles in Austria."[111] Furthermore, there was the matter of Austria's place within Europe: "The European Union's project for a broad, democratic and prosperous Europe, to which the Federal Government is unconditionally committed, is the best guarantee against a repetition of this darkest chapter of Austrian history."[112] Finally, the statement recognized "the singularity of the crimes of the Holocaust which are without precedent in history are an exhortation to permanent alertness against all forms of dictatorship and totalitarianism."[113]

While the document clearly reiterates the rhetorical foundation of Europe's founding, it failed to alleviate the apprehensions of Europe's leading politicians and prominent critics. Ironically, as in so many European documents, it included mention of the "dark period," Nazis and even the Holocaust—but with no express mention of Jews.[114]

For those attentive to political double-speak, the government's joint statement raised interesting contradictions. For instance, both parties affirmed the *federal government's* support of a Charter that neither signed. The Charter of European Political Parties for a Non-Racist Society prohibits political parties from pandering to prejudices related to race, ethnicity, national identity, and religion. Austria's prominent linguist, Ruth Wodak, contends that the parties' repeated reliance on the "federal government" to support EU values is no coincidence. She explains that the new government intentionally concealed its own refusal to move on seemingly progressive proposals by off-loading responsibility for their implementation on an amorphous federal bureaucracy.[115] Ponder, for instance, the federal government's commitment to a "self-scrutiny of the Nazi Socialist past." Given Haider's sizeable success in "dealing with the past," Wodak finds it telling that Nazi slave labor is the only issue to receive the document's direct consideration.[116]

It reads, "As regards the *question* of forced labour under the National Socialist regime, the Federal Government will endeavour to arrive at *objective* solutions in the light of the intermediate report by the Austrian commission of historians, while having regard to the primary responsibility of the companies concerned."[117] Wodak explains how this statement de-contextualizes demands pertaining to restitution: "restitution is restricted to slave labour, prisoners of war (the *Wehrmacht*), and the Sudeten Germans." She continues, "Jews, Roma and Sinti and other victims are not mentioned."[118] Moreover, "objectivity" dictates that *Austrian* historians alone can provide a solution to the "question" for "concerned parties."

For Austria's political insiders, the message was clear: "The values of the European Union are not to be taken seriously. We can fool Europe by paying lip service to these values, but then we'll continue as before."[119] The EU was not, however, entirely fooled. It did not take the statement at face value. Instead, it supported the "bi-lateral" sanctions. Thus, bowing to pressures from within Austria, the EU, and the international community, Haider resigned as head of the FPÖ in February of 2000, within months of his having brought his party into government. Despite his apparent absence from the governing table, Haider continued to call the shots through his loyal successor, Vice-Chancellor Susanne Riess-Passer. At the party's convention that May 2000, she put any doubts of this to rest by stating "The FPÖ is the party of Jörg Haider."[120] Thus, with Haider's influence hardly diminished, the EU was in no position to claim a victory and as tensions escalated, it took another seven months before the EU rescinded its censure.

In singling out Austria, the EU had to contend with compelling criticisms. First, although Austria had not violated any specific rules, the EU still imposed (however indirectly) its sanctions with limited discussion. Nonetheless, while a specific meeting to address Austria's new government was never called, representatives from all the Member States were in attendance at Persson's high-profile Stockholm conference. They were present just as Austria's government was forming. The fact that the members *immediately* called for action following this event reveals their desire to symbolically establish Europe's common values in opposition to the Holocaust.[121] Austria, it seems, offered this opportunity—though, again, not without several complications.

In the absence of explicit infringements and rigorous open debate, it was difficult for the EU to emphasize Austria's failings as a democracy, especially as Haider was unanimously elected the year before to serve on the EU Committee of the Regions, a talking shop consulted by the Commission, Parliament, and the Council of Ministers and one devoted to key areas of EU regional policy. That particular decision came without even a whisper of dissent. As the noted historian Richard Mitten explains, "The representatives of the very states which have sanctioned Austria for forming a government of which Haider is not a member, voted one year earlier to accept him personally into an official EU body."[122] This was not the only inconsistency of note.

Charges of hypocrisy abounded. For some, the crisis proved an "irresistible" opportunity for Europe's political actors "to score moral points off foreign 'fascists.'"[123] Critics noted that the EU took no similar steps against Italy in 1994 when Silvio Berlusconi's government went into coalition with the National Alliance, a party unapologetically descended from Mussolini's Fascist party.[124] Indeed, Italy distinguished itself as one of the few Member States in which the far right maintained a continuous parliamentary presence in the postwar period.

Nonetheless, others explained the limitations of what they believed were facile comparisons. For Markovits in particular, the more compelling comparison to be made is with the United States and the federal government's imposition of reform on deeply reluctant southern states.[125] Still, Europe was a changed polity in the aftermath of the Amsterdam Treaty of 1997, an agreement that established a seemingly crucial foundation for EU efforts to undermine discrimination.

If the EU was negligent for failing to respond to the earlier threat posed by Italy's National Alliance party, ignoring Haider would not remedy the mistake.[126] National sovereignty was also not at issue—Austria was as free to choose Haider as the EU and its Member States were free to express their disapproval. Ignoring this, some suggested that the sanctions rendered national sovereignty "meaningless."[127] In sum, opponents of the EU's response were apt to overstate the severity of Europe's public rebukes and the diplomatic sanctions.[128]

Ironically, the Viennese Jewish community's response to this controversy was often overlooked though Haider had cast a pall over it for over a decade. According to the cultural anthropologist Matti Bunzl, Europe's intervention empowered the community to take unprecedented action. In April 2000, the Association for Jewish University Students rallied against the new government and was joined by the Israelitische Kultusgemeinde (IKG), the central registry and official governing body of Vienna's Jewish community. "The demonstration marked the first time Vienna's Jewish community took to the streets to protest postwar Austria's political realities."[129]

One of the community's leaders, Martin Engelberg, made clear that Austria's EU membership provided a rhetorical fillip for Jewish protest. Months earlier, at an IKG meeting to address Jewish concerns about the new governing coalition, Engelberg assumed the *bema* of the city's main synagogue. As he stood before the congregants, he rendered the European dimension of the challenges and opportunities they faced explicit. He said "In ten years, there will be no Austrian currency, no foreign policy, and the domestic policy will be the domestic policy of the EU."[130] As Bunzl explains, this meant that Austria's Jews "were no longer the abject citizens of the Austrian nation-state" but instead "citizens of the New Europe."[131] Whether this "new Europe" will afford Austria's Jews (and others) the "potent protection against virulent nationalism and the threat of anti-Semitism" remains to be seen, but Bunzl demonstrates that the rhetoric of integrated Europe afforded Austria's Jews hope.[132]

Regardless of one's viewpoint, the EU was clearly in unchartered waters—its principle focus had never been the promotion of parliamentary democracy and human rights throughout Europe. That (official) task belongs to the Council of Europe (COE), Europe's oldest pan-European institution. Founded in 1949, the COE comprises over forty nation states that ratified the European Convention on Human Rights (ECHR) to affirm an express commitment to non-discrimination. Additionally, the case law generated by the Council's European Court of Human Rights (ECtHR) has been influential for the ECJ, not least because the latter Court has made clear that its chief focus has not been on human rights.

With Amsterdam newly in force and Austria not having expressly violated its provisions, Portugal's former Prime Minister and then EU President (Antonio Gutterres) requested assistance from the ECtHR and not the ECJ. This choice suggests that Judt was likely correct that Europe's elite had little confidence in EU institutions to determine whether the Union's controversial sanctions against Austria had served their stated purpose. Gutterres was eager for closure. Austria was threatening to veto the upcoming Nice Treaty that entailed institutional reform for the EU. There was also the European single currency to consider. Danish opponents of the euro pointed to the Austrian debacle to suggest that continuing integration undermined state sovereignty. Action became necessary.

The President of the ECtHR appointed "three wise men" to deliver a report concerning the FPÖ's political evolution and "the Austrian Government's commitment to the common European values, in particular concerning the rights of minorities, refugees and immigrants."[133] The men were notified that their conclusions would inform "the fourteen's" re-examination of their bilateral relations with Austria's government. The panel concluded that the FPÖ was "populist" and sometimes employed language that was xenophobic, racist, and "trivialized" Nazism. Yet, they also observed, "several political groupings using similar language in Europe."[134]

The report found Austria's record on minorities, refugees, and immigrants no worse than any other EU Member State. To the contrary, it suggested Austria might sometimes prove a positive example for others to follow. For instance, it "ratified the European Convention on Human Rights in 1958 and is the only country in which the Convention enjoys full constitutional rank."[135] In addition, Austria received the highest per capita number of refugees from the former Yugoslavia of any of the Member States, including those (like Sweden and Denmark) that profess a strong commitment to human rights.[136] Ironically these seemingly benevolent northern states frequently adopted the most draconian restrictions on immigrants, refugees, and asylum seekers in the midst of genocide in the Balkans.

Indeed, according to the UN High Commissioner for Refugees, in 1999, Austria ranked sixth in the EU, after Germany the United Kingdom, the Netherlands, Belgium, and France in accepting asylum seekers.[137] Notwithstanding the FPÖ's xenophobic rhetoric, the "three wise men" found that the new government did not deviate from the principles and substantive outcomes of its predecessors.[138]

Under the circumstances, the report concluded that *continuing* the sanctions would prove "counterproductive" and should thus end.[139] "The measures have already stirred up nationalist feelings in the country, as they have in some cases been wrongly understood as sanctions directed against Austrian citizens."[140]

In reaching this conclusion, the investigation was in no way condemnatory of "the fourteen" whose actions it praised for positively energizing civil society. The report credited them with heightening an awareness of crucial common European values and intensifying the Austrian Government's efforts to defend them. In moving forward, the report recommended the development of a Human Rights office that might enlarge the EUMC in Vienna. This suggestion was largely ignored until—as we will see—the EUMC endured a legitimacy crisis of its own in 2003. Days after the report's release, "the fourteen" informed Austria that they were lifting the sanctions.

CONCLUSION

Europe's short-lived censure of Austria may have served notice to some on the far right and demonstrated a rhetorical commitment to Europe's common values, but it also set an opaque and feeble precedent for future moves against discrimination. Recall that the final settlement came not from within the EU (e.g., by the ECJ, Council or Commission) but outside of it—from the COE. This may have been one of the EU's first highly publicized missteps against discrimination but it was not to be its last. According to Robert Wistrich, one of Europe's more astute observers, "Austria, it seems, has the misfortune of presenting a politically correct target—as well as a convenient deflection from uncomfortable realities."[141] One of these was (and would be) the persistent presence of a far right coalition within the European Parliament. Another challenge, and one readily apparent from Sweden and the other side of the political aisle, concerns the presumption of "best practices," despite evidence to the contrary. As the next chapter demonstrates, this myopic view wrecked havoc on and helped discredit the EUMC.

The Council's swift adoption in 2000 of a Race Directive was a way to signal the EU's commitment to fighting racism in the aftermath of the Haider debacle and the plethora of restrictions taken by the Member States to reduce migration.[142] As Mark Bell, a leading EU legal scholar explains: "Paradoxically, the restrictive trend of EU immigration policies acted as a catalyst for EU policy on combating racism."[143] He continues: "The perception of 'Fortress Europe' galvanized national and European civil society into transnational action for anti-racism policies at the EU level, so as to ameliorate the effects of immigration policies."[144] What consequences, if any, this directive and similar EU anti-discrimination measures might have for European Jews is the focus of our next section.

NOTES

1. David Saltiel, "Austria: Crossroads or Roadblock in a New Europe," *Mediterranean Quarterly* (Spring 2000): 44.

2. See Anton Pelinka, *Austria: Out of the Shadow of the Past* (Boulder, 1998), 131.

3. Allan Pred, *Even in Sweden: Racisms, racialized spaces and the popular geographical imagination* (Berkeley, Calif., 2000), 83, note 42.

4. Detlaf Jahn and Anne-Sofie Storsved, "Legitimacy through Referendum? The Nearly Successful Domino-Strategy of the EU-Referendums in Austria, Finland, Sweden and Norway," *West European Politics* 18, no. 4 (1995): 18–37.

5. Per Ahlmark, "Anti-Semitism, Anti-Americanism, Anti-Zionism: Is There a Connection?" (Paper presented at an International Conference at Yad Vashem, Jerusalem, 11 Aug. 2004), 7–8.

6. Anders Lange, et al., *Utsatthet för etnisk och politiskt relaterat våld hot m m, spridning av rasistisk och antirasistisk propaganda samt attityder till demokrati m m bland skolelever* (Stockholm, 1997).

7. Maciej Zaremba, "Rashygien i folkhemmet: 60,000 steriliserades," *Dagens Nyheter*, 20 Aug. 1997, 1.

8. Pred, *Even in Sweden*, Chapter 2, note 110.

9. Ibid.

10. See, e.g., Roger Cohen, "The (Not So) Neutrals of World War II," *New York Times*, 26 Jan. 1997; Warren Hoge, "The Swedish Dilemma: The Immigrant Ghetto," *New York Times*, 6 Oct. 1998.

11. Warren Hoge, "Sweden, Once the World's Conscience, Now Drifts," *New York Times*, 10 Aug. 1998, A4.

12. Ibid.

13. The editors of one of Sweden's leading evening papers, *Aftonbladet,* aptly illustrated this when, one week after 9/11, they declared, "The US is the greatest mass murderer of our time." This gall was not lost on Bruce Thornton who exclaimed, "this from the country that sat out World War II and traded with the *real* champion of mass murder, Nazi Germany." See Bruce S. Thornton, *Decline and Fall: Europe's Slow-motion Suicide* (New York, 2007), 125.

14. Stéphane Bruchfeld and Paul A. Levine, *Tell ye your children: A book about the Holocaust in Europe 1933–1945* (Stockholm, 1998), back cover, emphasis added.

15. The second conference, held in 2001, was entitled, "Combating Intolerance." The third, "Truth, Justice and Reconciliation," transpired the following year. The last such forum, "Preventing Genocide," convened in 2004. After considering the first conference, we will consider the last one below.

16. Malgorzata Pakier and Bo Stråth, "A European memory?" in *A European Memory? Contested Histories and Politics of Remembrance*, edited by Malgorzata Pakier and Bo Stråth (New York, 2010), 1–20.

17. "Declaration of the Stockholm International Forum on the Holocaust" (Delivered at Stockholm International Forum on Education, Remembrance and Research, Stockholm, 29 Jan. 2000).

18. Göran Persson, "Prime Minister Göran Persson Speech in the Riksdag" in *The Living History Project: Information on the Holocaust. An information packet* (Stockholm, 1998), 2.

19. Ibid., 1.

20. The Swedish Government, "Project Plan for the Living History Project" in *The Living History Project: Information on the Holocaust. An information packet* (Stockholm, 1998), 1, emphasis added.

21. Göran Persson, "Speech by Prime Minister Göran Persson at the Memorial Service for the Victims of the Holocaust" (Stockholm, 2004).

22. The Swedish Government, "Project Plan," 2.

23. Bruchfeld and Levine, *Tell ye your children*.

24. Ibid., 69.

25. Swedish Educational Broadcasting, *Förintelsen's Barn Sweden* (Stockholm, 1998).

26. Bruchfeld and Levine, *Tell ye your children*, 3.

27. Hans Lindberg, *Svensk flyktingpolitik under internationellt tryck 1936–1941, Sverige under andra världskriget* (Stockholm, 1973).

28. David Glück, Aaron Neuman, and Jacqueline Stare, *Sveriges judar, deras historia, tro och traditioner* (Stockholm, 1997).

29. Raul Hilberg, *The Destruction of the European Jews* (Chicago, 1961), 31.

30. Steven Koblik, David Mel Paul, and Margareta Paul, *The Stones Cry Out: Sweden's Response to the Persecution of the Jews, 1933–1945* (New York, 1988).

31. Ibid., 42, emphasis added.

32. Ibid., 50–1.

33. Ibid., 63.

34. Ingvar Svanberg and Mattias Tydén, *Tusen år av invandring* (Stockholm, 1992), 273; See also Svanberg and Tydén, *Sverige och förintelsen: debatt och dokument om Europas judar 1933–1945* (Stockholm, 1997).

35. Svanberg and Tydén, *Tusen år*, 275, author's translation.

36. Bruchfeld and Levine, *Tell ye your children*, 19.

37. Ibid., 23, emphasis added.

38. Quoted in Denis Nordin, *A Swedish Dilemma: A Liberal European Nation's Struggle with Racism and Xenophobia, 1990–2000* (Lanham, Md., 2005), 19.

39. Bruchfeld and Levine, *Tell ye your children*, 19, emphasis added.

40. Koblik, Paul, and Paul, *The Stones*, 23.

41. Maria-Pia Boëthius, *Heder och samvete: Sverige och andra världskriget* (Stockholm, 1992), 119, author's translation.

42. Bruchfeld and Levine, *Tell ye your children*, 4.

43. Nordin, *A Swedish Dilemma*, 19.

44. "Sweden followed Nazi marriage laws," *The Local: Swedish News in English,*

4 Apr. 2006.

45. Bruchfeld and Levine, *Tell ye your children*, 7.

46. Lindberg, *Svensk flyktingpolitik*.

47. See, for instance, Henrik Bachner, *Återkomsten: Antisemitism i Sverige efter 1945* (Stockholm, 2000); Lena Berggren, *Nationell Upplysning: Drag i den svenska Antisemitismens idéhistoria* (Stockholm, 1999); and Svanberg and Tydén, *Tusen År*.

48. European Commission, "A European Union Contribution to the OSCE anti-Semitism Conference" (Paper presented at the Organization for Security and Cooperation in Europe anti-Semitism Conference, Vienna, 19–20 June 2003), 8.

49. European Union Monitoring Centre on Racism and Xenophobia, *Racism and Xenophobia in the EU Member States—Trends, Developments and Good Practice* (Vienna, 2004), 17; European Union Agency for Fundamental Rights, *Anti-Semitism: Summary overview of the situation in the European Union 2001–2008* (Vienna, 2009), 13.

50. Jonas Ring and Scarlett Morgantau, *Anti-Semitic, Homophobic, Islamophobic and Xenophobic Tendencies among the Young* (Stockholm, 2004)

51. Ibid., 68.

52. Quoted in Richard Mitten, "Austria all Black and Blue: Jörg Haider, the European Sactions, and the Political Crisis in Austria" in *The Haider Phenomenon in Austria*, edited by Ruth Wodak and Anton Pelinka (New Brunswick, N.J., 2002), 190.

53. Ring and Morgantau, *Anti-Semitic*, 70.

54. Henrik Bachner and Jonas Ring, *Antisemitiska attityder och föreställningar i Sverige* (Stockholm, 2006).

55. Ibid., 9.

56. Ibid.

57. Mitten, "Austria," 190.

58. TT/, Persson: "Attitudes to Jews 'Shameful,'" *The Local: Sweden's News in English*, 14 Mar. 2006.

59. "Swedish anti-Semitism Revealed," *The Local: Swedish News in English*, 14 Mar. 2006.

60. Quoted in Walter Manoschek, "FPÖ, ÖVP, and Austria's Nazi Past" in *The Haider Phenomenon in Austria*, 8.

61. See, e.g., Hans-Georg, "Haider's Revolution or the Future Has Just Begun" in *Austria in the European Union*, edited by Günter Bischof, Anton Pelinka and Michael Gehler (New Brunswick, 2002), 118–43.

62. Andrei S. Markovits, "Austrian Exceptionalism: Haider, the European Union, the Austrian Past and Present" in *The Haider Phenomenon in Austria*, 116.

63. Robert S. Wistrich, *A Lethal Obsession: Anti-Semitism from Antiquity to the Global Jihad* (New York, 2010), 224.

64. Wistrich, *Anti-Zionism and Antisemitism: The Case of Bruno Kreisky* (Jerusalem, 2007), 9.

65. Manoschek, "FPÖ," 7.

66. Wistrich, *A Lethal Obsession,* 222.

67. Tom Segev, *Simon Wiesenthal: The Life and Legends* (New York, 2010).

68. Wistrich, *A Lethal Obsession*, 226.

69. Manoschek, "FPÖ," 13.

70. David Art, "Reacting to the Radical Right: Lessons from Germany and Austria," *Party Politics* 13, no. 3 (2007): 341–42.

71. Matti Bunzl, "Austrian Zionism and the Jews of the New Europe," *Jewish Social Studies* 9, no. 2 (2003): 162.

72. Anti-Defamation League, *Joerg Haider: The Rise of an Austrian Extreme Rightist* (2004), http://archive.adl.org/backgrounders/joerg_haider.html.
73. Jacques Le Rider, "Diary of a Trip to Vienna: Jörg Haider's Austria," in *Euroskepticism*, edited by Ronald Tiersky (Lanham, Md., 2001), 240.
74. Anti-Defamation League, *Joerg Haider.*
75. Ibid.
76. Melanie A. Sully, *The Haider Phenomenon, East European monographs no. 484* (Boulder, Colo., 1997), 68.
77. Robert S. Wistrich, "Haider and His Critics," *Commentary* 109, no. 4 (2000): 31.
78. Manoschek, "FPÖ," 7.
79. Decisions are the legal equivalent of advice given to governments. They are the weakest instruments in the EU's legislative arsenal. See note 14 in the next chapter for the distinctions between decisions, directives and regulations.
80. Anton Pelinka, "The FPÖ in the European Context," in *The Haider Phenomenon in Austria*, 215.
81. Andrei S. Markovits, "Austrian Exceptionalism: Haider, the European Union, the Austrian Past and Present," in *The Haider Phenomenon in Austria*, 115.
82. Ibid., 116.
83. Andrei S. Markovits and Anson Rabinbach, "Why Waldheim Won in Austria." *Dissent* 33 (1986): 409.
84. Joint Four-Nation Declaration. 1943. The Moscow Conference: October 1943. Yale Law School: The Avalon Project.
85. Richard Mitten, "Austria all Black and Blue," 232.
86. Joint Four-Nation Declaration. The Moscow Conference: October 1943. Yale Law School: The Avalon Project.
87. Robert Knight, "'Neutrality,' not Sympathy: Jews in Post-War Austria" in *Austrians and Jews in the Twentieth Century*, edited by Robert. S. Wistrich (New York, 1992), 224.
88. Austria's Chancellory. *Red-white-red-book; descriptions, documents and proofs to the antecedents and history of the occupation of Austria, from official sources* (Vienna, 1947).
89. Stefan Berger, "Remembering the Second World War in Western Europe: 1945–2005" in *A European Memory? Contested Histories and Politics of Remembrance*, edited by Małgorzata Pakier and Bo Stråth (New York, 2010), 119–36.
90. Richard Mitten, "Jews and Other Victims: The 'Jewish Questions' and Discourses of Victimhood in Postwar Austria" in *Austria in the European Union*, edited by Günter Bischof, Anton Pelinka, and Michael Gehler (Brunswick, N.J., 2002), 223–70.
91. Bunzl, "Austrian Zionism," 162.
92. Anton Pelinka, *Austria: Out of the Shadow of the Past* (Boulder, Colo., 1998), 20.
93. Michael Gehler, "'Preventive Hammer Blow' or Boomerang: The EU 'Sanction' Measures against Austria 2000" in *Austria in the European Union*, 188.
94. European Parliament resolution on the result of the legislative elections in Austria and the proposal to form a coalition government between the ÖVP (Austrian People's Party) and the FPÖ (Austrian Freedom Party), OJ C 309, 03.02.2000, 87–88.
95. Anton Pelinka, "The FPÖ in the European Context," 223.
96. See, for instance, Markovits, "Austrian Exceptionalism," 97.
97. Council Regulation (EC) No 1035/97 of 2 June 1997 establishing a European

Monitoring Centre on Racism and Xenophobia, OJ C 194, 25.06.1997.

98. Ibid., emphasis added.

99. Treaty of Amsterdam amending the Treaty on European Union, the Treaties Establishing the European Communities and Certain Related Acts, OJ C 340, 10.11.1997.

100. Tony Judt, "Tale from the Vienna Woods," *New York Review of Books*, 23 Mar. 2000, 8–9.

101. European Commission, *Eurobarometer 61*. (Brussels, 2004).

102. European Commission, *Eurobarometer 57: Executive Summary—Discrimination in Europe* (Brussels, 2003), 4.

103. European Commission, *Special Eurobarometer 296—Discrimination in the European Union: Perceptions, Experiences and Attitudes* (Brussels, 2008), 22; Compare with European Commission, *EU Citizenship Report 2010: Dismantling the obstacles to EU citizens' rights* (Brussels, 2010).

104. R. Amy Elman, *Sexual Equality in an Integrated Europe: Virtual Equality* (New York, 2007).

105. Luc Bondy, "Austria and Europe," *New York Review of Books*, 27 Apr. 2000, 7.

106. Judt, "Tale from the Vienna Woods," 8–9.

107. Markovits, "Austrian Exceptionalism," 97.

108. Bondy, "Austria and Europe," 7.

109. Wistrich, "Haider and His Critics," 34.

110. Ruth Wodak provides a full translation of this document in her appendix. See Ruth Wodak, "Discourse and Politics: The Rhetoric of Exclusion" in *The Haider Phenomenon in Austria*, 33–58, for appendix see 52–8.

111. Quoted in ibid., 52.

112. Quoted in ibid., 54.

113. Ibid.

114. Ibid., 33–58. Nearly fifteen years later, the EU's official statement for International Holocaust Memorial Day made no mention of Jews. See Chapter Five.

115. Ibid., 43.

116. Ibid., 44.

117. Quoted in ibid., 54–5, emphasis added.

118. Ibid., 44–5.

119. Pelinka, "The FPÖ in the European Context," 227.

120. Quoted in Manoschek, "FPÖ," 153.

121. Jenny Wüstenberg and David Art, "Using the Past in the Nazi Successor States from 1945 to the Present," *Annals of the American Academy* (2008): 82–3.

122. Mitten, "Austria," 2.

123. Judt, "Tale from the Vienna Woods," 8–9.

124. Andrew Nagorski, "The Politics of Guilt: Austria's Bigot, Europe's Burden," *Foreign Affairs* 79 no. 3 (2000):18–22.

125. Markovits, "Austrian Exceptionalism."

126. Ibid.

127. Saltiel, "Austria: Crossroads," 52.

128. Marc Marjé Howard, "Can Populism Be Suppressed in a Democracy? Austria, Germany, and the European Union," *East European Politics and Societies* 14, no. 2 (2000): 31.

129. Bunzl, "Austrian Zionism," 166.

130. Quoted in Ibid.

131. Ibid.

132. Ibid., 167.

133. Martti Ahtisaari, Jochen Frowein, and Marcelino Orejo. *Report by Martti Ahtisaari, Jochen Frowein and Marcelino Orejo* (Strasbourg, 2000), 1. Mr. Ahtisaari was Finland's former president. The second appointee was Mr. Frowein, a German attorney and former Vice-President of the Council of Europe's Commission of Human Rights. Not least, Mr. Oreja, was a Spanish former foreign minister and prior member of the European Commission.

134. Ibid., 27.

135. Ibid., 5.

136. Ibid., 10.

137. Ibid., 11.

138. Ibid., 14.

139. Ibid., 33.

140. Ibid.

141. Wistrich, "Haider and His Critics," 34.

142. Mark Bell, *Anti-Discrimination Law and the European Union* (Oxford, 2004), 74.

143 Ibid., 67.

144. Ibid.

CHAPTER THREE

The 2000 Directives and Additional EU Remedies

The Race Directive, regarded by many as a "milestone" and "essential tool" in the fight against race and ethnic based discrimination,[1] provided no clarity about the meaning its central terms. According to the Directive's sixth recital, this was intentional. The Directive states: "The European Union rejects theories which attempt to determine the existence of separate human races and acknowledges that the very concept (of race) is a social construction."[2] Emphasizing "race's" social construction might exempt us from believing "in its reality in some scientific or objective sense,"[3] but there is more to consider. This section explores the EU's reticence to define the prejudices its Directive seeks to counter and considers the consequences of this legislation and an additional directive (the Framework Directive)[4] passed the same year. To this end, it examines the EU's own assessments of its more recent efforts to counter antisemitism in the aftermath of 9/11.

Whatever the benefits of the EU's initial reluctance to define either race or ethnicity, overlooking the ways in which ignoring and/or refusing to identify group traits can leave a people vulnerable and/or without a cherished aspect of their own identity.[5] In particular, Jews (like Blacks) have sometimes been willing to accept the historically poisonous terminology of race within legal contexts that allow protection.

Consider *Shaare Tefila Congregation v. Cobb*, a 1987 United States Supreme Court case that involved the desecration of a synagogue, a growing occurrence in Europe. In the United States, congregants insisted that although they are not a racially distinct group, they should be entitled to protection against racial discrimination because others treat them as though they are distinctive.[6] The Supreme Court agreed. In its unanimous decision, it held that American Jews are, like other ethnic groups, protected from racial discrimination, a decision that preceded the UN's 1998 resolution recognizing antisemitism as a form of racism.[7]

For the U.S. legal scholar Martha Minow, the Jews in *Shaare Tefila Congregation v. Cobb* "demonstrated their reluctance to have a difference identified in a way that they themselves could not control, while simultaneously expressing their desire for protection against having that difference assigned to them by others."[8] She further notes: "To gain this protection, the petitioners had to identify themselves through the very category they rejected."[9] Minow calls this conundrum "the dilemma of difference" and though her focus has been on historically oppressed groups within the United States; her insights extend to Jews throughout Europe as well.[10]

For Europe's Jews, the Race Directive provides redress only in those circumstances where there is the willingness and ability to demonstrate that anti-Jewish bias derives from others treating Jews as if they are racially (or ethnically) distinct. Legal precedent for this may derive, in part, from the UN's recognition that antisemitism is a form of racism. However, when the European Parliament first called upon the Council in 1993 to adopt a Directive to combat racism, xenophobia, antisemitism and "other forms of religious intolerance," it became clear that their rubric of racism did not include discrimination against Jews. For these MEPs, Jews were a religious group and not an ethnic or racial one,[11] a position in keeping with a resistance among Jews to racial distinctions and one informed by antisemitism's protean character.

After the Holocaust, the social stigma attached to explicit racism meant even the most flagrant antisemites began concealing their racist intent.[12] In consequence, antisemitism is increasingly manifest as a political antagonism against those connected to Israel (the Jewish state) through blood, conviction or faith.

Ironically, however, the particular omission of religion from the Race Directive poses a challenge for those Jews who observe that the prejudice they encounter involves the often-inextricable combination of racial, cultural, ethnic, and religious discrimination. By contrast, for the EU and most Member States, "anti-discrimination law conceives of claimants as possessing a singular set of social characteristics: for example, inclusion in the category of 'black' or inclusion in the category 'woman,'" each in ways that exclude the other.[13] Despite recent efforts to resolve the legal chasms posed by "intersectionality" and "multi-discrimination," Jews have been largely absent from these discussions. With limited attention to the ways in which Jews are a people whose identity and resulting discrimination rests at the intersections of ethnicity, race, culture, and religion, future remedies fastened to even the most seemingly progressive "racial" discourse are likely to fall short.

Against the background of these concerns, one might wonder if the Framework Directive offers Jews better redress.[14] That directive, also passed in 2000, prohibits "any direct or indirect discrimination based on religion or belief, disability, age or sexual orientation."[15] Although this legislation stipulates protection for observant (i.e., religious) Jews, it comes no closer to providing recognition for the multiple discriminations they and others suffer. For instance, the Directive offers little to secular Jews and/or those unable to demonstrate that the discrimination against them was religious in character. Moreover, while the Race Directive extends protection to the public arenas of education, housing, and access to other goods and services, the Framework Directive covers only the labor market.

With different discriminations deriving varied levels of protection (i.e., only race and gender discrimination are recognized *outside employment*), a hierarchy of oppression has developed. The EU's institutionalization of this hierarchy is clear when one considers, for example, that only the Race Directive (and not the Framework Directive) requires that Member States establish a body for the promotion of equal treatment. This division of responsibilities and the compound character of anti-Jewish prejudice provide a partial explanation for the relatively limited attention extended by the EU to the problem of antisemitism.

That the EU's adoption of the Charter of Fundamental Rights failed to correct this uneven course is unsurprising given its narrow scope. The Charter does not establish any new power or task for the Community or the Union, "or modify powers and tasks defined in the Treaties."[16] Indeed, the Commission itself has no general power to intervene against fundamental rights violations. Passed in December 2000 (and incorporated into the Treaty years later), its objective is to make more visible to the Union's citizens the fundamental rights that they *already enjoy* at the European level. For Europe's Jews (and other minorities), whose history with basic rights has often been short lived, disputed and/or denied, imagining that rights are to be enjoyed (as opposed to protected) can be a challenge.

In the summer of 2001, months after the EU celebrated its two new Directives and its Fundamental Rights Charter, antisemitism reached new depths under the guise of anti-racism at the UN's World Conference Against Racism (WCAR).[17] The EU helped sponsor this event, often referred to by its location, Durban, South Africa. Antisemitic leaflets littered the proceedings. Alongside anti-racist materials, the notorious antisemitic fabrication, *The Protocols of Zion*, was on sale in the exhibition tent. Flyers of Jews in Nazi regalia were commonplace as were those with favourable depictions of Hitler. There was one in which Hitler asks, "What if I had Won?" Beneath this query, the subheading, of "bad things" states, "I wouldn't have allowed the making of the new beetle." More ominously, beneath the assertion of "good things" it states, "there would be no Israel and no Palestinian's blood shed."[18]

"In the new Manichean vision born of 'anti-racism,'" Wistrich explains, "Jewish victims have been mutated into 'executioners'; the right to self-defense is turned into an act of 'imperial' expansionism, while the existence of a Jewish state itself becomes a questionable manifestation of exclusivity and 'racist' particularism."[19] That many antisemites now gather beneath the banner of anti-racism to denounce the right of Jews (alone) to have their own state warrants its own extended book, but it may be naïve to expect that Europeans who previously denied Jews a right to have their lives would then support Jewish self-determination in the form of statehood.

Outside the UN conference hall, at one point, thousands of South African Muslim demonstrators marched with banners proclaiming, "Hitler should have finished the job"—a slogan gaining prominence across the Member States in an effort to affirm, downplay, or deny the Nazi slaughter of Europe's Jews.[20] This poisonous ideology proved so invasive that the Jewish Centre in Durban was forced to close its doors, the U.S. and Israeli delegations left in disgust, and many of those Jews still in attendance expressed concern for their own safety.

Joëlle Fiss, then chair of the European Union of Jewish Students (EUJS), chronicled the WCAR in a diary she maintained throughout her stay. In an organized session on antisemitism stormed by dozens of hecklers, she and her peers were called murderers of Palestinians and told, "You don't belong to the human race."[21] Worse, none of the UN officials bothered to intervene, much less condemn this cascade of cruelties. And, while most of the self-identified anti-racists did not participate in this virtual pogrom, they also did nothing to prevent it. Years later, Fiss writes that because of Durban, "today's younger generation of Diaspora Jews no longer suffered from any existential threat"—Durban served to remind them "hatred can surface with no prior notice."[22] Rather than expose the antisemitic outbursts of this conference, many political activists and journalists depicted these as legitimate criticisms of "Zionism" and Israel. Sweden's "anti-racist" magazine, *Mana*, not only epitomized this bias, its subsequent "Hate Israel" headlines cast suicide bombers in a favourable light.[23]

A couple of days after this virulently antisemitic UN "human rights" conference concluded, nineteen Muslim men flew two planes into the World Trade Center in New York, and yet, like the Orwellian rhetoric that reigned at Durban, rumours spread that this murderous attack was a "Zionist plot." Allegedly, the lives of several thousand Jews had been spared because they were tipped off to stay at home that day.[24] Books such as Thierry Meyssan's

9/11: L'Effroyable imposture (9/11: The big lie)[25] and Andreas von Bülow's *Die CIA und der 11. September* (The CIA and September 11)[26] climbed European best-sellers lists by insinuating a covert connection between the Israeli Mossad and the U.S. Central Intelligence Agency (CIA), agencies alleged to have orchestrated the event. Neither author was a noted "extremist." Meyssan, an openly gay activist, worked with the centre-left to expose France's far right. Von Bülow was also respected; a former state-secretary in the German Federal Ministry of Defence, he had served as an SPD member of the German parliament from 1969 to 1994. Von Bülow's book became a *Der Spiegel* best seller and Meyssan's work enjoyed even greater commercial success. After only two weeks on France's best-seller list, *The Big Lie* became the highest-grossing book in Europe in a single week.

The powerful impact of such antisemitic propaganda cannot be discounted and its success is, in part, evidenced in the surveys that reveal a public willing to believe that Israel was behind 9/11. When, for instance, Swedes were asked whether "Israel was involved in the 9/11 terror attacks on the U.S.," respondents were evenly divided between those (47%) who rejected this statement completely and others who (at 46%) had no opinion.[27]

It appears to have mattered little that the man who commandeered one of the planes, the Egyptian Mohammad Atta, coordinated the attack from Germany, where he had lived since 1992. What may have mattered less is that the original (1993) World Trade Center bombers confessed that they targeted New York because of its large Jewish population. As one insisted, "Most of the people working in the World Trade Centre are Jews."[28]

Nonetheless, the anti-Jewish dimensions of the 9/11 slaughters have been variously ignored and/or denied. Even the U.S. *9/11 Commission Report* makes no mention of Osama Bin Laden's antisemitism though it does note Mohamed Atta's virulent hatred of Jews and his admiration of Hitler. The failure to address Bin Laden's animus against Jews is especially startling as he made it clear that his antisemitism was the central purpose of his attacks.[29] Such jihadi Jew-hating explains why a growing number of National Socialists, like Britain's David Myatt, have proposed alliances with Islamic militants. In "The National-Socialist Guide to Understanding Islam," Myatt insists on a "genuine and worthwhile cooperation" with Muslims who "are also fighting the dishonor which is Zionism."[30]

Protean in quality, antisemitism adopts the idiom of its day.[31] With the emergence of nation-states and the diminishing power of Europe's churches in the nineteenth and twentieth centuries, the religious demonology of Jews of past morphed into a nationalistic "science" that cast Jews as a distinctive race during the Third Reich. Lest one forget, as Europe's first state to sponsor an institute for the study of racial science in Europe, Sweden played no minor role.

What scientific appeal antisemitism now lacks it has gained in transnational currency, tempting both left leaning cosmopolitans and religiously observant communities through slick references to Jews as the material and moral culprits of globalization.[32] This perspective helps explains why, in 2002, a representative survey of Germans found that 20 percent considered Jews responsible for the world's major conflicts.[33] A year later, a European-wide survey concerning war in Iraq revealed that 59 percent of its respondents ranked the Jewish state—Israel—first among nations as a threat to world peace.[34] With these attitudes seemingly unhindered by the EU's earlier efforts to combat racism, one may wonder about the promise of its efforts.

THE EU POST–9/11

In the immediate wake of September 11, 2001, EU officials were primarily concerned that hostility toward Islam would increase but shortly after implementing a monitoring process throughout the Member States that resulted in three separate reports, the EUMC found it necessary to carry out a detailed investigation into the prevalence of antisemitism.[35] The Centre recognized that while "Jews are rather well integrated economically, socially and culturally in the Member States. . .the attacks in New York and Washington on September 11 and the conflict in the Middle East have contributed to an atmosphere in Europe, which gives latent anti-Semitism and hate and incitement a new strength and power of seduction."[36] The Centre also observed, "Anti-Semitic conspiracy theories are spreading over the Internet, which provides a cheap vehicle for the distribution of hate."[37]

Interestingly, the Centre's *final* report on antisemitism conspicuously excludes reference to the role that the UN's Durban conference (against racism) may have played in promoting this bigotry. Although researchers in the draft report stressed this connection,[38] the Centre expunged it from the final report.[39] This was not, as we will note, the only difference to emerge between these documents.

As one of the only Member States to maintain meticulous records on antisemitism through frequent studies of general political attitudes, Germany offers crucial insights into the escalation of anti-Jewish sentiment throughout the EU—particularly after 9/11. The Sigmund Freud Institute in Frankfurt found a significant increase in those who agreed with the statement: "I can understand well that some people feel unpleasant about Jews." In 1999, 20 percent agreed with the statement. In 2002, 36 percent did.[40] Reports of antisemitic violence also increased during this period, from 18 offences in 2001 to 28 the following year.[41]

Antisemitism was, clearly, in no way limited to Germany; there were increased physical attacks on Jewish property—and individuals—throughout Europe. In Denmark, Islamic political organizations distributed Durban-like flyers from websites containing comments like "And kill them, wherever you find them, and expel them from where they expel you."[42] The parallels between such statements and those aired by Nazi propagandists throughout the Middle East and North Africa are impossible to ignore. In July of 1942, "Kill the Jews Before They Kill You" was the program title of Voice of Free Arabism.[43] As we will later note, similar statements gained prominence in Sweden.

In France, a country with Europe's largest Muslim and Jewish populations (at 5 million and 600,000 respectively), researchers found what press reports had documented sporadically for months prior; hundreds of antisemitic incidents including synagogue burnings and physical assaults. Such conditions led France's Chief Rabbi to acknowledge that because it was dangerous for Jewish men to wear their skullcaps, it would be safer if they not do so in public. Others throughout the EU came to similar conclusions.[44]

In November 2001, then president-elect of the European Jewish Congress (EJC), Michel Friedman, told the German press that antisemitism was a priority issue for his organization and, in fearing increased collaboration between Islamic militants and right-wing extremists, efforts against antisemitism could no longer be effectively waged on a national level.[45] As the sole representative body of democratically elected Jewish communities throughout Europe, the EJC had worked with Member States, EU institutions and the COE to represent the common interests and concerns of approximately 2.5 million Jews across Europe since 1986. Twenty-five years later, transnational mobilization was more than a lofty ambition—it became a political necessity.

The Commission had reached a similar conclusion the same month but it emphasized, instead, the persistence of racist crimes and the rapid dissemination of Holocaust denial through the internet, including within those Member States that had restrictions against it.[46] By exploiting the legislative differences between the Member States, the body expressed concern that Holocaust deniers and others had the upper hand. Though it offered no concrete data on either "forum shopping" or the transnational dimensions of these crimes, the Commission stressed the need to both reinforce punitive measures and enhance judicial cooperation throughout the EU.[47]

To accomplish a more integrated approach to Holocaust denial while balancing the Union's commitments to free expression, the Commission proposed a Framework Decision.[48] After a turbulent and lengthy legislative history in which several states expressed their reservations about that Decision's compatibility with their domestic protections for free speech,[49] the legislation passed in 2008 (see below). The following year the EJC, which until then had only one office in Paris, opened its Brussels bureau. As we will now note, the intervening years were anything but kind.

On the heels of the Commission's proposed legislation to combat antisemitic propaganda, young men physically assaulted the Chief Rabbi in Brussels, the heart of the EU. This December event marked a terrible conclusion to 2001, an already appalling year. Within months synagogues, kosher restaurants, and Jewish bookshops throughout the city were set on fire and shattered by air rifles.[50] That spring, world Jewish leaders held emergency talks in Brussels to consider how best to stem such violence. According to the EJC, there were 300 anti-Jewish attacks across Europe in the three weeks that led up to its April 2002 meeting. Not only was a clear condemnation of these attacks needed from above, a more thorough account of antisemitism was in order.

Such was the incendiary climate that prompted the EU to emphasize its renewed commitment to fight antisemitism at a June 2003 OSCE Vienna meeting concerning antisemitism. After declaring that the EU "approaches anti-Semitism and racism as *interrelated* phenomena," the European Commission belatedly acknowledged, "Anti-Semitism is a painful part of our history. . .that requires certain *specific* approaches. The measures instigated and the lessons learnt from our experience of anti-Semitism have ensured that strategies to combat anti-Semitism will continue to form an important component of the EU's approach to combating racism, xenophobia and related intolerance."[51]

More specifically, the Commission insisted its "comprehensive and cohesive approach to tackling racism and anti-Semitism" would entail "mainstreaming" anti-racism efforts throughout the EU's programs and policies.[52] Thus, rather than thoroughly exploring or fundamentally changing its existing efforts, it chose a strategy that seemed to enhance its commitment to current positions.

In the EU, the notion of mainstreaming first extended to gender, not race, equality. According to the Commission, mainstreaming is a policy to promote "equality between men and women in all activities and policies at all levels," a goal that was reaffirmed by all Member States in their ratification of the 1997 Treaty of Amsterdam. Article 3(2) of that Treaty calls on Member

States to "eliminate inequalities and promote equality between women and men *in all the activities of the Union.*"[53] Later attempts to promote the principle of racial equality through mainstreaming similarly suggest that such efforts must be integrated and implemented throughout all Member State and EU institutions rather than just within offices established (at each of these levels) to promote equal opportunities. In sum, social justice became everyone's task but no one's responsibility.[54]

The same year that the Commission began "mainstreaming" its method for combating racism, its annual report on equality and non-discrimination neither mentioned the EUMC nor its efforts to address anti-Jewish discrimination.[55] This was a stunning omission considering that the EUMC had just initiated its first EU-wide study of antisemitism (see below) and annual reports are supposed to highlight the year's important developments. Nonetheless, this outcome was hardly surprising. Robert Wistrich, who had addressed the OSCE conference in 2003, detected reluctance among the Europeans "to deal with anti-Semitism as a distinct issue, preferring to address it under the general heading of racism, xenophobia discrimination."[56] Regarding the remarks of the Dutch chair, he noted "a barely concealed desire to get through the business with the Jews so that more 'politically correct' issues of countering racial discrimination and Islamophobia could be dealt with."[57] This desire to simply move on to other matters is far from unique. By 2005, the EUMC's own reports on "racist violence" contained no mention of antisemitism,[58] an odd omission considering that such violence accounted for a sizeable portion of crime in some states (see below). Moreover, weeks before the release of its report, the Centre had adopted a "working definition of antisemitism."

Despite the EU's earlier assurance that the prejudices of racism and antisemitism are *interrelated* phenomena, a chasm again emerged between them. Whether this resulted from the EU's sensitivities to antisemitism and a related belief that this bigotry requires a "specific" approach (in light of Europe's past) is doubtful, but this possibility is worth considering.

When the EU initiated its first EU-wide examination of antisemitism in 2002, the EUMC solicited national reports from each of the (then 15) Member States through its own Racism and Xenophobia Information Network (RAXEN). These reports covered a one-month period (May 15– June 15, 2002) and were then supplemented and synthesized into a European context by the internationally renowned Centre for Research on Antisemitism (CRA) in Berlin.

When the study appeared at last complete in October of 2003, researchers from the CRA observed that, in many cases, violent attacks against Jews arose from virulent anti-Zionism that cut across the entire political spectrum.[59] While researchers in both Austria and Sweden revealed similar findings about the broad appeal of antisemitism, those from the CRA also concluded that "the anti-Semitic incidents in the monitoring period were committed above all either by right-wing extremists or radical Islamists or young Muslims mostly of Arab descent, who are often themselves potential victims of exclusion and racism."[60]

The CRA's focus on Muslim perpetrators and anti-Zionist organizations so unsettled the EUMC that it, in turn, responded by repeatedly requesting that the researchers alter their conclusions. In a letter to the CRA, the EU Centre pleaded for the removal of "divisive statements." It explained: "The EUMC must be seen bringing groups together, not as acting divisively."[61] However, in its efforts to conceal the identity of those who had been persecuting Jews, the Centre failed to grasp the divisiveness of its own actions. In addition to implying that the social exclusion of one group (e.g., young Muslim men) exempts it from responsibility for bigotry against another (e.g., Jews), the Centre's patronizing posture (of tolerance of some antisemitism) undermines Muslims by imposing a moral and political segregation on them. In consequence, "politicians and policymakers. . .too afraid to confront us Muslims with our illusions" actually perpetuate "injustice and human suffering."[62] Manfred Gerstenfeld identifies this elitist behaviour as "humanitarian racism," a "mirror image of the white supremacist variety." He explains, "Humanitarian racists consider—usually without saying so explicitly—that only white people can be fully responsible for their actions. . . ."[63] What results from this bias, however unintentionally, is a confusion between victims and the criminals who persecute them.

When the researchers in Berlin refused to accommodate the EUMC's political agenda, the EU's Centre shelved the report in November of 2003, insisting that it was methodologically unsound. In particular, the EUMC contended that the period covered in the investigation was too short and that the report was never intended for publication. Infuriated by these misrepresentations, the CRA's researchers went to the press. News of the decision to suppress the report first surfaced in the *Financial Times* and the subsequent public outcry included a swift call from several MEPs for the report's release.[64] The World Jewish Congress (WJC) and Jewish communities throughout Europe, in turn, released the original "draft" of the report on the Internet that December. Denmark's TV2 also posted the report on its European news website. In the open air of debate, the report and its attempted suppression pointed to two crucial and inextricably linked facts: the unpleasant reality that exists for Jews on the streets of Europe and the EUMC's reluctance to confront it.[65]

In early 2004, the EUMC was embarrassed and on the defensive. Its director (Beate Winkler) and chair (Bob Purkiss) issued a joint press release that acknowledged their diminished credibility. Noting that the scandal "presents the strongest challenge for the EUMC since its foundation," they promised a more thorough report by March of 2004.[66] That final report would, they said; differ from the initial draft in three ways. First, it would provide data through October of 2003, extending the original research by three months. Second, it would include the perceptions of Jewish leaders across the region and, last, it would contain recommendations for addressing antisemitism in Europe.

The final, lengthier EUMC study often reiterated and expounded upon the main points of the initial one. Nevertheless, in presenting the European Parliament with an abbreviated version of the report, Winkler issued a widely circulated statement that contradicted the final report's key findings. That statement read:

> Although it is not easy to generalize, the largest group [of perpetrators] appears to be young, disaffected white European[s], often stimulated by extreme right wing groups. A further source of antisemitism in some countries was young people of North African Muslim extraction. Traditionally, antisemitic groups on the extreme right played a part in stirring up opinion.[67]

While the data do not discount the involvement of far right perpetrators, they nonetheless suggest that, in some states, this segment reduced their involvement with antisemitism. In France, for example, researchers found that "the percentage of anti-Semitic violence attributable to the extreme-right was only 9 percent in 2002 (against 14 percent in 2001 and 68 percent in 1994)."[68]

Faced with Winkler's misleading summary of the final report, the CRA researcher Victor Weitzel acknowledged that the EUMC had consistently manipulated his findings to conform to this and other shibboleths. When, for example, he insisted on the "need to monitor the inflammatory language being used by the Arab press in Europe," Weitzel said, "This was changed to the 'minority press.'"[69]

The European Jewish Congress went further with its criticisms. It again accused the EU's watchdog agency of distorting the report's findings: "We cannot let it be said that the majority of anti-Semitic incidents come from young, disaffected white men. This is in complete contradiction with the facts recorded by the police."[70]

With most attention understandably focused on the suppression of the initial report and the Centre's misleading synopsis of the second, the differences between the reports can seem minor. They are not. To wit, the draft described a small public gathering of approximately 100 people in Stockholm to counter antisemitism and anti-Muslim prejudice. It was disrupted by between 100–150 demonstrators, shouting, "Kill the Jews!" and "We'll blow you up!" The draft report states, "Some attackers also went around aggressively asking people if they were Jewish. *It should be pointed out that there were also many young Swedish extreme left-wing people amongst the most aggressive participants.*"[71] While the draft thus emphasized the role of Sweden's extreme left-wing in fostering such violence, this (italicized) reference to it was deleted from the second report.[72] This was not the only omission to surface in the final report. Again, the case of Sweden is instructive. In the first report, the authors note that, in Sweden, the EU network "found no example of politicians speaking up against anti-Semitism." They continue, "The leftist party. . .announced a campaign against racism, mentioning xenophobia, homophobia and other forms of racism, but not anti-Semitism."[73] If one interprets the failure of Sweden's politicians to tackle antisemitism as a tacit acceptance of it, the EUMC and other EU institutions risk being similarly charged.

In deleting mention of the established left's failure to confront the problem of antisemitism and excluding evidence of its role in fomenting it, the EUMC's final report (and related statement) implies that opposition to the far right is, alone, a sufficient response to antisemitism. This position has special appeal to a left that "sees itself as immune from anti-Semitism, which it considers the exclusive province in the xenophobic right."[74] Yet, by ignoring the lefts' long-standing antisemitism, the EU's Centre obscured evidence that some of the greatest threats to Jews come from the left side of Europe's political aisle and its deepening alliances with others from across the political spectrum. Hannah Arendt's insights from the last century haunt us in this one, as when she observed that antisemitic sloganeering was a means by which an otherwise dissimilar collection of groups—Catholic clergy, the army, aristocracy, the haute-bourgeoisie, and the mob—cohered.[75]

In the midst of the controversy and related denials concerning antisemitism, it was clear that the EUMC was pursuing, whether half-heartedly or full-throttle, efforts against a prejudice it had yet to understand and never defined. According to Dina Porat, head of the Stephen Roth Institute at Tel Aviv University, this was not unusual. International bodies had long neglected their responsibility to address directly, much less define, antisemitism. Even after World War II, the term was absent from numerous treaties and agreements. Porat explains, "after the war all nations wished to start afresh by avoiding the pin pointing of former culprits or victims, and the former allies did not wish to insinuate that their war effort was in any way motivated by Jewish demands."[76] Nonetheless, without an adequate (read: explicit) definition of antisemitism, the EUMC acknowledged that its own pledge to monitor and analyze this prejudice had come up short. Only nine of the fifteen national (RAXEN) reports based their evaluation of antisemitism on an explicit definition of it and, of these, none used the same one. This methodology made thoughtful comparisons of the Member States virtually impossible.

Following a 2004 OSCE meeting in Berlin that forcefully condemned all manifestations of antisemitism, the EUMC invited Jewish organizations to assist it in formulating a "Working Definition of Antisemitism." Soon after, the EU's Centre presented the subsequent "working definition" to participants at a follow-up conference in Cordoba where it was immediately received, though *informally* adopted—a matter to which we will return. The definition reads: "Antisemitism is a certain perception of Jews, which may be expressed as hatred toward Jews. Rhetorical and physical manifestations of antisemitism are directed toward Jewish or non-Jewish individuals and/or their property, toward Jewish community institutions and religious facilities."[77]

In addition to informally adopting this working definition, the EUMC incorporated it into a single-page document that also provided "a practical guide for identifying incidents, collecting data, and supporting the implementation and enforcement of legislation dealing with antisemitism."[78] The Centre's guide makes clear that manifestations of antisemitism "could also target the state of Israel, conceived as a Jewish collectivity." It continues, "Antisemitism frequently charges Jews with conspiring to harm humanity, and it is often used to blame Jews for 'why things go wrong.'"[79]

The Centre provided examples for clarification, focusing first on the expression of this prejudice in public life more generally and then on the antisemitic idiom specifically targeting Israel. The Centre's guide notes that "holding Jews collectively responsible for actions in the state of Israel" and presenting caricatures of contemporary Israeli policy that draw comparisons to Nazi policy is antisemitic.[80] The guide explains that when criticism of Israel is similar to that levelled against any other country, such criticism cannot be regarded as antisemitic.[81] However, it also acknowledges that the application of "double standards" for Israel (i.e., standards not expected of any other democratic state) and/or "denying the Jewish people their right to self-determination (e.g., by claiming that the existence of a state of Israel is a racist endeavour)" is antisemitic. Per Ahlmark, Sweden's former deputy Prime Minister, bluntly explains, "If anti-Semites once aspired to live in a world rid of Jews, today anti-Semitism's goal is apparently a world cleansed of the Jewish state."[82] That is, antisemitism has moved from *Judenrein* to *Judenstaatrein*.

Expecting the working definition might oblige Member States to combat antisemitism,[83] Jewish organizations and various state actors (perhaps especially those based outside of Europe) hailed its 2005 adoption. For instance, when the U.S. Congress passed the Global Anti-Semitism Review Act of 2004, in response to rising antisemitism worldwide, it mandated a one-time investigation into antisemitic acts. The authors of that report then adopted the EUMC's working definition for their research.[84] When Canadian Members of Parliament passed a resolution to combat antisemitism in 2007, they too cited the EUMC's authoritative definition, as did the Australian Online Hate Prevention Institute (OHPI) when it was established in 2012 to combat cyber hate.

Nonetheless, in 2008, the American Jewish Committee's European Forum on Anti-Semitism in Berlin found that "many Jewish community and NGO leaders involved in monitoring antisemitism remain(ed) unaware of the working definition or have been hampered by its existence to date only in English."[85] This might explain why Britain's All-Party Parliamentary Inquiry into Anti-Semitism appears to be one of the only European groups to have taken the definition to heart. To enhance the European public's knowledge of this definition, the American Jewish Committee (AJC) translated it into over two dozen languages and made it readily available through its Forum website. One would have thought that this was the responsibility of the EU's Centre and not a non-governmental organization, particularly one based outside of the EU.

Rather than translate the working definition for adoption throughout the Member States, the EUMC disseminated its English-only text principally to its Racism and Xenophobia Information Network (RAXEN) and did little else to promote it. So much for the EU's purported efforts to mainstream efforts against discrimination. In fact, following its adoption, the working definition of antisemitism appears in none of the EUMC's annual reports. This is an especially telling omission as the Centre insists its reports are designed to offer an overview of important advances against discrimination. The fact that the Centre neither translated nor advanced the working definition underscores the limitations of its *informal* adoption and the

Centre's ambivalence to see it implemented. In 2013, the official agency withdrew reference to the document from its website. (See Appendix for the text of the document).

According to an official for the Fundamental Rights Agency (the FRA, formerly known as the EUMC), the definition was merely "a work in progress."[86] As such, it required testing and further comment from throughout the Union before its practical use and effectiveness could be established and supported fully.[87] Yet, by repeatedly ignoring the working definition of antisemitism, its effectiveness could not be determined. Moreover, it is difficult to remedy a violation that has not been defined, much less acknowledged. Conditions deteriorated further when, in 2006, the EUMC (together with the Commission and the Austrian government) scheduled a conference entitled "Racism, Xenophobia and the Media." European officials responded with "regret" after Israel's ambassador to Austria refused to attend upon finding that references to antisemitism (as a form of racism) had been deleted from the initial conference program.[88] Once again, the EUMC had passed on an opportunity to share the working definition. Instead EU officials extended a last-minute invitation to a board member from the European Jewish Center for Information after Israeli diplomats stated their concern that there were no Jewish panellists.[89]

When the EUMC was renamed the European Union Agency for Fundamental Rights (FRA) in 2007, it came no closer to acknowledging, much less revising and/or supporting the working definition of antisemitism—a shortcoming that persists. Consider the FRA's brief summary overview of antisemitism in 2009[90] and, again, in 2011.[91] While in both reports the FRA laments that most Member States have neither official nor unofficial statistics on antisemitic incidents because their authorities have yet to define the problem, it nowhere mentions the EUMC's earlier adoption of a working definition that might resolve this conundrum. In consequence, the FRA revisits—without the least irony—the methodological quandaries that stem from reporting a problem one has yet to define.

Far from being discredited for its anaemic research as well as its inconsistent and dispiriting response to antisemitism, the EUMC's powers were expanded in the midst of the controversies that surrounded it. Less than a month after the storm over Centre's suppression of its first report on antisemitism, the European Council met for its routine (2003) December summit. Once assembled, the various heads of state and governments together stressed "the importance of human rights data collection and analysis" and agreed "to extend its mandate to make it a Human Rights Agency."[92]

It was as if the Centre's publicized shortcomings provided a momentum that the Council earlier lacked when, in its summit in 1999, it had considered the establishment of a human rights oriented agency.[93] In early 2004, the Commission launched a "public consultation" and shortly thereafter concluded that the Centre's remit would include additional responsibilities and fundamental rights.[94] This expansion marked a bold move—especially given the EU was on the cusp of enlarging by another ten Member States that May.[95] Fallout over the Centre's 2003 reports on antisemitism and its later deletion of Jewish voices from its 2006 conference program on racism led neither to recriminations nor a reconsideration of the Centre's revised and expanded remit.

The FRA has the same objectives and essential tasks (collecting and analyzing data and providing advice and enhanced consciousness via reports and opinions) as the EUMC, but these have been extended from "racism, xenophobia and related intolerance" (e.g., antisemitism) to involve all of the "thematic areas" (through 2012) covered by the Charter of Fundamental Rights. These are:

- discrimination based on sex, race or ethnic origin, religion, or belief, disability, age or sexual orientation, and against persons belonging to minorities;
- compensation of victims, prevention of crime and related aspects relevant to the security of citizens;
- protection of children, including the rights of the child;
- immigration and integration of migrants;
- asylum;
- visa and border control;
- participation in the Union's democratic functioning;
- human rights issues relating to the information society; and
- access to efficient and independent justice

In addition, the Council claims it reaffirmed the EU's commitment to the Charter through the 2008 Framework Decision by requesting that the same (criminal racist and antisemitic) behaviour constitutes a common offence in all Member States.[96] Following the Decision's passage, the FRA embraced the legislation as "an important tool for the EU-wide condemnation of racist and xenophobic crime," but expressed disappointment that it does not cover crimes against "other vulnerable social groups, such as the LGBT community and the disabled."[97]

Article 1(1) of the Decision stipulates four *intentional* transgressions that Member States are expected to punish. These are:

(a) publicly inciting to violence or hatred directed against a group of persons or a member of such a group defined by reference to race, colour, religion, descent or national or ethnic origin;

(b) the commission of an act referred to in point (a) by public dissemination or distribution of tracts, pictures or other material;

(c) publicly condoning, denying or grossly trivialising crimes of genocide, crimes against humanity and war crimes as defined in Articles 6, 7 and 8 of the Statute of the International Criminal Court, directed against a group of persons or a member of such a group defined by reference to race, colour, religion, descent or national or ethnic origin when the conduct is carried out in a manner likely to incite to violence or hatred against such a group or a member of such a group;

(d) publicly condoning, denying or grossly trivialising the crimes defined in Article 6 of the Charter of the International Military Tribunal appended to the London Agreement of 8 August 1945, directed against a group of persons or a member of such a group defined by reference to race, colour, religion, descent or national or ethnic origin when the conduct is carried out in a manner likely to incite to violence or hatred against such a group or a member of such a group.

The Military Tribunal noted in the last paragraph (d) of this statement pertains to Nuremberg and thus seems to directly reference the *Shoah*. For this reason, one notes an express condemnation of Holocaust denial and revisionism. Those found in violation of the Decision are to receive no less than one year and no more than three years of imprisonment for their wrongdoings, a penalty intended to be effective, proportionate and dissuasive. Member States had until 2010 to adopt the legislation and an analysis of its limited results came in late 2013. The continued discussion helps explain why.

To accommodate the persistent concerns of several Member States about its over-reach and potential challenges to free expression, the Decision allowed for several significant exceptions. First, the Decision "is *limited to* combating *particularly serious forms of racism and xenophobia* by means of criminal law" (Paragraph 6, emphasis added). Hence Article 1(2) explicitly permits Member States to criminalize only conduct "which is either carried out in a manner *likely* to disturb public order or which is threatening, abusive or insulting" (emphasis added). With no clear EU guidelines on what constitutes "public order," "insulting," "abusive," or "threatening," Laurent Pech suggests national authorities are "free to decide when, for instance, a statement denying the Holocaust becomes likely to disturb the public order."[98] This, he warns, might lead to "the distressing possibility of a person being extradited for having engaged in lawful conduct in his/her country of residence but constitutive of a racist offense in another EU member State."[99]

As states step in where transnational institutions fear to tread, the EU's Framework Decision could exacerbate the legislative disparities it sought to remedy. Additionally, Laurent and others worry that the Decision's restrictions on free expression could lead to greater ones tomorrow,[100] a concern better known as the known as the "slippery slope effect."

Perhaps the most contentious and significant exception turns on Article 7(2):

> This Framework Decision shall not have the effect of requiring Member States to take measures in contradiction to fundamental principles relating to freedom of association and freedom of expression, in particular freedom of the press and the freedom of expression in other media as they result from constitutional traditions or rules governing the rights and responsibilities of, and the procedural guarantees for, the press or other media where these rules relate to the determination or limitation of liability.[101]

Considering that all Member States have legislation outlawing hate speech and a majority of them "have long considered that the fundamental right to freedom of expression *inter alia* precludes the criminalization of Holocaust denial per se,"[102] it is unlikely their governments will incorporate, much less implement, those provisions of the Decision that might afford Jews further protection. Indeed, three years after the Decision was adopted, an impatient Moshe Kantor, the President of the European Jewish Congress (EJC), insisted that not one Member State adopted reforms in keeping with this ambition.[103] Considering that the heaviest tolls for Europe's toleration of hate speech and genocide have been born by its Jewish communities, Kantor's frustration is warranted.

While time and space constraints preclude a more comprehensive view of the Framework Decision, it is sufficient to stress that the above-noted "escape clause" and enduring conflicts over freedom's requirements, suggest that Member States will continue to enjoy considerable latitude in implementing the Decision's ambiguous aspirations. According to Jenia Iontcheva Turner, this may have been the Council's intent from the start. That is, rather than an effective sanction in the arsenal against antisemitism and other prejudices, the Framework Decision may best be understood as a "tool to express the Union's commitment to human rights and equal treatment."[104] Are these separate? If Turner is correct and "the EU is using the Framework Decision primarily to make a statement about the values for which it stands,"[105] the question is: how do we measure its commitment to these values? The fact that we are often asked to accept (and even appreciate) the "expressive function" of laws independent of their other measureable consequences suggests the impossibility of knowing what the consequences are. However, it might also suggest a reluctance to learn more about these outcomes. More to the point, on the matter of antisemitism, one is often struck by the disinclination to dig deep.

CONCLUSION

In the absence of any marked success for its initial responsibilities, it is ironic that the newly established FRA is expected to enhance awareness of all fundamental rights and counter discrimination in an even larger EU. Announcement of the FRA's 2007 opening thus left the EJC sceptical. It cautioned:

> Critics have argued that the new agency is too similar to the Council of Europe, which lacked the authority to enforce decisions that tracked human rights issues in Europe, and Jewish groups have expressed concern that the Fundamental Rights Agency would spend less time focusing on anti-Semitism than did its predecessor.[106]

Two years later, in 2009, an FRA official whose previous work addressed antisemitism confirmed this concern by suggesting that the Agency's expanded charges might, in part, account for its relative neglect of anti-semitism.[107] This view is hardly compelling given that, in the EUMC, Jewish concerns were rarely, if ever, paramount.

When, in 2008, the EU pursued its largest and most comprehensive survey of 23,500 people from various immigrant and ethnic groups throughout the then-twenty-seven Member States on the extent and nature of, and appropriate response to, discrimination—Jews were once again excluded. This time the FRA stated their numbers were too small.[108] According to the Agency, (minority) groups had to reach an overall size of at least 5 percent of the population to obtain sufficiency for the random sampling required for this ambitious survey.[109] This particular explanation and survey design appears reasonable until one realizes that, in some Member States (e.g., in France and Sweden's south), a hefty fraction of racist acts are directed against Jews.[110] Indeed, in 2009 alone, more than half of all the hate crimes in Malmö (Sweden) were antisemitic. That year, over 400 such acts were registered with that city's authorities,[111] as elsewhere and in the past—many of these were perpetrated by Arabs and Muslim immigrants.

When then considering antisemitism's emergence within Europe's Muslim communities, in 2009, the FRA asserts that it is likely "directly linked with the Israeli-Palestinian conflict."[112] By proffering this (as yet untested) explanation, the Agency helps perpetuate the widespread myth that antisemitism among Muslims results from (recent) Mideast conflicts—a position that ignores both this community's collaborationist past and its persistent antisemitism, both of which preceded Israel's founding.[113] No wonder then that the FRA concedes that "some research evidence" exists to suggest that Muslim antisemitism has also "acquired a presence independent of underlying national conflicts."[114] Nonetheless, the FRA's explanatory emphasis on "the conflict"—with no effort taken to historicize it—implies a retreat from the EUMC's 2005 position. That view, as expressed in its working definition of antisemitism, recognizes that the demonization of Israel and Zionism frequently masks Jew hating.[115] Moreover, holding Jews throughout the world collectively responsible for Israel's action(s) is antisemitic.[116]

Although the FRA appears to have more recently departed from its emphasis on "the conflict," its findings from a recent summary overview of antisemitism throughout the EU remain discouraging. There are two reasons for concern. First the Agency concedes that it is still unable to offer sufficient and comparable data covering the period from 2001–2009. Second, it nonetheless found "available official data indicate an increase in anti-Semitic activity in 2009."[117]

By early 2010, the FRA publicly recognized the need for comparable data on the experiences and views of Jews throughout Europe and proposed an entirely separate and more focused study on the extent to which they are subject to discrimination and harassment. Through an online questionnaire directed toward self-identified Jewish men and women, the Agency endeavors to capture the "experiences and perceptions of discrimination. . .in key areas of social life." These include "education, housing, health, and employment as well as experiences and perceptions of hate crimes and hate speech, and in addition, awareness of available legal remedies."[118]

Yet, unlike its comprehensive 2008 survey of minorities throughout all of the then twenty-seven Member States that excluded Jews, the 2013 survey covered only eight Member States (i.e., Belgium, France, Germany, Greece, Hungary, Latvia, Sweden, and the United Kingdom). These, the Agency avers, were "selected based on the estimated size of their Jewish populations and/or to ensure coverage of various regions of the EU, to reflect historical developments and their effects on the communities they surveyed."[119] The methodological underpinnings of this survey, while ambiguous, could mark a move in the right direction. However, the past suggests there might be few reasons to be especially sanguine about the political consequences of this work. The initial findings, presented during the 4th International Conference of the Global Forum for Combatting Antisemitism (28–30 May 2013), provided an ominous glimpse into current conditions and the future for Jews in Europe. In addition to enduring antisemitic harassment and discrimination, between 40 and 50% of respondents from three of the eight Member States (Belgium, France, and Hungary) stated they had considered emigrating from their country of residence because they did not feel safe.[120]

NOTES

1. See, for instance, European Network Against Racism (ENAR), *Response of the European Network Against Racism (ENAR)—Five year report on the application of the Directive* (Brussels, 2005), 2.

2. Council Directive 2000/43/EC of 29 June 2000 implementing the principle of equal treatment between persons irrespective of racial or ethnic origin. OJ L 180, 19.07.2000.

3. Geoff Eley, "The Trouble with 'Race': Migrancy, Cultural Difference, and the Remaking of Europe" in *After the Nazi Racial State: Difference and Democracy in Germany and Europe*, edited by Rita C. K. Chin (Ann Arbor, Mich., 2009), 175.

4. Council Directive 2000/78/EC of 27 November 2000 establishing a general framework for equal treatment in employment and occupation. OJ L 303, 02.12.2000.

5. Martha Minow, "The Supreme Court, 1986 Term: Forward: Justice Engendered," *Harvard Law Review* 101, no. 1 (1987): 12.

6. Naomi W. Cohen, "Shaare Tefila Congregation v. Cobb: A New Departure in American Jewish Defense?," *Jewish History* 3 no. 1 (1988): 95–108.

7. United Nations General Assembly Resolution 623 Measures to combat racial discrimination, xenophobia and related intolerance, 9 Dec. 1998, point 17.

8. Minow, "Supreme Court," 20.

9. Ibid.

10. See also Minow, *Making All the Difference: Inclusion, Exclusion, and American Law* (Ithaca, N.Y., 1990); Like Minow, Kenneth L. Marcus is a legal scholar concerned with the challenges that attend the dilemma of difference in the United States. But, in addition to focusing most on (U.S.) Jews, he offers a compelling account of how Britain's Supreme Court endeavored to resolve the dilemma of difference. See his *Jewish Identity and Civil Rights in America* (New York, 2010), Chapter 1.

11. Erica Howard, *The EU Race Directive: Developing the Protection against Racial Discrimination within the EU* (London, 2010), 98.

12. Marcus, *Jewish Identity*, 11.

13. Sarah Hannett, "Equality at the Intersections: The Legislative and Judicial Failure to Tackle Multiple Discrimination," *Oxford Journal of Legal Studies* 23, no. 1 (2003): 66.

14. This legislation, Council Directive 2000/78/EC. OJ L 303, 2.12.00, is not to be

confused with the Framework Decision. That was adopted by the Council in 2008 and will be later addressed. Such decisions generally function as advice given to governments while directives are binding and introduce broad objectives that call on Member States to implement them, each in its own way. Regulations are also binding in law and Member States automatically incorporate them into their national legal systems. To reiterate, directives are binding and allow states flexibility in their implementation.

15. Ibid., Para 12.

16. Charter of Fundamental Rights of the European Union, OJ C 83, 30.03.2010, Article 51, 2.

17. Robert S. Wistrich, *A Lethal Obsession. Anti-Semitism from Antiquity to the Global Jihad* (New York: 2010), Chapter 13; Malka Marcovich, *Les Nations Désunies: Comment l'ONU enterre les Droits de l'Homme* (Paris, 2008).

18. For this image and analyses, see Coordination Française pour le Lobby Européen des Femmes, and Mouvement pour l'Abolition de la Pornographie et de toutes formes de violences sexuelles et discrimination sexistes, *Durban et après* (Paris: 2001), 16. Additional examples may be found through ICARE, Internet Centre Anti-racism Europe (www.icare.to).

19. Robert S. Wistrich, *European Anti-Semitism Reinvents Itself* (New York, 2005), 42.

20. Abraham Cooper, "Hate Hits the Mainstream," *Los Angeles Times*, 16 Dec. 2001.

21. Joëlle Fiss, *The Durban Diaries: What really happened at the UN Conference against racism in Durban (2001)* (New York and Brussels, 2008), online http://www.ajc.org/atf/cf/%7B42d75369-d582-4380-8395-d25925b85eaf%7D/THEDURBANDIARIES.PDF, 24–5.

22. Ibid., 43.

23. Henrik Bachner, "Political Cultures of Denial? Antisemitism in Sweden and Scandinavia" in *Politics and Resentment: Antisemitism and Counter-Cosmopolitanism in the European Union*, edited by Lars Rensmann and Julius H. Schoeps (Leiden and Boston, 2010), 346.

24. Joseph Lelyveld, "All Suicide Bombers are Not Alike," *New York Times Magazine*, 28 Oct. 2001, 53.

25. Thierry Meyssan, *9/11: The Big Lie* (London, 2002).

26. Andreas von Bülow, *Die CIA und der 11* (Munich, 2003).

27. Bachner, "Political Cultures of Denial?," 349.

28. Quoted in Matthias Küntzel, *Jihad and Jew-Hatred: Islamism, Nazism and the Roots of 9/11* (New York, 2007), 128.

29. Ibid., 132–33.

30. Quoted in Mark Weitzman, *Magical Logic: Globalization, Conspiracy Theory, and the Shoah* (Posen Papers in Contemporary Antisemitism, no. 10, Jerusalem, 2008), 9–10.

31. Daniel Goldhagen, "The Globalization of Anti-Semitism" (paper read at Montreal International Conference on Global Anti-Semitism, Montreal, 14–16 Mar. 2004).

32. Ibid.

33. Küntzel, *Jihad and Jew-Hatred*, 145.

34. European Commission, *Eurobarometer 151: Iraq and Peace in the World*. (Brussels, 2003), 78.

35. Werner Bergman and Juliane Wetzel, *Manifestations of anti-Semitism in the*

European Union: First Synthesis Report (Vienna, 2003), Preface.

36. Ibid.

37. Ibid. See also the Online Hate Prevention Institute (http://ohpi.org.au), an organization dedicated to monitoring and combating the now exponential increase of antisemitism throughout myriad social networks (e.g., Facebook, Twitter, and YouTube). What was previously limited to graffiti in niche publications, bathroom stalls, and city walls is so widely disseminated that Andre Oboler (the founder of the Online Hate Prevention Institute) warns, "the danger is not so much that people might read content inspired by anti-Semitism, but rather that they might be induced to accept it as a valid point of view, a fact of life, or something with which one may or may not agree, but not something whose dissemination one should oppose." See *Presentation of the Final Document of the Sub-Committee of Inquiry into Anti-Semitism* (Rome 2011), 304.

38. Ibid., 16.

39. Compare Bergman and Wetzel's *First Synthesis Report* with European Monitoring Centre on Racism and Xenophobia, *Manifestations of Anti-semitism in the EU 2002–2003: Based on information by the National Focal Points of the EUMC—RAXEN Information Network* (Vienna, 2004).

40. Ibid., 64.

41. Ibid., 16.

42. Bergman and Wetzel, *First Synthesis Report*, 45.

43. Jeffrey Herf, *Nazi Propaganda for the Arab World* (Ann Arbor, Mich., 2009), 125.

44. Years later, in 2012, local community leaders and the Israeli embassy in Copenhagen warned Jews there against wearing their kippot or any other religious symbols. Moreover, Israelis were advised against speaking Hebrew loudly, even in areas they perceived as safe. See Maureen Shamee, "Jews In Copenhagen Are Being Warned Not To Wear Religious Symbols In Public," *European Jewish Press*, 13 Dec. 2012, online http://www.ejpress.org/article/64006. Martin Schain observes, "there is probably no synagogue in Europe that is not plagued by problems of security, and many have locked doors, with admission only by appointment" (e-mail message to author, 12 Feb. 2012).

45. Manfred Gerstenfeld, *Europe's Crumbling Myths: The Post-Holocaust Origins of Today's Anti-Semitism* (Jerusalem, 2003), 17–18.

46. At that point, ten of the then twenty-seven Member States had such prohibitions. They were Austria, Belgium, the Czech Republic, France, Germany, Lithuania, Poland, Romania, Slovakia and Spain. See Michael Whine, "Expanding Holocaust Denial and Legislation Against It" in *Extreme Speech and Democracy*, edited by Ivan Hare and James Weinstein (Oxford, 2009), 538–56.

47. Jenia Iontcheva Turner, "The Expressive Dimension of EU Criminal Law," *American Journal of Comparative Law* 60, no. 2 (2012): 555–84.

48. Proposal for a Council Framework Decision on Combating Racism and Xenophobia, COM (2001), 664 final.

49. Mark Bell, *Racism and Equality in the European Union* (Oxford, 2008), Chapter 8; Erik Bleich, *The Freedom to Be Racist?: How the United States and Europe Struggle to Preserve Freedom and Combat Racism* (New York, 2011); Turner, "Expressive Dimension of EU Criminal Law."

50. Bergman and Wetzel, *First Synthesis Report*, 41.

51. European Commission, "A European Union Contribution to the OSCE anti-Semitism Conference" (paper read at Organization for Security and Cooperation in

Europe anti-Semitism Conference, Vienna, 19 June 2003), 2, emphasis added.
  52. Ibid., 3–4.
  53. Treaty of Amsterdam amending the Treaty on European Union, the Treaties Establishing the European Communities and Certain Related Acts, OJ C 340 10.11.1997, 12, emphasis added.
  54. R. Amy Elman, *Sexual Equality in an Integrated Europe: Virtual Equality* (New York, 2007), Chapter 5.
  55. European Commission., *Annual Report on Equality and Non-Discrimination 2003: Towards Diversity* (Brussels, 2003).
  56. Robert S. Wistrich, "Fighting Antisemitism," *Midstream* 50, no. 2 (2004):22.
  57. Ibid.
  58. European Commission, *Equality and Non-Discrimination: Annual Report 2005* (Brussels, 2005).
  59. Bergman and Wetzel, *First Synthesis Report,* 29.
  60. Ibid., 7.
  61. Hannah Cleaver, "Race report team 'told to change findings on Muslims,'" *Telegraph*, 27 Nov. 2003.
  62. Ayaan Hirsi Ali, *The Caged Virgin: An Emancipation Proclamation for Women and Islam* (New York, 2006), 16.
  63. Manfred Gerstenfeld, *Behind the Humanitarian Mask: The Nordic Countries, Israel, and the Jews* (Jerusalem, 2008), 23.
  64. Bertrand Benoit, "EU racism group shelves anti-Semitism study," *Financial Times*, 22 Nov. 2003, 9.
  65. Daniel Pipes, "Locus of Euro-hate," *Jerusalem Post*, 10 Dec. 2003.
  66. Bob Purkiss and Beate Winkler, *EUMC Media Release, Issue 194-03-03-12-01-EN*. EUMC, 2 Dec. 2003, online http://eumc.eu.int/eumc/material/pub/FT/MR-194-03-03-12-01-EN.pdf.
  67. Beate Winkler, Presentation on 31 March 2004 in the European Parliament (paper read at Parliamentary Session, Strasbourg, 31 Mar. 2004).
  68. European Monitoring Centre on Racism and Xenophobia, *Manifestations of Anti-Semitism in the EU 2002–2003*, 21.
  69. Quoted in Ambrose Evans-Pritchard, "EU 'covered up' attacks on Jews by young Muslims," *Daily Telegraph*, 1 Apr. 2004.
  70. Ibid.
  71. Bergman and Wetzel, *First Synthesis Report,* 93, emphasis added.
  72. European Monitoring Centre on Racism and Xenophobia, *Manifestations of Anti-semitism in the EU 2002–2003*, 188.
  73. Bergman and Wetzel, *First Synthesis Report,* 95.
  74. Emanuele Ottolenghi, "Making Sense of European Anti-Semitism," *Human Rights Review* 8, no. 2 (2007):107.
  75. Hannah Arendt, *The Origins of Totalitarianism* (New York, 1979), 10.
  76. Dina Porat, *The Road that Led to an Internationally Accepted Definition of Antisemitism* (Tel Aviv, 2006), 12.
  77. European Union Monitoring Centre, *Working Definition of Antisemitism* (Vienna, 2005). For the full text of the definition, see Appendix.
  78. Ibid.
  79. Ibid.
  80. Ibid.
  81. Still, Israel receives more than its fair share of criticism, a point evidenced by comparing casualties since World War II. Since then, 25 million people were killed in

internal conflicts, of them, 8,000 in the Israel-Palestinian conflict—ranking it 46th in a list of victims. Nonetheless, the UN and other international groups have condemned Israel more than all the other nations combined. See Walter Laqueur, *The Changing Face of Antisemitism: From Ancient Times to the Present Day* (New York, 2006), 8. For an analysis of the UN's institutionalized anti-Zionism, see Wistrich, *A Lethal Obsession*, Chapter 13.

82. Quoted in Yair Sheleg, "A World Cleansed of the Jewish State," *Haaretz*, 18 Apr. 2002.

83. See, for instance, Porat, *The Road*, 16.

84. United States Department of State. *Contemporary Global Anti-Semitism. A Report Provided to the United States Congress* (Washington, D.C., 2008), online http://purl.access.gpo.gov/GPO/LPS92553.

85. European Forum on Antisemitism. "Working Definition of Antisemitism," accessed 26 Nov. 2009, online http://www.european-forum-on-antisemitism.org /working-definition-of-antisemitism/.

86. Alexander Pollak (Programme Manager for Social Research, Fundamental Rights Agency), in discussion with author, Vienna, 28 May 2009.

87. Ibid.

88. Herb Keinon, "EU 'regrets' Israeli snub of racism conference," *Jerusalem Post*, 21 May 2006.

89. Ibid.

90. European Union Agency for Fundamental Rights, *Anti-Semitism: Summary overview of the situation in the European Union 2001–2008* (Vienna, 2009).

91. European Union Agency for Fundamental Rights (FRA), *Anti-Semitism: Summary overview of the situation in the European Union 2001–2010* (Vienna, 2011).

92. European Council, "Presidency Conclusions," 12–13 December, 5381/03, (Brussels, 2003), 27.

93. European Council, "Presidency Conclusions," 3–4 June, 150/99 REV 1, (Cologne, 1999), para 46.

94. Proposal for a Council Decision implementing Regulation (EC) No 168 as regards the adoption of a Multiannual Framework for the European Union Agency for Fundamental Rights for 2007–2012, COM(2007) 515 final.

95. Erica Howard, "The European Union Agency for Fundamental Rights," *European Human Rights Law Reporter*, no. 4 (2006): 453.

96. Council Framework Decision 2008/913/JHA of 28 November 2008 on combating certain forms of racism and xenophobia by means of criminal law, OJ L 328 6.12.2008.

97. Democracy and Human Rights Education in Europe (DARE), "FRA welcomes new EU Framework Decision on combating racism and xenophobia," accessed 2 Mar. 2013, http://dare-network.blogspot.com/2008/12/fra-welcomes-new-eu-framework-decision.html.

98. Laurent Pech, "The Law of Holocaust Denial in Europe: Towards a (qualified) EU-wide Criminal Prohibition" in *Genocide Denials and the Law*, edited by Ludovic Hennebel and Thomas Hochmann (Oxford, 2011), 230.

99. Ibid., 231.

100. Erik Bleich, *The Freedom to Be Racist?: How the United States and Europe Struggle to Preserve Freedom and Combat Racism* (New York and Oxford, 2011), 135.

101. Council Framework Decision 2008/913/JHA of 28 November 2008 on combating certain forms of racism and xenophobia by means of criminal law, OJ L

328 6.12.2008, emphasis added.
   102. Pech, "Law of Holocaust Denial in Europe," 185.
   103. Moshe Kantor, "Dealing with Europe's Soul, Not Just Economies," *Jerusalem Post*, 6 Dec. 2011.
   104. Jenia Iontcheva Turner, "The Expressive Dimension of EU Criminal Law, *"American Journal of Comparative Law* 60, no. 2 (2012): 557.
   105. Ibid., 572.
   106. World Jewish Congress, "EU human rights watchdog opens in Vienna," accessed 26 Nov. 2009, http://www.worldjewishcongress.org/en/main/showNews /id/6685?print=true.
   107. Alexander Pollak (Programme Manager for Social Research, Fundamental Rights Agency), in discussion with author, Vienna, 28 May 2009.
   108. European Union Agency for Fundamental Rights, *EU-MIDIS: European Union Minorities and Discrimination Survey* (Vienna, 2009).
   109. European Union Agency for Fundamental Rights, *Memo—Mapping discrimination in Europe European Union Minorities and Discrimination Survey (EU-MIDIS)* (Vienna, 2009), 6.
   110. Wistrich, *European Anti-Semitism Reinvents Itself*, 100. Consider, e.g., the Netherlands where Jews comprise only 0.25 per cent of the population. There a Dutch online watchdog agency (Meldpunt Discriminatie Internet or MDI) disclosed that 26 per cent of the (943) complaints they received in 2012 concerned antisemitism. MDI monitors racism and racial incitement on the Internet in the Netherlands. See Jewish Telegraph Agency News, "Watchdog: 25% of Dutch online hate speech complaints concern anti-Semitism," *Haaretz*, 5 Jan. 2013. According to the Scottish government, in 2012 Jews in Scotland were 20 times more likely to be attacked because of their faith than Christians, and several times more likely than Muslims. Marcus Dysch, "Attacks on Scottish Jews Rise," Jewish Chronicle Online, http://www.thejc.com /news/uk-news/109032/attacks-scottish-jews-rise; accessed 4 Aug. 2013.
   111. "Wiesenthal Center slams Sweden for 'Jewish tax,'" *The Local*, 15 Mar. 2011.
   112. European Union Agency for Fundamental Rights, *Anti-Semitism: Summary overview of the situation in the European Union 2001–2008*, 24.
   113. Meir Litvak and Ester Webman, *From Empathy to Denial: Arab Responses to the Holocaust* (New York, 2009); Matthias Küntzel, *Jihad and Jew-Hatred: Islamism, Nazism and the Roots of 9/11* (New York, 2007); Jeffrey Herf, *Nazi Propaganda for the Arab World* (Ann Arbor, Mich., 2009).
   114. European Union Agency for Fundamental Rights, *Anti-Semitism: Summary overview of the situation in the European Union 2001–2008*, 24.
   115. See, for instance, Edward Kaplan and Charles Small, "Anti-Israel Sentiment Predicts Anti-Semitism in Europe," *Journal of Conflict Resolution* 50, no. 4 (2006): 548–61.
   116. Edward Kaplan and Charles Small substantiated the connection between antisemitism and anti-Israel sentiment in their detailed study of 5,000 European citizens throughout ten states. They found that while one can certainly be critical of Israeli policies without being antisemitic; those with extreme anti-Israel sentiments were roughly six times more likely to harbour antisemitic views than those who do not share such sentiments. In sum, whether the accusation is "Jews have too much power in our country" or "Jews don't care what happens to anyone but their own kind," the fraction of respondents who agree with such stereotypic statements consistently increases in relation to their anti-Israel positions. Ibid.

117. European Union Agency for Fundamental Rights (FRA), *Anti-Semitism: Summary overview of the situation in the European Union 2001–2010* (Vienna, 2011), 31.

118. Ibid., 3.

119. European Union Agency for Fundamental Rights (FRA), FRA *Survey of Jewish people's experiences and perceptions of antisemitism.* Accessed 2 Mar. 2012 online http://fra.europa.eu/sites/default/files/fra_uploads/2029-FRA-2012-factsheet-jewish-population-survey_EN.pdf.

120. Communication of Ms. Sandra de Waele, First Counsellor, Head of Political and Press Section of the European Union delegation in Israel at the 4th International Conference of the Global Forum for Combatting Antisemitism, 28–30 May 2013, Jerusalem.

CHAPTER FOUR

Member States Post–9/11

Have Member States replicated (and thus reinforced) the EU's shortcomings in addressing antisemitism or have they overcome its limitations in the aftermath of 9/11? That is, do Sweden and Austria, the states that are the focus of this study, regard the threat of antisemitism as more than the rabble of the far right? Do they deny, ignore, and/or excuse anti-Jewish hatred when the perpetrators are Muslim and/or of the left? Not least, has the adoption of new anti-discrimination legislation made a difference for Jews in the Member States or are those charged with their implementation negligent? Adopted in 2000, all Member States had three years to transpose both the Race and Framework Directives. Because we have had a decade to witness the repercussions of these and other EU initiatives, it is time to consider their consequences within the Member States and, again, we begin with Sweden.

SWEDEN

When, in the wake of 9/11, it became clearer that antisemitism was not exclusive to neo-Nazis and others of the far right, Sweden's officials were every bit as reticent as their EU counterparts to acknowledge this fact. Having just received accolades for their state-sponsored Holocaust education initiatives, few Swedes recognized antisemitism as a contemporary Swedish problem, to say nothing of the prejudice being more prevalent among Sweden's Muslims.[1] In consequence, the persistent verbal and physical attacks by Arab and Muslim men against those they identified as Jews continued unabated,[2] effectively reducing synagogue attendance. In addition to assaults and death threats, Sweden's synagogues and Jewish cemeteries were desecrated in Stockholm, Gothenburg, and Malmö—in metropolitan areas where a majority of Jews live.[3] One "artist" even used the resulting terror as a backdrop for his agitprop, by placing cans he illustrated with a Magen David and the label "Zyclon B" outside the cemetery.[4] The climate became so harsh that reports of Swedish Jews leaving for Israel became less remarkable.[5] For those who stay, few feel safe wearing yarmulkes or Magen David pendants in public.[6]

By 2006, the *European Jewish Press* reported that Sweden's Jewish communities were spending a quarter of their budgets on extensive security as no Jewish social, religious or cultural event can take place without it.[7] Five years later, after state authorities remained unresponsive to the constant need Jews had for security; the Simon Wiesenthal Center excoriated this Member State for making the community pay the equivalent of a "Jewish tax." Rabbi Abraham Cooper, the Center's Associate Dean, stated "It is long overdue that the Swedish authorities assume the costs of the security of the Jewish institutions."[8] Even Sweden's Committee against Anti-Semitism (*Svenska Kommittén Mot Antisemitism, SKMA*) operates from an undisclosed location in Stockholm. Visitors are often screened before obtaining access to the organization's office.[9]

The relative silence of Swedes to such conditions compelled Mikael Tossavainen, a Swedish historian, to pen a brief study for the SKMA entitled, *The Denied Hatred: Anti-Semitism among Muslims and Arabs in Sweden*. He explains: "Unlike the anti-Semitism that traditionally finds expression in Nazi circles—[antisemitism among Arabs and Muslims] is not mentioned or in any way stressed in the public debate. On the contrary, it is actively hushed up, excused or even denied in the media, and the political, academic and intellectual establishment."[10] These elite operate at significant remove from the majority of the country's Arabs and Muslims who live in the poorer segregated suburbs of Sweden's larger cities. Tossavainen's in-depth interviews with teachers from these segregated school districts offered insight into a poisonous public sphere that many, it seems, have chosen to deny.

For those whom Tossavainen interviewed, 9/11 proved a watershed event. Shocked teachers reported that students "gathered spontaneously and cheered after September 11. In Rinkeby [a notoriously impoverished Stockholm suburb], one such student group gathered outside school on September 12, 2001, and shouted 'Death to Jews!' 'Death to America!'"[11] Only a year earlier Sweden had hosted its international conference on Holocaust remembrance, yet official assertions of "never again" swiftly succumbed to silence.

The country renowned for its Holocaust education initiatives (whatever their quality) now has teachers unable to implement their lesson plans on this subject. Holocaust survivors, like Judith Popinski, are less likely to share their stories with students, particularly in schools with large Muslim populations. The disrespect is overwhelming. "Malmö reminds me of the anti-Semitism I felt as a child in Poland before the war," Popinski explains.[12] Whether Arab and Muslim students obstruct instruction by insisting that Jewish genocide is Zionist propaganda or they praise Hitler for his murderous regime, these youth often insist that Jews use the Holocaust to extract sympathy for Israel—a perspective reminiscent of Haider in 1999 and one so often echoed in the pages of Sweden's daily newspapers that, in 2006, 14 percent of Swedes fully or partially agreed that "Jews exploit the Holocaust for financial and political purposes."[13]

Those tempted to attribute the antisemitic attitudes of Muslim and Arab minorities to their segregated communities will also find Sweden's elite openly expressing similar viewpoints—often as a means of pandering to a large minority whose interests they then claim to represent. For example, when two politicians sought to ingratiate themselves to the Muslims of Rosengärd (a downtrodden district of Malmö within walking distance of the city's centre), they attended the inauguration of a public library exhibit on Israel entitled "Expulsion and Terror" and there legitimized suicide bombing. One, from the Conservative Party, insisted that killing Jewish children was justified while the other, a Social Democrat, said bombing Jewish civilians was self-defence.[14] In Sweden, such statements are hardly provocative.

When Sweden's first Social Democratic woman leader, Mona Sahlin, marched under the banners of Hamas at an ostensibly pro-immigrant demonstration that culminated with the burning of Israeli flags during the war in Gaza, it seems she assumed the resulting photos would prove a greater asset than liability. Although Hamas governs Gaza under Sharia, promotes a Charter that calls for Israel's "obliteration" and is expressly identified by the EU as a terrorist organization, Sahlin—a self-proclaimed feminist—was undeterred from publicly embracing the group. Such dalliances with Hamas are, after all, *de rigeur* for Sweden's elite and its support for Hamas seems undiminished by the annihilationist jihad the organization advocates. Rare is the public intellectual who, like Norway's Eirik Eiglad, questions the left's tolerance of "radical Islam's misogyny, patriarchy, homophobia; its religious totalitarianism; its anti-intellectualism, anti-secularism and anti-socialism; its contempt for individualism and its truly poisonous anti-Semitism."[15]

Following the 2006 electoral victory of Hamas, Swedish authorities issued visas to the party's representatives who, in turn, met with several Swedish parliamentarians. The visas also offered Hamas a welcome mat on which it could wipe the blood of its crimes from its feet before entering into Europe's borderless Schengen region and into Germany.[16] Once there, a frustrated Prime Minister Merkel made clear that the organization was unwelcome.[17]

If, in Sweden, politicians calibrate the lethal sentiments of Hamas for wider audiences to project a seemingly more moderate profile (e.g., a simple photo-op for immigrants' rights), they assume an alternate posture at the transnational level, in part because the EU bans contacts with the organization. Thus, when Israel accused Sweden of breaching EU policy when the

Nordic government held the rotating European presidency in 2009, Sweden issued a robust denial of the allegation.[18]

The ideological chameleonic cultivated by Sahlin and others is on full public display at demonstrations where "Hamas flags and headbands . . . [are] spotted next to banners supporting communist groups and feminist causes,"[19] yet Sahlin is no ordinary Swedish politician and the Social Democrats are no ordinary party. First, the party has had the longest period of social democratic rule anywhere. It was only after nearly a century that, in 2010, an opposition centre-right government had been re-elected after serving a full term. Following this centre-right victory, Sahlin stepped down as party chair, but it would be foolish to dismiss the enduring influence of either the woman or her party. Sahlin is keenly adept at moving from incendiary anti-Israel demonstrations to Jewish communities so scorched by antisemitism that their members are making *aliyah*.[20] Such skill undoubtedly contributed to her emergence as the first woman to chair the Social Democrats. And, as Göran Persson's protégé, Sahlin's credentials extend beyond the small Nordic state.

In addition to having headed her country's commission against racism and xenophobia for the 1997 European Year against Racism, Sahlin appeared before the OSCE's above-mentioned Berlin Conference on Anti-Semitism in 2004. There, as then Minister of Justice, she professed Sweden's firm opposition to antisemitism and championed the Living History Project (and related efforts) as a model to which others should aspire.[21] If, by that time, it was becoming clear that these efforts had done little more than bolster her country's reputation, Sahlin gave no hint of it.

One of the most ubiquitous tropes among Swedes is to deny antisemitism's (domestic) existence altogether.[22] Jan Guillou, one of the country's best-selling authors and journalists, is notorious for this tact. In the leading Social Democratic evening paper, *Aftonbladet*, he dismissed contemporary antisemitism as an anachronism used by Israel to evoke sympathy for suspect policies.[23] In 2006, the Left Party (formerly the Communist Party) echoed this position in an Orwellian policy document entitled "Racism and Anti-racism." After claiming that prejudice against Jews poses no problem, it posits that contemporary antisemitism is a bigotry spread by "Jewish-Israeli fascism" against Arabs and Muslims.[24] Such claims remind one that the politics of antisemitism involve charging Jews with the very crimes being carried out against them.[25]

Still others in Sweden acknowledge antisemitism, but dismiss it as rational—especially when Muslims express it. The work of Jan Samuelson, the late professor of religious history, epitomises this position. His article, "It is Permitted to Hate Jews," excused Islamic antisemitism as understandable, reasonable, and justified.[26] Published by the country's largest Social Democratic daily (*Dagens Nyheter, DN*), Samuelson's article proved so egregious that the EUMC referred to it in its final report on antisemitism. However, without the slightest irony, the EU agency then declared: "With the exception of ongoing traditional antisemitic propaganda published by the extreme right and ultra-nationalist groups, published statements with a specific anti-Jewish or antisemitic content are rare in mainstream media."[27] By implying that Sweden's antisemitism is an "extreme right" phenomenon, the EUMC ignored three key facts. First, the surge of anti-Jewish attacks came largely from the country's Muslim and Arab population. Second, Samuelson's sympathies were neither far right nor xenophobic. Last, *DN* is Sweden's mainstream media. If Samuelson's position was antithetical to this mainstream, it was in the clarity of its tone and not its content.

Sweden's masterful public relations (e.g., its Living History Forum) might help explain how it has managed to remain largely unscathed by charges of antisemitism, but the left's dominance and ties to Europe's larger ideological divide also conceals a bigotry so often associated with the right that the country's left is able to indulge in and ignore its own antisemitism. Manfred Gerstenfeld explains that the military defeat of the Nazis led to a public purge of its European (though not Middle Eastern) adherents whereas the incremental demise of Communist regimes spared its supporters from having to seriously confront the crimes against humanity associated with its name.[28] His insights account for the dearth of Swedish research on the left's antisemitism[29] and explains why the few works that buck this trend go largely ignored.[30] In consequence, onlookers often regard the left's opposition to right-wing racism and antisemitism as a sufficient guarantor of social justice.

The EUMC helped perpetuate this restricted view when it expunged (from its 2004 final report on antisemitism) references to the extreme left's role in violent attacks against Jews in Sweden. In addition, the Centre deleted reference to Swedish Nazis who enthusiastically applauded Islamic anti-semites.[31] While this toxic collaboration remains a growing concern among Jewish leaders throughout Europe, the EUMC also failed to note the political establishment's silence in the face of these conditions and on-going prejudice.

When, on rare occasions, Sweden's elite discusses antisemitism, they often do so with reference to a grab bag of other prejudices with little regard for the factors that serve to distinguish them. For example, in studying the "anti-social behaviour" of the country's youth, researchers from the National Council for Crime Prevention placed antisemitism along a broad spectrum that also considered homophobia, Islamophobia, and xenophobia.[32] Years later, in 2011, Sweden's centre-right Minister of Integration, Erik Ullenhag, tasked the Living History Forum with charting Swedish antisemitism and Islamophobia, insisting that both are particularly virulent forms of hatred because they are "ideologized." The persistent reluctance to address antisemitism without reference to Islamophobia does not operate in the reverse. That is, it is possible to address discrimination against Muslims without having to also address antisemitism.

While Sweden's elite and the EU officials who monitor antisemitism often appear reticent to fully acknowledge the problem, others—like Israel's former ambassador to Sweden—have had little choice. During his tenure as Israel's Ambassador to Sweden (December 2002–April 2004), Zvi Mazel became internationally known for disconnecting electricity to a Stockholm museum installation that was associated with and foreshadowed the Living History Forum's last (2004) international conference, "Preventing Genocide." The exhibit, "Snow White and the Madness of Truth," featured a small white sailboat floating in a fountain of red water. Its sail featured a smiling photograph of a suicide bomber who (three months earlier) murdered twenty-two Israeli Jews and Arabs in a Haifa restaurant.

With the pools of blood barely dry in Haifa, the Israeli government requested that the incendiary exhibit be dismantled and the Swedes, in turn, assured them that this would happen.[33] When the ambassador discovered that Sweden had reneged on its promise, he simply pulled the electric plug on this work, insisting it glorified suicide bombing and thus served as "an affront to the grieving families."[34]

For then-ambassador Mazel, the Museum fiasco typified the country's tolerance of rabid antisemitism and followed "dozens of anti-Israeli and anti-Jewish events in Sweden,"[35] while for the retired Swedish diplomat, Sverker Åström, Israel's request was reminiscent of the pressure the Third Reich exerted on Sweden to censor expressions of anti-Nazism.[36] Both men brought considerable experience to their claims. No stranger to hostility, Mazel served five years in Egypt before coming to Sweden. He nonetheless admits to having been stunned to find that "Sweden is among the most severely anti-Semitic places" with "daily agitations in the media to kill Jews"[37]—a point to which we will return.

Having effectively transformed ambassador Mazel and the state of Israel (not to mention Jews as a collective) into contemporary Nazis, Åström's position, issued in the daily *Svenska Dagbladet*, was as evasive as it was incredulous. After all, Åström was a member of Sweden's Nazi party in 1935. From 1936–1937, he studied international law and politics in Nazi Germany. After returning to Sweden, he became a prominent Social Democrat, serving as his country's permanent United Nations representative. Like his Austrian UN colleague, Kurt Waldheim, Åström claims to have forgotten his past. "It might sound strange," he said in a *DN* interview in 2002, "but I have no real recollection of Nazi influences."[38] How ironic then that Åström's views on Israel and its purported Nazism saturated Sweden's mainstream news and cultural magazines two years later.[39] Not only did he go unchallenged, he was soon after feted as a leading advocate for gay rights in Sweden, though he had not come out until the year before, at 87. This last honor provides added irony as Åström embraced an ideology that led to the destruction of gay Gentile men, as well as all Jews, within Nazi occupied Europe. With no outcry, the Swedish public joined Åström in forgetting the past. On the heels of the Museum scandal and related lies, the Swedish government convened the first major intergovernmental conference on genocide since the UN issued its Convention against it in 1948. It would be its fourth and last Living History Forum event.

Soon after the 2004 museum scandal, the Wiesenthal Center petitioned the Swedish government to take a substantive step during its conference on preventing genocide and declare suicide bombing "a crime against humanity," a position adopted in 2002 by Amnesty International and Human Rights Watch, both frequent critics of Israel. In July 2002, Amnesty International found "the attacks against civilians by Palestinian armed groups are widespread, systematic and in pursuit of an explicit policy to attack civilians. . . ." that "constitute crimes against humanity."[40] By September of the same year, even Yasser Arafat publicly condemned suicide bombings, if only "to preserve the *higher national interest* of the Palestinian people."[41] Later that fall, Human Rights Watch released a report that found "Palestinians who launch suicide attacks against Israeli civilians are guilty of 'crimes against humanity.'"[42] As the organization's executive director, Kenneth Roth, stated: "The people who carry out suicide bombings are not martyrs, they're war criminals, and so are the people who help to plan such attacks."[43]

A similar denunciation of suicide bombing by Sweden's government would have been consistent with the conference's express commitment to explore "seriously and actively. . .action against genocidal threats, mass murders, deadly conflicts, ethnic cleansing as well as genocidal ideologies and incitement to genocide."[44] Instead, the Swedish government ignored the Wiesenthal Center's request and championed "Snow White's" veneration of murder-suicide under the rubric of artistic freedom. Whether this obstinacy can be attributed, in part, to the ideological inroads made by the European Council of Fatwa and Research (ECFR) is impossible to know, but it is worth pointing out that ECFR met in Stockholm months prior to the 2004 conference with a clear objective—to mute the outrage that had mounted against suicide bombings. Tellingly, the conference was entitled "Jihad and Denying its Connection to Terror." The event was hosted by Stockholm's Great Mosque and featured Sheikh Yousef Al-Qaradhawi, who insisted that suicide bombings are acts of resistance, not terrorism.[45] One would expect nothing less from a man whose more recent broadcasts request that Allah not spare a single Jew—"Oh Allah, count their numbers and kill them, down to the very last one."[46]

Sweden's commitment to countering genocide appeared as precarious as its enthusiasm for free expression remained robust—at least as far as the leeway it extended to the Stockholm Great Mosque for its incitement to murder Jews. In late November 2005, almost a year after the Swedish government penned its 2004 Declaration to prevent genocide, a Swedish radio news program (*Dagens Eko*) reported on antisemitic cassette tapes it had purchased at the mosque's bookshop. On one, a voice in Arabic proclaimed "Oh God exterminate the Jews!"[47] Although the police immediately seized the tapes at the behest of Göran Lambertz, then Chancellor of Justice, the radio program insisted these were source materials and refused to formally relinquish them.

As Sweden's only government-appointed prosecutor with the sole power to take legal action in cases concerning freedom of speech and the press, Chancellor Lambertz dropped his investigation (in mid-December) because, he said, he could not access crucial evidence. A search of the mosque's bookshop and warehouse failed to locate the same tapes that the radio aired. In a January 2nd interview on Swedish Radio (on the same slow news day he issued his formal written decision), the then Chancellor of Justice explained "it would probably be hard to achieve a conviction partly because it may be difficult to ascertain who is responsible for the tapes."[48] While Lambertz conceded (in writing) that it would have been possible for the government to "seize" the material, he insists that doing this would have been "disproportionate" and even "unthinkable"—conclusions he never bothered to explain.[49] However, in a private interview, Lambertz attributed his reluctance to pursue the case to an unnamed legal mentor from Uppsala University who insisted that a case against the Great Mosque could not be won and was thus not worth pursuing.[50] When asked whether he dropped other cases he believed he could not win, he declined but claimed winning was important. Leaders from Sweden's Jewish community were astonished by Lambertz's decision and feared the government's refusal to act would send "the wrong signals" and reveal "an attitude of resignation and passivity."[51]

Worse, Lambertz's written legal decision concerning the Great Mosque codified Samuelson's above-noted position in his article, "It is Permitted to Hate Jews." While the former Chancellor of Justice concedes that exhortations to kill Jews (e.g., on a Nazi poster in downtown Stockholm) *could* be interpreted as racial incitement under Swedish law, he insisted the mosque's antisemites be judged differently.[52] In a ruling reminiscent of Sheikh Qaradhawi's defense of suicide bombings (aka "martyrdom operations") as "acts of resistance," Lambertz found the threats of extermination emanating from the Great Mosque "permissible" because such "battle cries and invectives are a commonplace feature of the rhetoric surrounding the [Middle East] conflict."[53]

Had Lambertz complied, instead, with his country's express commitment to the 2004 OSCE Berlin Declaration, he could have proclaimed "unambiguously that international developments or political issues, including those in Israel or elsewhere in the Middle East, never justify anti-Semitism."[54] He might also have embraced the EU's repeated calls to counter racial incitement by pursuing effective, proportionate and dissuasive penalties. But, without agreement among the Member States on how best to impose these penalties,[55] the EU's remedies were (and still are) of little practical import to the Chancellor's office. Indeed, Lambertz insisted they were inapplicable.[56]

Instead, Lambertz's justification for not punishing those calling for the murder of Jews read as a textbook example from the EUMC's practical guide identifying antisemitism. That guide recognizes, as antisemitism, "Calling for, aiding, or justifying the killing or harming of Jews in the name of a radical ideology or an extremist view of religion."[57]

Years later, Lambertz did not waiver from this position and he explained that calling for the obliteration of Israel and/or the killing of Israelis is acceptable though calling for the murder of *Swedish* Jews "would be obviously criminal."[58] This distinction treats "genocidal antisemitism as if it were acceptable as part of the Israeli-Palestinian conflict."[59] Yet, the former Chancellor of Justice's rationalization contravenes none of the EU's legislative efforts against antisemitism because, for all of the protection against race and/or ethnic discrimination that the race and framework directives claim to offer, they exempt a difference of treatment based in nationality. Israelis are not EU nationals. Moreover, while Jews may be EU nationals, those in Sweden were, from the perspective of that state, regarded by the Great Mosque as representatives of Israel and, as such, could be legally threatened with death.

While the EUMC's largely-ignored working definition of antisemitism acknowledged that the prejudice may be manifest in targeting the state of Israel, conceived as a Jewish identity, the (race and framework) Directives' explicit exemption of nationality as a protective status renders (Europe's) Jews vulnerable and without a *legal* foundation for challenging contemporary expressions of antisemitism. That is because "the new anti-Semitism does not discriminate against Jews as individuals on account of their race. Instead, it is centred on Israel, and the denial to the Jewish people alone of the right to self-determination."[60]

In consequence, "If one mentions Palestine in hate speeches and calls for mass murder against Jews, one risks nothing in Sweden," a position that nullifies the government's earlier rhetoric against antisemitism and its related call for action against genocide. [61] Drawing on Europe's past, Ilya Meyer writes, "Here is a case in which Hitler's racist supremacy descendants are expressing the very same sentiments albeit in a different language, and the result is, once again, a politically correct shrug of public indifference."[62] Whatever the shortcomings of the EU and its Member States, we are not, however, in the 1930s and 1940s. This time there was substantial *domestic* legal precedent to interdict antisemitic incitement. The Chancellor of Justice chose to ignore it.

Lambertz's reasoning in early 2006 marked a significant departure from Swedish legal precedent involving the successful prosecution of Radio Islam's Ahmed Rami, in 1990, on seventeen counts of antisemitic incitement. Despite repeated efforts by Rami's legal defence and outspoken supporters to likewise mitigate his culpability by attributing his antisemitic rants to robust invectives inspired by the Middle East, Rami was incarcerated for six months and his radio station closed by Lambertz's predecessor. Rami's followers now flock to the Internet but, according to Bachner, his support among well-known journalists, intellectuals and academics generally receded following his conviction.[63] This outcome might, in part, explain why Lambertz ignored the Court's (earlier) judgment in this celebrated Swedish case.

Moreover, Lambertz selectively invoked the European Court of Human Rights (ECtHR) and its imposition of freedom of expression. Insisting "Swedish law should be interpreted in light of the requirements the ECHR [European Convention on Human Rights] imposes on freedom of expression," he nowhere noted that this freedom (in Article 10) had been restricted to protect the public order and the rights of others.[64]

More specifically, Sweden's Chancellor of Justice disregarded two of the ECtHR's then most recent Article 10 rulings. The first of these, in 2003, involved the notorious French Holocaust denier, Roger Garaudy. Here the Court established limits to freedom of expression and it was both unanimous and unambiguous that Holocaust denial does not enjoy the protection of Article 10. After finding that such denial is "one of the most serious forms of racial defamation of Jews and of incitement to hatred of them," the Court concluded that such "acts" pose a "serious threat to public order" and are thus "incompatible with democracy and human rights because they infringe the rights of others."[65] The following year, it similarly reasoned that hate speech "is incompatible with the values of the Convention, notably tolerance, social peace and non-discrimination."[66] This second ruling involved Mark Anthony Norwood, an organizer from Britain's far right National Party. Norwood placed a poster in his window containing a photograph of the (U.S.) Twin Towers engulfed in flames with the words "Islam out of Britain—Protect the British People."[67] The Court ruled "that the words and images on the poster amounted to a public expression of attack on all Muslims in the United Kingdom" and for this reason was unprotected by the European Convention on Human Rights (Article 10).[68]

Had he chosen to, Lambertz could have similarly concluded that the exhortations emanating from the Great Mosque amounted to an attack on all Jews in Sweden and could not thus merit the Convention's protection. Instead, his refusal to condemn the Great Mosque's incitement was consistent with the European Council for Fatwa and Research's position and paralleled his government's earlier disinclination to denounce suicide bombing as a "crime against humanity." Furthermore, by taking this stance Lambertz overlooked the precedent of a Court whose rulings he claimed to follow.

By the end of 2006, Sweden's enthusiasm for free expression proved as feeble as its 2004 pledge to counter genocide. When, for instance, the Swedish Democrats (a far right party) posted the now-famous Danish cartoons of the Muslim prophet Mohammed on their website in early 2006, the Ministry of Foreign Affairs instructed the Internet provider to close the site. When then Minister of Foreign Affairs, Laila Freivalds, insisted her office had intervened without her knowledge, the press revealed evidence of her involvement. Freivalds subsequently resigned in disgrace—less because she had curbed "provocative" speech than because she had initially misled the public about it. Still, with the world's focus on Denmark, perhaps few were aware that Scandinavians were, in general, under threat. In early 2006, Islamic militants torched Danish, Swedish, and Norwegian embassies in Syria. As well, armed mobs belonging to Fatah, along with Hamas, invaded and occupied the EU office in Gaza and threatened to murder Scandinavians there for insulting Islam.

The government's closure of the far right's website distinguished Sweden as the first Western state to block the re-publication of the caricatures of Mohammed. As a bewildered Swedish press confronted a government initially unable to account for the usurpation of its own press freedom act, no one referenced European law and the requirement it imposes concerning freedom of expression. Instead, the government dressed its capitulation to Jihadist threats beneath a cloak of tolerance and pluralistic sensitivity.

Sweden's Muslim Council embraced the government's action and claimed "The Danish cartoons are a provocation against Muslims all over the world and can't be seen as a statement of freedom of speech even with good will."[69] Far from contradicting this position, Lars Leijonbor, leader of the Liberal Party, explained: "For once, the Swedish parties are very much in agreement. We want the best possible relationship with the Muslim world."[70] Should the price of that relationship involve denying, ignoring and/or accepting antisemitism, Sweden's political elite appears ready to have Jews pay for it. Robert Wistrich explains, "Behind the legal formalism and the usual sophistry about free speech also lay electoral considerations in a Swedish society where half a million Muslims heavily outnumbered Jews by more than twenty-five to one."[71] With upcoming elections, Sweden's politicians were clearly courting Muslim votes in 2006.

Three years later, Swedish politicians again capitulated—this time stating that mounting security concerns forced them to ban spectators from a Davis Cup tennis match between Sweden and Israel. After enlisting a thousand police officers, helicopters, and police vehicles on loan from Denmark to prevent the rioting of seven thousand demonstrators (including Islamists, neo-Nazis, and left-wing activists) gathered in Malmö's main square at a "Stop the Match" protest, authorities claimed they were unable to protect 4,000 nonviolent sports spectators (among them Israelis and Jews). Still others, like the left-wing members of the city's council, insisted that the mere presence of Israeli players in the stadium was "a provocation against Arabs living in Malmö."[72]

Regardless of their emphasis, the authorities reneged on the strong police presence necessary to ensure protection to athletes and their spectators, a position that fell short of previous enhanced efforts requested by the EU to combat hooliganism.[73] In addition to underscoring a double standard for Jews and Israelis, the Swedish based Israeli journalist David Stavrou wondered, "If a few threats on a relatively minor sporting event can empty a 4,000 seat arena, just imagine what a real terrorist attack would do to Swedish society."[74]

For those inclined to regard the Davis Cup decision as less a concession to terrorism than the result of a successful boycott against Israel for its alleged human rights violations,[75] Stavrou offers a historical corrective. Sweden, he notes, willingly participated (and won twenty medals) in the 1936 Berlin Olympics under Hitler and it also competed in the 1968 Mexico City Olympic Games, days after the government there killed hundreds of demonstrating students. More recently, Sweden competed in the Beijing games, despite China's massive human-rights violations. While these facts do not necessarily invalidate current claims for boycotts in general, Stavrou explains that the logic of Sweden's avid anti-Zionists "imply that Israel is worse than Nazi Germany and that Israeli policies brought about events more severe than. . . the Mexican Tlateloco Massacre and the events of Tiananmen Square all combined!"[76] Aware of the antisemitic character that girds such claims, he asks readers to discern the context and quality of the arguments against Sweden hosting Israeli athletes.

The protests surrounding the Davis Cup marked the third time within a month that Sweden retreated from protecting its (Jewish) citizens from angry mobs. January 2009 opened with repeated arsonist attacks against Jewish congregations in the country's southern region and vandalism of the Israeli embassy in Stockholm. After leaders from the Jewish community demanded that politicians take a stand against the escalating violence, Sweden's Minister of Integration and Gender posted a brief statement to the government's website that condemned the fire bombings, but printed sources suggest she (and the Jewish community) met with silence from the media. No one stepped in to fill this void. To the contrary, Malmö's police disbanded a peaceful pro-Israeli demonstration of nearly 200 after merely thirty-five minutes when twice as many stone and bottle-throwing counter-demonstrators arrived and began screaming "Hitler, Hitler," "Juden Raus," "Bloody Jews," "Death to Israel," and "*Itbach al yahoud*" (Arabic, Death to Jews).[77] The Director of the Wiesenthal's Center for International Relations, Shimon Samuels, denounced the "pogrom-style" conditions as dire and called for "a full state investigation into Malmö police behavior, the prosecution of those responsible, and an apology to the Swedish Jewish targets."[78] He too was ignored.

Hostility against Jews in general and Israel in particular reached a fevered pitch months later when Sweden's officials again embraced press freedom, this time by insisting that their reverence for it prevented them from criticizing *Aftonbladet* for an article suggesting that Israeli Defense Forces trafficked in the organs of murdered Palestinians. The reporter, Donald Boström, used the 2009 arrest of a Jewish businessman in the United States as a pretext to revive his discredited allegations from his earlier book, *Inshallah: The Conflict Between Israel and Palestine.*[79] Reminiscent of accounts Goebbels might have penned in recycling the trope that Jews abduct and murder children for their blood, Boström's modern-day blood libel (entitled "Our Sons are Plundered for Their Organs") stirred international controversy, particularly after he admitted that he lacked evidence to substantiate his libelous assertions.[80] The Palestinians he identified as his story's sources denied making the claims he attributed to them.

Writing for the *Wall Street Journal*, Andrea Levin explains, "in the classic mode of conspiracy theorists" the article "linked a criminal New Jersey group—that included several Jews—engaged in organ-trafficking, to sweeping charges against Israel's supposedly unethical medical establishment."[81] Others, like the Middle East and international affairs expert Gerald Steinberg, emphasized that the Swedish government had long funded the anti-Zionist groups that promote the kind of libel that incites anti-Israeli hatred. For Steinberg, the *Aftonbladet* article was but one example of Israel's demonization, one consistent with what Israel's (former) ambassador Mazel faced years earlier.[82]

After Sweden's Ambassador to Israel at that time, Elisabet Borsiin-Bonnier, swiftly denounced Boström's article as "shocking and appalling" on the Embassy website, her foreign ministry immediately disavowed her position in public. Sweden's Conservative Foreign Minister Carl Bildt rebuked her, explaining his country supports fully "constitutionally protected free speech."[83] In turn, the Left Party (previously Sweden's Communist Party) insisted the government recall Ambassador Borsiin-Bonnier to Stockholm, where she would be educated in free speech fundamentals. Not to be upstaged, the Social Democrats demanded an official inquiry into her handling of her website statement.[84]

In addition to emphasizing the hypocrisy inherent in reproaching Borsiin-Bonnier for her statement in the name of "free speech," critics stressed that press freedom should not prevent officials from speaking out against hate speech, but rather obliged leaders to do so.[85] Indeed, Sweden appears to have departed from its own (and the EU's) position (as earlier expressed in venues to counter racism) that leaders must publicly condemn a politics against hate.

Moreover, commentators throughout Europe recalled Sweden's earlier and very different position regarding caricatures of Mohammad. As the Austrian daily *Die Presse* remarked, "When it was a matter of the Mohammad caricatures, the Swedish foreign minister sent a letter of protest to the Danish government."[86] Concerned by *Aftonbladet's* incitement against Jews and Israel, Italy's foreign minister and seasoned Eurocrat, Franco Frattini, also entered into the debate.[87]

This particular row between Sweden and Israel assumed a more pronounced European dimension because Sweden had just assumed the rotating European presidency (June–December 2009) and the EU had just adopted the 2008 Framework Decision, rendering the *intentional* public incitement to discrimination, violence, or hatred a crime. According to Jacques Barrot, the Vice President of the European Commission, the 2008 Framework Decision was established to "ensure comparable racist and xenophobic behaviour is made a criminal defense in all Member States by laying down a common definition and by approximating sanctions."[88]

Yet, Sweden paid little heed to the Framework Decision, perhaps with good reason. In addition to being under no obligation to implement it until 2010, the Decision's expectation that one establish the speaker's intention to cause harm proves a Sisyphean task. Nonetheless, the EU (like the ECtHR before it) was distancing itself—however ineffectively—from free speech fundamentalism. It is within this context that Sweden's more obstreperous and often inconsistent position on free expression and *Aftonbladet* may be understood.

In the run-up to Sweden's hosting a meeting of the Council of Ministers, Frattini announced that he had met with his Swedish counterpart, Carl Bildt, to forge an EU resolution to strongly condemn antisemitism. The next day Sweden's Foreign Ministry denied that the two ministers had discussed the matter and, instead, attributed Frattini's statement to an "Italian misunder-standing."[89] An unrelenting Frattini countered, "We're morally obligated to reiterate that there is no room for anti-Semitism. . . . but since there won't be any formal conclusions from the [Council] meeting, it won't be included in any [EU] document."[90] Sweden's then conservative Prime Minister Reinfeldt followed with a press conference. There he insisted, "We cannot be asked by anyone to contravene the Swedish constitution, and this is something we will also not do within the European Union."[91] How an EU-level condemnation of antisemitism would have undermined Sweden's constitution remains unclear.

Two months after the Swedish government insisted that its reverence for press freedom prevented it from even commenting on anything in the media (relating to antisemitism); its officials adamantly condemned an *Aftonbladet* editorial. The column, by Jimmie Åkesson, leader of the Swedish Democrats, claimed that Islam poses the "greatest foreign threat" to Sweden since World War II.[92] That piece met with immediate charges of racism from all political parties, including the Social Democrats.

While Prime Minister Reinfeldt was careful not to condemn the paper's decision to publish his political rival's column, he nevertheless voiced his clear opposition to the op-ed, abandoning his government's earlier position that Sweden's laws and norms prevented any politician from interfering with the press. Rather than insisting that his government's condemnation would impinge on freedom of speech as he had with Boström's article demonizing Israel, the Prime Minister appropriately countered Åkesson's assertions. He furthermore refrained from offering Muslims a sobering discourse on press freedom following *Aftonbladet's* tirade against Islam.

In condemning both real and perceived slights against Islam with an alacrity that has been altogether lacking for Jews, Sweden's political elite has also rarely held Muslims to account for their incitements against Jews. This finding was also echoed in a 2010 OSCE report on antisemitism that concluded:

> There seems to be little debate among civil society representatives or Government authorities with whom we met that the primary sources of anti-Jewish attacks today stem from the country's Muslim population. Yet, there is a reluctance to identify this, perhaps as one of our interlocutors suggested, so as not to contribute still further to the anti-immigrant sentiment among the population.[93]

While the Chancellor of Justice's earlier decisions on incitement and the government's wavering positions regarding press freedom epitomize this problem, additional examples also underscore Sweden's double standard. Consider, for instance, the government's position on suicide bombings during its 2004 conference on genocide.

A year after the OSCE issued its critical report concerning Sweden's disinclination to identify the primary sources of antisemitism; the Minister of Integration offered a simultaneous condemnation of both antisemitism and Islamophobia. Together with the Chair of the Council of the Jewish Communities, the President of the Muslim Council and a smattering of academics, the anodyne statement (entitled "We Must Fight Hatred Together") promised another government investigation by the Living History Forum. As if there was a need to start from scratch, the new investigation promises to "identify the presence of anti-Semitism and Islamophobia attitudes, and the reasons for them."[94] Conspicuously absent from the statement was any mention of the fact that Muslims have been the primary perpetrators of anti-Jewish attacks.

In sum, Sweden has replicated the EU's persistent shortcomings (these have included denying, ignoring, and/or rationalizing antisemitism), while overlooking those EU measures that might ameliorate it. For instance, this Member State might have demonstrated best practice by affirming the rhetoric of the EUMC's working definition of antisemitism and utilizing the Centre's guide against it. In this way it might have condemned Åström's malicious assertion that Israel's request that Sweden dismantle an inflammatory museum exhibit is comparable to the censorious Third Reich. "Drawing comparisons of contemporary Israeli policy to that of the Nazis" is antisemitic, according to the EUMC's under-utilized guide.[95] Had Sweden emphasized this particular insight, it might have also more forcefully countered similar comparisons issued by the Davis Cup Boycotters. Instead, the state's capitulation to these agitators may have emboldened them.

The arsonist attacks on Sweden's Jewish congregations continue and, in contrast to the European Commission's 2008 position that the Mideast conflict "can never be a reason for anti-Semitism,"[96] one cannot overlook the lasting effects of Lambert's apologetics. When, for instance, the Pew Forum, an American research center, released its 2011 report on religious conflicts worldwide (between 2006 and 2009), it found Sweden was one of only four Member States (the others were Bulgaria, Denmark, and the UK) where religious conflicts increased most.[97]

If Sweden appears to be changing course, it may be less because it has come to appreciate its shortcomings than because others from outside the EU have done so for them. According to *Svensk Dagbladet*, it was only after fierce international criticism mounted from non-EU actors like the OSCE and the Wiesenthal Center, a U.S.-based Jewish rights group, that the government agreed to a one-time 2012 expenditure of four million kronor ($630,000) to increase security and reduce the vulnerability of the country's Jewish communities.[98]

The Minister of Integration, Erik Ullenhag, explained, "I am concerned that there is a picture outside of Sweden that we have not taken the threat to Jews seriously. We have on several occasions received criticism from international representatives for not doing enough against anti-Semitism."[99] Months later, Ullenhag met with Hannah Rosenthal, a special U.S. envoy sent by the Obama administration to combat antisemitism. Following that meeting, Ullenhag issued a public rebuke of Malmö's notoriously antisemitic Mayor Ilmar Reepalu for his recurring statements against Jews, including that Sweden's Jews had engaged in a nationalist conspiracy against the country's Muslims. "These statements," the minister said, "not only have a negative impact on the image of Malmö but the entire country's credibility in these issues."[100] When Reepalu later announced he would relinquish his position in advance of the 2014 election cycle, the mayor maintained that his comments about Jews had been misunderstood and he insisted that he had initiated the meeting with envoy Rosenthal to discuss antisemitism, an account Rosenthal denies.[101]

With Sweden's reputation of paramount concern to its government officials, it is doubtful that either its single expenditure to protect Jews or Reepalu's resignation signal a substantive shift in state policy. Indeed, Reepalu's Social Democratic colleagues appear more concerned with how the charges of antisemitism have "marred" Reepalu's legacy than with the in-security Jews experienced during his reign.[102]

Shortly after Reepalu's resignation, the Social Democrats elected Omar Mustafa to their Stockholm governing board despite his desreputable tenure as spokesman for Sweden's Islamic society. After considerable public oputrage followed an exposé revealing his organization's sexism, homo-phobia, and antisemitism, the party reconsidered his appoitment and Mustafa resigned. Among his most troubling public positions was his defense of the Jew-hating Qaradhawi as "balanced." Had Sweden's elites taken a more pro-active position against the virulent antisemitism endured by Jews in Malmö and elsewhere, the four million euro investment in stepped-up security might not have been necessary and another political scandal might have been averted. Whether Austria's record proves any less disappointing is the question we next reflect on as we consider Europe's integration and its consequences on its Member States.

AUSTRIA

In turning to Austria, we employ the three key queries that framed our analysis of Sweden. First, has Austria relegated antisemitism to the rabble of the far right, away from more respectable political quarters? Is this Member State relatively unresponsive to antisemitism when its perpetrators are Muslim and/or left-affiliated? Last, what (if any) are the consequences of integration for Austria's policies and have the EU's post–9/11 initiatives to counter antisemitism mattered to Austrian Jews? I address each query in the order asked.

To begin, a pervasive and deep hostility against Jews has long been such an unrelenting fact of Austrian public life that relegating antisemitism to a single segment of the political spectrum makes little sense. One need only recall that Austria's Social Democrats (SPÖ) both courted ex-Nazis and entered into coalition with the far right (FPÖ) and so too did its conservative mainstream counterpart, the People's Party (ÖVP). A high-ranking Social Democrat elucidated the political calculus of his party's "social partnership" (or "extreme opportunism") when he said, "If the gassed Jew could vote, I would be ready to speak at election meetings about the crimes of the Nazis. But unfortunately we need the votes of those who gassed them."[103] The rela-tive strength of Austria's unrepentant electorate continues and cannot be discounted.

Europe's intervention in 2000 may have helped facilitate the FPÖ's electoral decline in 2002, when the party suffered its worst electoral performance since 1986 (capturing only 10 percent of the national vote), but Haiderism itself survived. Weeks prior to Haider's regional comeback in 2004, analysts doubted his political resilience.[104] In addition to having uttered one too many provocative statements, Haider's reverence for Nazi labor policies and the *Waffen SS* was audacious and augmented by his refusal to show remorse. Yet, this defiance appealed both to the Austrian electorate and accentuated Haider's standing abroad. At home, Haider enjoyed steadfast support from Austria's largest newspaper, *Kronen Zeitung.* Its popular columnist, Richard Nimmerichter, referred to him as "an unfaltering representative of the truth and indispensable ally of the little man."[105] Somewhat more surprising perhaps is that Sweden's gay male press expressed similar sentiments. Following (international) revelations that Haider relished the company and love of other men while projecting a more conventional image of a married (heterosexual) man, it eulogized Haider as someone who "dared to tell the truth" though he was "*seen by his critics* as a dangerous racist and demagogue."[106] What bit of Haider's truth telling merits this statement remains a mystery.

In 2004, just four years before his inebriated death from a car crash, Haider emerged victorious at the local level in Corinthia where he was reappointed as Governor with 42 percent voting FPÖ (and 4 percent fewer favoring the SPÖ). Emboldened by this success and wishing to project a somewhat more moderate image as his party expanded its neo-Nazi connections, Haider and several of his former colleagues established a new party the following year.[107] They called it the Alliance for the Future of Austria (BZÖ).

By September 2008, Haider's new Alliance party garnered 11 percent in federal elections while the FPÖ won 18 percent under new leadership. Having campaigned to defend the rights of "real Austrians," the BZÖ and FPÖ outpolled conservatives (who won 25.6 percent). Together they handed the Social Democrats (with 29.7 percent of the vote) their worst showing in postwar history and the FPÖ took Vienna, a once solid bastion of the worker's movement. While the far right came within a hair behind the SPÖ, the FPÖ remains the strongest party nationwide among voters under thirty.

With this clout, the FPÖ's Martin Graf garnered enough votes within the parliament's right flank (109 of 156 MPs) to become one of two of its deputy presidents. A steadfast member of the Burschenschaft Olympia, a fraternity with long-standing Nazi associations (whose past members included Adolph Eichmann, Rudolph Hess, and Heinrich Himmler), Graf's ascendance elicited outrage from the Jewish community. In advance of the parliament's vote, Vienna's concentration camp survivors met with Austrian MPs and asked them to withhold their endorsement of Graf. After the MPs rebuffed the survivors, the Jewish Religious Community in Vienna released a public statement. It warned Austrian lawmakers had "made a symbolic decision which can lead to a further strengthening of the right-wing extremist camp and which shows little sensibility for Austrian history and the tragic results of German nationalism."[108] Graf's toxic brand of politics had been brewing for some time.

In 2005, Graf's fraternity, Olympia, further distinguished itself as extremist when it contravened Austria's law on Holocaust denial by inviting Britain's notorious denier David Irving to lecture. Five years prior, Irving had launched and lost a libel suit in Britain against the American scholar Deborah Lipstadt and her publisher (Penguin Books) for having labeled him "one of the most dangerous spokespersons for Holocaust denial."[109] With this reputation, Irving solidified his standing as an international cult figure among neo-Nazis and, thus, became an appealing illicit speaker for Olympia's members. In addition to successive restrictions and prohibitions on Irving in Italy, South Africa, and Canada, Irving had an outstanding Austrian arrest warrant from 1989 for his earlier denials, among them that Auschwitz had no gas chambers.

As Europe's first Member State to prohibit Holocaust denial—well in advance of the EU's adoption of the 2008 Framework Decision—Austrian authorities were able to apprehend a defiant Irving while he was en route to his Olympia address. Austria's law extends to "whoever denies, grossly plays down, approves or tries to excuse the National Socialist genocide or other National Socialist crimes against humanity in a print publication, in broadcast or other media."[110] Not only does it not require intent, it carries up to ten years in prison for those who transgress it.

Irving was sentenced to three years in 2006 for falsifying history and although he served only thirteen months before Austria expelled him, his trial and subsequent sentence generated immediate and intense debate within Austria and abroad. In Austria, the prominent sociologist, Christian Fleck, insisted in the leading daily *Der Standard* that Irving was punished for an "opinion crime" that was "unworthy of a democracy."[111] Fleck's plea to "Let Irving Speak" may have struck a sympathetic chord among free speech advocates and others opposed to the law that led to Irving's arrest, but the denier and his most avid defenders had hardly proven paragons of "free speech." In fact, Irving offered to suspend his libel case against Lipstadt if, in addition to issuing him an apology, she would agree to have all of her books destroyed. Words clearly matter, and for the columnist Hans Rauscher and other Austrian public intellectuals, Holocaust denial is not an opinion but an act that undermines democracy by minimizing Nazism's evils,[112] a position codified both by the ECtHR's 2003 *Garaudy* decision and then by the EU's 2008 Framework legislation.

For Austrian political scientist Fritz Plasser, Irving's conviction held "strong symbolic meaning" for a country intent on showing the world it had "fundamentally changed" since the Nazi era.[113] But, in early 2006, the sentence may have held limited appeal for those less interested in Austria's past than with its "evenhandedness" concerning European restrictions on free speech.[114] The American political scientist, Erik Bleich, explains, "The Irving trial took place. . .at the peak of the Danish Cartoon Controversy, during which many Europeans vociferously defended the freedom to publish material deemed deeply offensive and possibly harmful to Muslims."[115] For Bleich and other Americans, including Lipstadt, the difference in treatment displayed rank unfairness. Lipstadt, an outspoken free speech advocate, wrote "to jail someone for denying the Holocaust, while supporting the right of cartoonists to lampoon other religions, smacks of a double standard."[116] However, for the Austrian political analyst Anton Pelinka and many of his European colleagues, the comparison is questionable. "As unwise and ill-advised as the cartoons may have been, and are," Pelinka insisted, "fighting the Holocaust revisionists has nothing to do with religious and other liberal freedoms but with facing Europe's greatest nightmare."[117]

While the vast majority of Austrian political leaders praised Irving's conviction as consistent with Austrian law,[118] the far right's opposition to the prohibition continued, especially as the efforts to enforce it did not diminish. From 1999–2006, Austrian authorities had secured the criminal convictions of over two hundred deniers,[119] verdicts in keeping with ECtHR (not ECJ) precedent. This record may have enhanced Austria's international standing as it weighed in on European-wide debates in favor of the above-noted 2008 Framework Decision criminalizing Holocaust denial, but it proved an irritant to its adversaries.

During the 2008 national campaign, the FPÖ's leadership both responded to its base and broadened its appeal by demonstrating a talent for ideological twister. That is, Graf half-heartedly denounced racism, antisemitism, and "all crimes committed in the name of a misguided ideology while simultaneously defending his membership in Olympia."[120] This political performance served Graf and his party well in the elections as they garnered just below 18 percent of the vote.

After the far right's impressive showing, Nick Griffin, the leader of Britain's Nationalist Party (BNP, a "white only party"),[121] sent his personal congratulations to the FPÖ's new leader, Heinz Christian Strache. Griffin was impressed by Strache's ability to generate sizeable neo-Nazi crowds at rallies where Hitler salutes were clearly visible.[122] A year before the election, photos surfaced that showed Strache taking part in paramilitary exercises in the 1980s. Then, on the eve of a Memorial day for the victims of Nazis (May 5, 2007), Strache called for the remembrance of "all victims of every war,"[123] a seemingly banal statement that in effect denies the particular historical reality of the Nazis and thus rejects political responsibility for the consequences of antisemitism. Such campaigning led Griffin to write, "We in Britain are impressed to see that you have been able to combine principled nationalism with electoral success. We are sure that this gives you a good springboard for the European elections and we hope very much that we will be able to join you in a successful nationalist block in Brussels next year."[124] Months later, the BNP celebrated its own victory after it became the first fascist party in British history to gain a seat within the European Parliament—a success that resulted in no small measure from a change in that Member State's election rules.

The FPÖ's European campaign met with similar success. Austria's far right took 17.7 percent of the 2009 vote and the FPÖ sent two members to Brussels. There they met counterparts from the BNP, France's National Front, and a clutch of other far-right parties. Although this alliance fell shy of the 25 MEPs (from at least seven Member States) needed to establish an official political grouping in parliament and access to EU funding, ignoring the potential of this coalition would be misguided. If nothing else, these parties have helped widen the range of acceptable political discourse, particularly in the aftermath of the downward economic spiral that began the same year.

During his European campaign, Strache called on Austrians to oppose Turkey and Israel's accession to the EU. An outraged Social Democratic Chancellor, Werner Faymann, characterized this request as disgraceful nonsense that was intended to "serve anti-Semitic prejudices" because Israel is not a candidate for accession.[125] Moreover, while the anti-Muslim tenor of Strache's opposition to Turkey's membership is obvious, one must not overlook the antisemitic dimensions of this case as well. Turkey's accession talks clearly informed FPÖ posters exclaiming "The West in Christian hands," but this anti-Muslim slur also coincided with routine references to "Jewish influence" in Turkey's state and civil society. Indeed, FPÖ propagandists insisted Turkey's secular founder, Kemal Ataturk, tried to "conceal his alleged Jewish roots."[126] Despite these and related statements, the antisemitic dimensions of the campaign against Turkey have consistently been ignored.[127]

Maligning both Jews and Muslims proved an effective campaign strategy, but as the Stephen Roth Institute notes, the FPÖ's leadership was less than unequivocal about some of its anti-Muslim propaganda. For instance, when one of its campaigning politicians, Susanne Winter, insisted that the Prophet Mohamed penned the Koran during "epileptic bouts" and referred to him as a "child molester" for marrying a six-year-old, "some German and Austrian neo-Nazis applauded this statement, but the majority rejected it as a provocation 'on behalf of Zionism.'"[128] Winter was placed under police protection after Muslim fundamentalists threatened to murder her and, in 2009, the Justice Department in Vienna charged her with "incitement and degradation of religious symbols" (*Verhetzung und Herabwürdigung religiöser Symbole*). She received a fine (of approximately $31,000) and a suspended sentence.

The occasional rejection by FPÖ elites of anti-Arab and anti-Islamic slander may stem less from any repudiation of bigotry than political affinity. Antisemitism is, after all, a powerful means by which otherwise disparate groups cohere.[129] Recall, for instance, our earlier discussion of the renewed efforts to restore Nazi-Islamic alliances.[130] As early as 1921, Islamicists admired Nazis for their anti-Zionist stance,[131] a position no less palpable at radical left and Islamicist demonstrations decades later. When in 2010, these groups converged to organize a 10,000 strong pro-Hamas demonstration, placards called on Hitler to "wake up," a slogan the centre-left newspaper, *Falter*, merely characterized as strange.[132] The antisemitic overtone of anti-Zionism is similarly held and equally unmistakable in the words of Mahmud Abbas (aka Abu Mazen), the current and seemingly more moderate President of the Palestinian Authority. The same year, Abbas insisted he was ready to accept a third party (e.g., NATO) to supervise the implementation of a peace agreement with Israel on the condition that he would "not accept the presence of Jews in these forces or a [single] Israeli on the Land of Palestine."[133] A year later, his ambassador to Washington restated this position when asked about the rights of minorities in a Palestinian state.[134] Such rhetoric may render the Palestinians alluring allies for Europe's far right,[135] but Haider came to this conclusion years earlier.

In the mid-1990s, Haider hailed his own party as "the PLO of Austria," a nod to the Palestinian Liberation Organization's express call (as articulated in its Charter) for the "liquidation of the Zionist presence." Kreisky had similarly expressed his sympathy for the PLO in 1978. That year, in an interview with the Dutch daily, *Trouw*, he condemned Israeli politicians (whom he called "Östjuden") as the world's most hated and unpopular. Kreisky went on to assert, "They are as unpleasant as the Africans, who are also quarrelsome people,"[136] a position that likely resonated with Haider and his later followers.

Those tempted to suggest that Strache's FPÖ changed course when he signed a 2010 "Jerusalem Declaration" affirming Israel's right to exist might consider how he used the occasion to simultaneously stoke anti-Islamic sentiment and antisemitism.[137] In addition to posing with Israeli paratroopers while vowing to defend Israel against its Arab enemies, Strache stood at Yad Vashem's Hall of Remembrance (where the ashes of Holocaust victims are kept) appearing to don a *kippah*. A closer look revealed that he wore a *Biertönnchen*, a red, blue, and black cap that identified him as a lifelong member of Vandalia, a far-right fraternity long associated with Pan-German nationalism and antisemitism.[138] Captured on Austrian television, this gesture at Israel's official Holocaust Museum sent a clear signal to his base and was in keeping with the antics of Haider, his predecessor.[139]

Although the FPÖ's political fortunes derive from its persistent positions and mobilization, it continued to garner legitimacy from Austria's political establishment, not least in the aftermath of Haider's death in late 2008. With over 30,000 mourners attending his funeral, the occasion became a day of national mourning, one covered live by the state's broadcaster (ORF).

At Haider's funeral, in an astonishing show of political solidarity that covered Austria's entire ideological spectrum, one politician after another praised Haider as the consummate politician. Encouraging Austrians to pay their tribute, then Chancellor Alfred Gusenbauer, a Social Democrat, claimed that Haider "had an excellent feeling for what needs to be changed,"[140] a puzzling remark given the FPÖ leader's long-standing ambition to break the Social Democrats and their hold on power. Barbara Prammer, the country's first woman president of the parliament and an outspoken advocate for women's rights, credited Haider with having changed her country's political landscape—implying it was for the better. The former Green Party chair, Alexander Van der Bellen, referred to Haider as "an exceptional politician" and the conservative vice chancellor, Wilhelm Moterer, insisted that he "deserves great respect."[141]

As the ink dried on Haider's October 2008 obituary and the Israeli press commented on the "absence of an intellectually honest appraisal of Europe's most significant right-wing extremist,"[142] an infuriated former FPÖ MP (Karlheinz Klement) insisted that once all Jews were dead, "a sense of relief and satisfaction" would overtake the "German speaking world."[143]

Months later, the Alliance party won 45.6 percent of the vote in Carinthia's local elections. Haider's widow attributed the outcome to her late husband's political achievements and the media concurred by dubbing the election a "posthumous triumph." This outcome came as no surprise to the Austrian political scientist, Stephan Grigat. In 2003 he predicted, "The normal state of post-Nazi society in Austria would remain even without Jörg Haider." He elaborated, "the terrible thing is not so much the success of extremists, but the way they are courted by conservatives and Social Democrats."[144]

Following the reverential embrace of Haider's venomous political bequest and his posthumous electoral "triumph," a German-based correspondent for the *Jerusalem Post* asked "Is Austria largely Haider?"[145] Given the unsettling circumstances that ensued, it seemed an appropriate question. Like Grigat and others, the journalist cast blame at the feet of Austria's political elite.

Michael Rendi, then Austria's ambassador to Israel, responded to the correspondent's query with a cascade of evidence to counter the notion of thriving Haiderism. After noting Austria's strong bilateral relations with Israel, Rendi cited the establishment of the National Fund of the Republic of Austria for Victims of National Socialism, noting it had processed over 60,000 applications with payments of over 450 million euros to the victims of that regime. The tide had clearly turned since 1982 when, as chair of the youth wing of the Social Democratic Party, Fritz Edlinger explicitly opposed such payments. In his letter to Vienna's Jewish Community that year, Edlinger wrote, "Instead of constantly directing cheap and superficial appeals to Austria's guilty conscience and demanding compensation from Austria's population, you should rather look more critically at the political development of the state of Israel that you defend uncritically." He concluded, "Until you are ready to do that, I deny absolutely your moral right to pass judgment on and make public declarations about the activities of Austrian organizations."[146] In essence, Edlinger cast Austria's Jews as un-Austrian (political and economic) exploiters of the Holocaust, a position antithetical to the later efforts underscored by Rendi who insisted Austria was confronting its past.

Not surprisingly, Rendi hailed Austria's stringent laws against Holocaust denial and its engagement with relevant international discussions to counter antisemitism at the EU level and beyond. Not only did Austria assume a leadership role in the adoption of the Framework Decision to counter Holocaust denial, the state could also boast success in reducing it. Austria's polling firm, GfK, revealed that only 6 percent of the population believed that there was no historic proof that the Holocaust happened, a significantly lower figure than the 15 percent of Austrians surveyed in 1979.[147] Though the firm did not release the details of its methodology, the decline is notable—if only because of the increase in doubt that followed Sweden's Holocaust programming four years earlier.

Insisting that remembrance of the *Shoah* is ever present among Austrians, Rendi declared that his country was honored to assume its role as President of the Task Force for International Cooperation on Holocaust Education, Remembrance and Research (ITF).[148] Although one might expect ambassador Rendi to emphasize his country's international efforts to combat antisemitism, his barbed tone was somewhat surprising. "It is legitimate to criticize a country if there is reason and substance," he wrote, "but it is unfair to apply incorrect stereotypes about Austria as a whole."[149] This attempt to place Austria's critics on the defensive seems misplaced given the correspondent's initial query stemmed less from stereotypes than from an effort to understand the unanimous accolades extended to Haider by political allies and presumed opponents alike. To argue, as Rendi then did, that attendance at Haider's funeral was mere "protocol" overlooks the substantive support Austria's politicians extended, however unintentionally, to Haiderism.

In general, the pro-Haider sentiment expressed by Austria's political elite contrasted sharply with the tenor of Austria's communiqués as this Member State assumed leadership of the ITF earlier the same year. Seven decades had passed since *Kristallnacht* (November 9–10, 1938), when rioters in Austria and Germany destroyed synagogues and other Jewish owned property in a prelude to the destruction of European Jewry. As the newly inducted Task Force Chair, Ambassador Ferdinand Trauttmansdorff recalled the significance of 2008 and emphasized Austria's special commitment to coordinate efforts against antisemitism. Together with the Council of Europe, the ITF was to lead Austria and other countries in a new direction.

"What we need is a genuine culture of remembrance, a targeted and exemplary remembrance of the causes and sheer unthinkable effects of National Socialism," argued Austria's State Secretary Hans Winkler. "In addition to an unbiased engagement with the facts of the past," he insisted, "it is also necessary to show all victims and cases of injustice the due respect and sympathy. We must become aware of our history and learn for the present and the future."[150]

When, in December of 2008, the ITF held its plenary meeting within the Austrian Parliament, Prammer, who two months earlier eulogized Haider, issued the conference's opening remarks. In addition to reiterating Winkler's statement, she chastised Austria's "political class" for failing to confront uncomfortable truths.[151] While one doubts she had herself in mind, Graf's ascent and the parliament's indifference to those survivors who organized against him deserve mention. Months prior to that meeting, Austria's former Chancellor, Franz Vranitzky, gave a lecture in which he described how Social

Democratic functionaries had requested that he *not* speak to efforts against fascism and antisemitism at electoral meetings.[152]

The chasm between the respect Austria's politicians accord the far right and their insistence that their compatriots engage in a "genuine culture of remembrance" is bridged, in part, by witnessing how they calibrate their acceptance of Haiderism for a national audience while taking a more critical posture for an international one. Like Sweden's Minister Ullenhag, Winkler made clear that "raising awareness of the holocaust. . .is. . .highly acknowledged at the international level."[153] However, in Austria, condemnations of contemporary antisemitism can carry heavy electoral costs at the domestic level.

The electoral appeal of antisemitism both suggests the absence of moral leadership and the persistent success of FPÖ politicians like Barbara Rosenkranz. Her opposition to Austria's Holocaust denial legislation, ten children, and marriage to the notorious Horst Rosenkranz, a leading member of Austria's banned neo-Nazi (NDP) party, earned her the moniker of "Reich mother." In 2010, she received support for her presidential bid from *Kronen Zeitung.* The paper's publisher, Hans Dichland, described her as "a courageous mother who would make a good president for Austria."[154]

Asked by a television interviewer about whether she believed that the Nazis murdered millions of Jews—a stock query for FPÖ candidates—Rosenkranz responded that freedom of expression permits one to hold many "bizarre" positions. Although she would later distance herself from this comment, her equivocation had its desired effect. She came in second with 15 percent of the vote, losing to Heinz Fischer—an independent who won 80 percent in an election in which voter turnout was at a historic low of 54 percent.

More important than Rosenkranz's bid for Austria's honorific presidential post was the FPÖ's success in local elections in Vienna the same year. There the Social Democratic Party lost its majority (with 44 percent) and the Conservatives received their lowest percentage in history (with 13 percent). By contrast, the FPÖ won over a quarter of the electorate (with nearly 26 percent), essentially doubling their local seats.

Thus, it is on the international stage, rather than the domestic one, that Austria's politicians (like their Swedish and EU counterparts) offer unequivocal condemnations of antisemitism, often by focusing specifically on the Nazism of past. For example, on the 65th anniversary of the liberation of Auschwitz, in 2010, the Social Democratic Chancellor, Werner Faymann, visited the Polish death camp. Insisting that "The terrible crimes against humanity committed by the murderous regime of the Third Reich on the basis of anti-human ideology should never be forgotten," he added, "The legacy of history and the task of our generation is the continued development of democracy and, where necessary, the protection of people and resources of the democratic state." Moreover, he declared that such a state would "prevent any reoccurrence of the crimes of past."[155] The further the Holocaust recedes into history, the greater the opportunity to exploit it for a redemptive narrative.

To mark this same occasion, the Chancellor's conservative counterpart, Foreign Minister Michael Spindelegger, turned from Auschwitz's liberation and presented a candid consideration of the present. He remarked, "Anti-Semitism is not a thing of the past. The grim face of anti-Semitism and racism is often apparent nowadays. There can be no tolerance of it in Austria." With this, he insisted that Austria has an "obligation to increase public consciousness of the greatest murder of a people in history and to raise our children to be tolerant and respectful of human rights."[156]

However, when debates later ensued over whether to revoke surviving honorary titles to Adolf Hitler in Austrian towns, Spindelegger was less strident. Following a vote to remove the honorary citizenship Amstetten (a town 100 kilometers west of Vienna) bestowed to Hitler in 1938, the FPÖ alone abstained. With its eye on the Chancellorship in 2013, Pelinka remarked that the FPÖ was signaling voters that, "the party's radical pan-German core has not weakened."[157] It was an astute observation, one that might also explain Spindelegger's sudden disinterest in confronting the "grim face" of antisemitism. Instead, as we will soon note, he proposed resolving the debate *in camera*, a daunting task for a state whose every misdeed is often under a scope and seen as similar to its untenable past.

This controversy took on an international dimension at a joint press conference held by Strache and France's National Front Leader, Marine Le Pen, in Strasbourg. When an attending Austrian journalist asked Le Pen what she thought of the FPÖ's abstention, Strache insisted the query was tantamount to tarnishing Austria's image abroad. When Spindelegger subsequently responded: "This is an Austrian debate that should be discussed in Austria and...not internationalized,"[158] the Green Party construed the Foreign Minister's comments as proof that he was—as the ÖVP's leader—considering a coalition with the FPÖ. Spindelegger formally rejected this possibility. After all, over a decade earlier, that alliance elicited international scorn and Europe's rebuke.

Still, for a Member State once subject to the sanctions of its EU peers, it is remarkable how little we know about Austria's successes and/or short-comings concerning antisemitism. One the one hand, the resilience and unrelenting antisemitism of Austria's far right suggests this Member State is impervious to change, notwithstanding Europe's earlier interventions. On the other hand, Austria's apparent success in prosecuting and reducing Holocaust denial in advance of EU efforts to do the same is impossible to ignore. Similarly, one might take solace from the decrease in the number of *official* recorded incidents of antisemitism—from 23 in 2008 to 12 in 2009. However, unofficial accounts suggest an increase from 46 incidents in 2008 to 200 in 2009.[159]

Although caution is required when dealing with such small numbers, the marked difference between the official and unofficial tallies stems in large part from the authorities' near exclusive reliance on right wing monitoring, an inadequate methodology given the virulent antisemitism sometimes rampant within the left and among Islamicists. Recall that in working together they turned out 10,000 anti-Israeli demonstrators in Vienna carrying countless antisemitic slogans and symbols in 2010. The event prompted the Viennese Jewish Community (the IKG) to file a complaint with the public prosecutor's office. Although we do not yet know the office's response, it is unlikely that this authority will strongly condemn these manifestations given the state's reluctance to monitor them.

Despite this methodological shortcoming and others, Austria is under no pressure to change. Its stated efforts to address antisemitism are in keeping with both Swedish and European standards. For years, the FRA has praised Sweden and Austria (along with France and Germany) for collecting "sufficient official criminal justice data allowing for a trend analysis of recorded anti-Semitic crimes."[160] The thin basis for this praise suggests that the EU agency expects little of its Member States; a matter that may be less troubling than it appears. Interpreted optimistically, it may be that in setting the bar so low, Member States are better encouraged to comply.

CONCLUSION

Over the past decade, Austria's attempt to enhance its international profile through Holocaust remembrance differed in one significant respect from Sweden's earlier efforts to do the same—it lacked the Nordic state's powerful connection to humanitarianism in the public conscience. Moreover, while the benevolent vision Swedes have of themselves appears proportionate to their international standing, the same cannot be said of Austrians.

By contrast, Austria's reputation as Europe's heavy is often at odds with the country's perception of itself as Nazism's "first victim," a misperception manifest in a unique opprobrium against (Austria's) Jews. Acutely aware of the ways in which Jewish survivors embodied the state's co-responsibility for the Holocaust, Vienna's Jewish Community (IKG) itself issued statements (as early as 1956) attesting to the ways the "very presence" of Austria's few Jews served as an "inconvenient" challenge to political parties and the country's founding myth.[161] As such, these survivors and their descendants have been "persistently constructed as an inherently antagonistic to the Austrian state"[162]—an identity complicated by European integration.

Understandably enthused by the ways that European identity offers Austrian Jews "potent protection against virulent nationalism and the threat of antisemitism,"[163] Bunzl and others might exaggerate the EU's protective capacity by overlooking Europe's reliance on Member States to implement it (i.e., protection). As realists remind us, and our Austrian and Swedish cases suggest, nation-states remain the *primary (though not exclusive)* unit for dispensing and protecting rights and privileges. Even Austria's most ambitious interventions against antisemitism that pertained to Holocaust denial had little to do with Europe's prodding or its precedent, in fact its prohibitions on Holocaust denial helped inform the EU's Framework Decision. Moreover, as Bleich makes clear, the vast majority of Austrian politicians who supported David Irving's (2006) sentencing did so because it was consistent with *Austrian*, not EU, law,[164] a point that signals the EU's modest leverage in ameliorating antisemitism.

There is perhaps no better illustration of the EU's limited powers than when Sweden's authorities issued visas (in 2006) to representatives from Hamas in clear defiance of the EU's ban on contact with the organization. Worse, this action proved in keeping with the government's persistent refusal to challenge those calling for the destruction of Jews. Consider, for instance, Sweden's earlier refusal to denounce suicide bombing at its international conference on genocide in 2004. Five years later, the Chancellor of Justice insisted that a (local) mosque's calls for the extermination of Jews did not constitute racial incitement but, instead, "commonplace" rhetorical "battle cries" from the Middle East. It is precisely this indifference to and acceptance of such hate mongering that inspired the EU's working definition of anti-semitism and other efforts—all of which Sweden has been able to ignore.

In the next (and last) section, we revisit the major findings of this work and reflect on recent developments at the transnational level to consider those steps that might enhance the effectiveness of EU and state measures against antisemitism.

NOTES

1. Mikael Tossavainen, *Det Förnekade Hatet—Antisemitism bland Muslimer och Araber i Sverige* (Stockholm, 2003); "Swedish anti-Semitism revealed," *The Local: Swedish News in English*, 14 Mar. 2006; Henrik Bachner, "Political Cultures of Denial? Antisemitism in Sweden and Scandinavia" in *Politics and Resentment: Antisemitism and Counter-Cosmopolitanism in the European Union*, edited by Lars Rensmann and Julius H. Schoeps (Leiden, 2010); See also note 10 below.

2. Mikael Tossavainen, "Arab and Muslim Anti-Semitism in Sweden," *Jewish Political Studies Review* 17, nos. 3–4 (2005): 115.

3. European Union Monitoring Centre on Racism and Xenophobia. *Racism and Xenophobia in the EU Member States—Trends, Developments and Good Practice EUMC Annual Report 2003/2004 Part 2* (Vienna, 2004), 191.

4. Erik Eiglad, *The Anti-Jewish Riots in Oslo* (Porsgrunn, 2010), 71.

5. Nick Meo, "Jews leave Swedish city after sharp rise in anti-Semitic hate crimes," *Telegraph*, 21 Feb. 2010; Cnaan Liphshiz, "Anti-Semitism, in Sweden? Depends who you're asking," *Haaretz.com*, 9 Nov. 2007.

6. Tossavainen, "Arab and Muslim Anti-Semitism in Sweden"; Lena Jersenius (Office Manager for Swedish Committee Against Antisemitism [SKMA]) in discussion with author, Stockholm, 25 May 2009.

7. Lisa Abramowicz et al, "The radical reinterpretation of incitement against Jews by the Chancellor of Justice in Sweden: EJP Publishes an Opinion written and signed by four Jewish Swedish personalities," *European Jewish Press*, 3 Apr. 2006.

8. "Wiesenthal Center slams Sweden for 'Jewish tax,'" *The Local: Swedish News in English*, 15 Mar. 2011.

9. Lena Jersenius (Office Manager for Swedish Committee Against Antisemitism [SKMA]) in discussion with author, Stockholm, 25 May 2009.

10. Tossavainen, *Det Förnekade Hatet*, 43–44, author's translation. This situation is especially concerning because, according to Henrik Bachner and Jonas Ring, antisemitism is twice as common among Muslim respondents than the Swedish population as a whole. See Henrik Bachner and Jonas Ring, *Antisemitiska attityder och föreställningar i Sverige* (Stockholm, 2006), 133. Nonetheless, the co-authors were circumspect about the representative dimensions of this finding because they had few Muslim respondents. Yet, well before their survey, Tossavainen had been careful to acknowledge the heterogeneous composition of Sweden's large Muslim community, noting, for instance, Muslims of non-Arab origin (e.g., those with families from Turkey and Bosnia) tend to be less antisemitic than others (e.g., from Iraq and Lebanon). See Tossavainen, *Det Förnekade Hatet*, 26.

11. Tossavainen, *Det Förnekade Hatet*, 25, author's translation. For those wondering how the death chants "Death to Jews" and "Death to America" are linked, Markovits writes, "One can easily write about European anti-Semitism without ever talking about anti-Americanism. The converse, I maintain, is impossible." Andrei Markovits, *Uncouth Nation: Why Europe Dislikes America* (Princeton, 2007), 151–52. Addditionally, drawing parallels to the protean dimensions of antisemitism, Markovits emphasizes anti-Americanism's antonymous character. Ibid., 24.

12. Quoted in Donald Snyder, "Jews reluctantly abandon Swedish city amid growing anti-Semitism," *Haaretz.com*, 11 July 210.

13. In Bachner, "Political Cultures of Denial?," 349–50.

14. Stephen Roth Institute, "Sweden" in *Annual Reports* (Tel Aviv, 2004), 6.

15. Eiglad, *The Anti-Jewish Riots in Oslo*, 78.

16. A year later, French President Nicolas Sarkozy welcomed Libyan dictator Muammar el-Qaddafi, to his country, coincidentally on December 10, International Human Rights day. Sarkozy's Human Rights Minister, Rama Yade, denounced this move and wrote: "Colonel Qaddafi must understand that our country is not a doormat on which a leader, terrorist or not, can come and wipe the blood of his crimes off his feet." Quoted in Mona Eltahawy, "Welcome mat for a dictator," *New York Times*, 14 Dec. 2007. Her remark comes to mind after Sweden hosted Hamas.

17. Lucia Kubosova, "MEPs to ask Belgium for Hamas visas," *EUobserver*, 18 May 2006.

18. Andrew Rettman, "Swedish-Israeli relations continue to deteriorate," *EUobserver*, 22 Sept. 2009.

19. Paulina Neuding, "Welcome to Ramallmö: How a tennis match sparked riots in Sweden," *Weekly Standard*, 13 Mar. 2009.

20. Meo, "Jews leave Swedish city after sharp rise in anti-Semitic hate crimes."

21. Mona Sahlin, "Legislative and Institutional Mechanisms and Governmental Action, Including Law Enforcement," PC.DEL13 11/04 (Stockholm, 2004).

22. Bachner, Political Cultures of Denial?

23. Tossavainen, *Det Förnekade Hatet*, 21, note 54.

24. Stephen Roth Institute, "Sweden" in *Annual Reports* (Tel Aviv, 2006), 3. This common claim excuses Arab antisemitism by suggesting that Arabs are also Semites. Bernard Lewis exposes two central flaws in this argument. First, he notes that the term "Semite" has no meaning when applied to groups as heterogeneous as Arabs and Jews. Indeed, he suggests that the use of this term is "itself a sign of racism and. . .either ignorance or bad faith." Second, he demonstrates that "anti-Semitism has never anywhere been concerned with anyone but Jews, and is therefore available to Arabs as to other people as an option should they choose it." See Bernard Lewis, *Semites and Anti-Semites: An Inquiry into the Conflict and Prejudice* (New York, 1987), 117. In fact, in 1942, the Nazis reassured their Arab allies that this was true. In a *New York Times* article filed in Stockholm, the Nazi Foreign Ministry issued the following statement, "We have never said the Arabs are inferior as a race. On the contrary, we have always pointed out the glorious historic past of the Arab people." See "Nazis Reassure Arabs—Antisemitism confined to Jews, Spokesman Explains," *New York Times*, 5 Nov. 1942, 2.

25. Ruth Wisse, "The Suicidal Passion," *Weekly Standard* 17, no. 10 (2011).

26. Quoted in Tossavainen, "Arab and Muslim Anti-Semitism in Sweden," 116. As we will see, Sweden's Chancellor of Justice, Göran Lambertz, then codified this position in a 2006 case concerning ethnic incitement against Jews.

27. European Union Monitoring Centre on Racism and Xenophobia. *Racism and Xenophobia in the EU Member States—Trends, Developments and Good Practice EUMC Annual Report 2003/2004 Part 2* (Vienna, 2004), 191.

28. Manfred Gerstenfeld, *Behind the Humanitarian Mask: The Nordic Countries, Israel, and the Jews* (Jerusalem, 2008), 28–29.

29. Mikael Tossavainen, "Arab and Muslim Anti-Semitism in Sweden," 116, n. 1.

30. One such work is Maria-Pia Boëthius, *Heder och Samvete: Sverige och andra världskriget* (Honor and conscience: Sweden and the Second World War) (Stockholm, 1992).

31. Werner Bergman and Juliane Wetzel, *Manifestations of anti-Semitism in the European Union: First Synthesis Report* (Vienna, 2003), 63.

32. See, for instance, Jonas Ring and Scarlett Morgentau, *Anti-Semitic, Homophobic, Islamophobic and Xenophobic Tendencies among the Young*

(Stockholm, 2005). For a critical analysis posed by such conflations, see Clemens Heni, *Antisemitism: A Specific Phenomenon* (Berlin, 2013). While Heni focuses most on Germany, Alvin H. Rosenfeld's anthology, *Resurgent Antisemitism: Global Perspectives* (Bloomington, Ind.: Indiana University Press, 2013) offers a broader lens for understanding the unique character of contemporary antisemitism. See, for example, Bernard Harrison's indispensible analysis of the distinction between "social prejudice" and antisemitism. Bernard Harrison, "Anti-Zionism, Antisemitism, and the Rhetorical Manipulation of Reality" in *Resurgent Antisemitism: Global Perspectives*.

33. Zvi Mazel (former Israeli ambassador to Sweden), in discussion with author, Jerusalem, 26 Mar. 2006.

34. Manfred Gerstenfeld, "Anti-Israelism and Anti-Semitism in Sweden: An Interview with Zvi Mazel," *Think Israel* (Jerusalem, 2007), http://www.think-israel.org/gerstenfeld.mazel.html.

35. Manfred Gerstenfeld, "An Interview with Zvi Mazel: Anti-Israelism and Anti-Semitism in Sweden" in *Behind the Humanitarian Mask: The Nordic Countries, Israel and the Jews* (Jerusalem, 2008), 86.

36. Amiram Barkat, "Jews in Sweden are afraid to be known as Jews," *Ha'aretz*, 10 Feb. 2004; Peter Carlberg, Anna-Lena Haverdahl, and Cordelia Edvardson, "Israel anklagar Sverige för svek," *Svenska Dagbladet*, 18 Jan. 2004.

37. Cnaan Liphshiz, "Anti-Semitism, in Sweden? Depends Who You're Asking," *Haaretz.com*, 9 Nov. 2007.

38. Quoted in Mats Wiklund, "Var mesta diplomat," *Dagens Nyheter*, 23 Mar. 2002, author's translation.

39. Bachner, "Political Cultures of Denial?," 337.

40. Associated Press, "Rights Group Condemns Palestinian Attacks; Suicide Bombings Are 'Crimes Against Humanity,' Amnesty International Says," *Washington Post*, 12 July 2002, A16.

41. "Arafat faction rejects attacks on Israel," *BBC News World Edition* online, 10 Sept. 2002, http:// news.bbc.co.uk/2/hi/middle_east/2248444.stm.

42. Quoted in CNN, "Human Rights Watch: Suicide bombers 'war criminals,'" *CNN.com/World*, 1 Nov. 2002, online http://edition.cnn.com/2002/WORLD/meast /11/01/human.rights.palestinians/.

43. Ibid.

44. "Declaration by the Stockholm International Forum 2004," *Prevent Genocide International*, 26–28 Jan. 2004, 6th recital, online http://www.preventgenocide.org/ prevent/conferences/StockholmDeclaration28Jan2004.htm.

45. Middle East Media Research Institute, "Al-Qaradhawi speaks in Favor of Suicide Operations at an Islamic Conference in Sweden," *MEMRI report* 542 (2003), http://www.memri.org/report/en/0/0/0/0/0/0/914.htm. Qaradhawi's enthusiastic embrace of suicide bombing is manifest, not least, in his having issued a separate fatwa permitting women to do them. See Paul Berman, *The Flight of the Intellectuals* (Brooklyn, 2010).

46. Quoted in Berman, *Flight of the Intellectuals*, 92. Berman characterized Qaradhawi as "someone who has outdone everyone else in rendering the concept of ritual suicide and terrorism acceptable and even admirable." Ibid., 189. This analysis that might explain his apparent impact on Sweden's political elite below.

47. Susanna Abramowicz, "Inquiry into anti-Semitic tapes dropped," *European Jewish Press*, 19 Jan. 2006.

48. Quoted in ibid.

49. Justitiekanslerns beslut, Decision Beslut 2006-01-02 2006-01-02; Dnr 6335-

05-33 6335-05-33, Stockholm, author's translation.

50. Göran Lambertz (Sweden's former Chancellor of Justice) in discussion with author, Stockholm, 9 June 2009.

51. Abramowicz, "Inquiry into anti-Semitic tapes dropped."

52. Göran Lambertz (Sweden's former Chancellor of Justice) in discussion with author, Stockholm, 9 June 2009.

53. Justitiekanslerns beslut, Decision Beslut 2006-01-02 2006-01-02; Dnr 6335-05-33 6335-05-33, Stockholm, author's translation.

54. Organization for Security and Co-operation in Europe, Berlin Declaration (Statement adopted at the Second OSCE Conference on Anti-Semitism, Berlin, 28–29 April 2004).

55. Franco Frattini, "The Need for a Unified Stance in Combating Racism and Xenophobia" (Paper presented at Seminar on Racism and Xenophobia, Vienna, 22 June 2006).

56. Göran Lambertz (Sweden's former Chancellor of Justice) in discussion with author, Stockholm, 9 June 2009.

57. European Union Monitoring Centre, *Working Definition of Antisemitism*, (Vienna, 2005).

58. Göran Lambertz (Sweden's former Chancellor of Justice) in discussion with author, Stockholm, 9 June 2009.

59. Robert S. Wistrich, *A Lethal Obsession: Anti-Semitism from Antiquity to the Global Jihad* (New York, 2010), 453.

60. Melanie Phillips, "The New Anti-Semitism" in *Those Who Forget the Past: The Question of Anti-Semitism*, edited by Ron Rosenbaum (New York, 2004), 252; see also Robert S. Wistrich, *From Ambivalence to Betrayal: The Left, the Jews, and Israel* (Lincoln, Neb., 2012).

61. Abramowicz et al, "The Radical Reinterpretation of Incitement against Jews by the Chancellor of Justice in Sweden."

62. Ilya Meyer, "Dhimmi Watch," *FrontPageMag.com*, 8 Apr. 2006.

63. Bachner, "Political Cultures of Denial?," 332.

64. Justitiekanslerns beslut, Decision Beslut 2006-01-02 2006-01-02; Dnr 6335-05-33 6335-05-33, Stockholm, author's translation. See, as well, the European Convention on Human Rights, available online http://www.echr.coe.int/NR/rdonlyres/D5CC24A7-DC13-4318-B457-5C9014916D7A/0/Convention_ENG.pdf.

65. *Garaudy v. France*, 2003.

66. *Norwood v. United Kingdom*, 2004.

67. The British far right is not, however, of one mind over such expressions. Indeed, more recently, it has expressed solidarity with Palestinians, in an effort to destroy Israel. See, for instance, New-Right London, "Justice for Palestinians A Vital British National Interest—Martin Webster" (YouTube, 2011).

68. *Norwood v. United Kingdom*, 2004.

69. "Preachers, fascists and cartoonists," *The Local: Swedish News in English*, 15 Feb. 2006.

70. "Swedish party leaders united on cartoon crisis," *The Local: Swedish News in English*, 6 Feb. 2006.

71. Wistrich, *A Lethal Obsession*, 453.

72. Lars Rensmann and Julius H. Schoeps, "Politics and resentment: Examining Antisemitism and counter-cosmopolitanism in the European Union and Beyond" in *Politics and Resentment: Antisemitism and Counter-Cosmopolitanism in the European Union*, edited by Lars Rensmann and Julius H. Schoeps (Leiden, 2010), 52.

73. See, for instance, European Commission, *The European Union and Sport* (Luxembourg, 2004).

74. David Stavrou, "Crowd ban 'risks bolstering extemists,'" *The Local: Swedish News in English*, 7 Mar. 2009.

75. See Neuding, "Welcome to Ramallmö."

76. Stavrou, "Crowd ban 'risks bolstering extemists.'"

77. "Jewish group calls on Swedish PM to investigate recent Malmö demonstration," *European Jewish Press*, 1 Feb. 2009.

78. Ibid.

79. Donald Boström, *Inshallah: Konflicten mellan Israel och Palestina* (Stockholm, 2001).

80. Boström, "Våra söner plunderas på sina organ," *Aftonbladet*, 17 Aug. 2009.

81. Andrea Levin, "Anatomy of a Swedish Blood Libel," *Wall Street Journal*, 14 Oct. 2009.

82. Gerald Steinberg, "Swedish government funds anti-Semitic NGOs," *Jerusalem Post*, 19 Aug. 2009.

83. Abraham Cooper, "The Free Press Defense: Sweden, Aftonbladet and What Wallenberg Would Think," *Huffington Post*, 1 Sept. 2009.

84. Matts Carblom, "E-post visar att ambassadör handlade på eget initiativ," *Dagens Nyheter*, 24 Aug. 2009.

85. See, e.g., Cooper, "Free Press Defense."

86. "Bad blood between EU and Israel," *Presseurop.eu*, 24 Aug. 2009.

87. Adar Primor, "Following inflammatory article, Sweden to demand EU condemn anti-Semitism," *Haaretz.com*, 31 Aug. 2009.

88. Jacques Barrot, "Racism and antisemitism have no place in the EU, nor elsewhere in the world" (Paper presented at Building Together the Future of Europe, European Parliament, Brussels, 30 Mar. 2009), 3.

89. Quoted in Herb Keinon, "Bildt: No plan to condemn anti-Semitism," *Jerusalem Post*, 31 Aug. 2009.

90. Quoted in Mikael Tossavainen, "The Aftonbladet Organ-Trafficking Affair: A Case Study," *Jewish Political Studies Review* 95, no 1 (2010).

91. Quoted in Keinon, "Bildt: No plan to condemn anti-Semitism."

92. Jimmie Åkesson, "Muslimerna är vårt största utländska hot," *Aftonbladet*, 19 Oct. 2009.

93. Andrew Baker, "Country Visit: Sweden Report of the Personal Represenative of the OSCE Chair-in-Office on Combatting Anti-Semitism June 13–16, 2010," OSCE.

94. Erik Ullenhag et al., "Vi måste bekämpa hatet ihop," *Svensk Dagbladet*, 14 May 2011, author's translation.

95. European Union Monitoring Centre, *Working Definition of Antisemitism*.

96. Franco Frattini, "Opening remarks for the second EC-Israel Seminar on the fight against racism, xenophobia and anti-Semitism" (Paper read at Israel Seminar on the Fight against Racism, Xenophobia and Anti-Semitism, Jerusalem, 22 Jan. 2008).

97. Pew Forum on Religion & Public Life, "Rising Restrictions on Religion" (Washington, 2011).

98. "Erik Ullenhag (FP): budgetsatsning för ökad säkerhet vid synagogor," *Svenska Dagbladet*, 5 Sept. 2011.

99. Ibid., author's translation.

100. Jewish Telegraph Agency, "Swedish minister rebukes Malmo mayor as 'ignorant and bigoted,'" 26 Apr. 2012.

101. Jewish Telegraph Agency, "Malmo mayor challenged on meeting with U.S. anti-Semitism envoy," 5 Mar. 2013.

102. "Anti-Semitism row 'could mar' Reepalu's legacy," *The Local: Swedish News in English*, 5 Feb. 2013.

103. Quoted in Karl Pfeifer, "Victim Compensation: Antisemitism and the Austrian Left," *Z Word*, 2008, http://www.hagalil.com/01/de/Europa.php?itemid =3034; See also Robert Knight, *Ich bin dafür, die Sache in die Länge zu ziehen. Wortprotokolle der österreichischen Bundesregierung von 1945–1952 über die Entschädigung der Juden* (Frankfurt, 1988), 197.

104. Richard Bernstein, "Today Carinthia, Tomorrow Vienna?," *New York Times*, 3 Mar. 2004.

105. Quoted in David Art, "Reacting to the Radial Right: Lessons from Germany and Austria," *Party Politics* 13, no. 3 (2007): 343.

106. Barbara Schmelz, "Jörg Haider levde dubbelliv," *QX*, 21 Oct. 2008, author's translation and emphasis added.

107. Art, "Reacting to the Radial Right," 345.

108. "Disputed Far-Rightist Elected to Top Post in Austrian Parliament," *Deutsche Welle*, http://www.dw-world.de, 28 Oct. 2008.

109. Deborah E. Lipstadt, *Denying the Holocaust: The Growing Assault on Truth and Memory* (New York, 1993), 181.

110. The National Socialism Prohibition Law of 1945, Amended in 1992. Available online at http://www.genocidepreventionnow.org.

111. Quoted in Erik Bleich, *The Freedom to Be Racist?: How the United States and Europe Struggle to Preserve Freedom and Combat Racism* (New York, 2011), 56.

112. Ibid.

113. Michael Adler, "British Holocaust denier Irving on trial in Austria," *European Jewish Press*, 19 Feb. 2006.

114. Bleich, *Freedom to Be Racist?*, 56.

115. Ibid., 56–57.

116. Quoted in ibid., 57.

117. Quoted in Adler, "British Holocaust denier Irving on trial in Austria."

118. Bleich, *Freedom to Be Racist?*, 57.

119. Michael Whine, "Expanding Holocaust Denial and Legislation Against It" in *Extreme Speech and Democracy*, edited by Ivan Hare and James Weinstein (Oxford, 2009), 549.

120. "Disputed Far-Rightist Elected to Top Post in Austrian Parliament," *Deutsche Welle*, http://www.dw-world.de, 28 Oct. 2008.

121. The BNP's constitution expressly "forbids blacks from being members and calls for the 'voluntary' repatriation of anyone descended from immigrants." Following Griffin's election to the EU Parliamentary in 2009, Britain's Equality and Human Rights Commission (a government bureau) challenged the Party for violating the UK Race Relations Act with its constitution and membership criteria.

122. Stephen Roth Institute, "Austria 2008/9" in *Annual Reports* (Tel Aviv), online http://www.tau.ac.il/Anti-Semitism/asw2008/austria.html.

123. Stephen Roth Institute, "Austria 2007" In *Annual Reports* (Tel Aviv), http://www.tau.ac.il /Anti-Semitism/asw2007/ austria.html.

124. Quoted in Billy Briggs, "The far right is on the march again: the rise of Fascism in Austria," *Daily Mail*, 14 Mar. 2009.

125. Sylvia Westall, "Austrian far-right leader isolated over Israel stance,"

Reuters Global News Journal, 20 May 2009.

126. Stephen Roth Institute, "Austria 2008/9" in *Annual Reports* (Tel Aviv), http://www.tau.ac.il/Anti-Semitism /asw2008/austria.html, 2.

127. See, for instance, Patrick R. Hugg, "Accession Aspirations Degenerate: A New Chapter For Turkey and the EU," *Washington University Global Studies Law Review* 9, no. 225 (2010): 225–81.

128. Stephen Roth Institute, "Austria 2008/9" in *Annual Reports* (Tel Aviv), online http://www.tau.ac.il/Anti-Semitism/asw2008/austria.html, 1.

129. Hannah Arendt, *The Origins of Totalitarianism* (New York, 1979), 10.

130. See, e.g., note 24.

131. Matthias Küntzel, *Jihad and Jew-Hatred: Islamism, Nazism and the Roots of 9/11* (New York, 2007), 28.

132. European Jewish Congress. *Antisemitism World Wide 2010: General Analysis,* edited by Roni Stauber (Tel Aviv, 2011), 9.

133. Quoted in Shmuel Trigano, "The Open Racism of the Future State of Palestine," Scholars for Peace in the Middle East (SPME*)*, 28 Oct. 2010, online http://spme.net/cgi-bin/articles.cgi?ID=7279.

134. "PLO official: Palestinians, Israelis must be totally separated," *Haaretz*, 14 Sept. 2011.

135. Rensmann and Schoeps, "Politics and resentment," 49–58.

136. Quoted in Karl Pfeifer, "Victim Compensation: Antisemitism and the Austrian Left."

137. Other extreme right European parties signed as well. They include Belgium's ultranationalist Vlaams Belang, Germany's Freedom Party, and the Sweden Democrats. According to Lena Posner-Körösi, president of Sweden's Official Council of Jewish Communities, the Sweden Democrats are a "neo-Nazi party." Quoted in Stefan Theil, "Europe's Extreme Righteous," *Newsweek*, 7 Mar. 2011.

138. Ibid.

139. Recall Haider's visit to the U.S. Holocaust Memorial Museum.

140. Quoted in Benjamin Weinthal, "Austrians praise deceased Nazi admirer Haider," *Jerusalem Post*, 19 Oct. 2008.

141. Quoted in ibid.

142. Weinthal, "Is Austria largely Haider?," *Jerusalem Post*, 12 Nov. 2008.

143. Quoted in Stephen Roth Institute, "Austria 2008/9" in *Annual Reports* (Tel Aviv) online http://www.tau.ac.il/Anti-Semitism/asw2008/austria.html.

144. Quoted in Benjamin Weinthal, "Haider's party scores 'posthumous triumph' for its founder," *Jerusalem Post*, 3 Mar. 2009.

145. Weinthal, "Is Austria largely Haider?".

146. Quoted in Karl Pfeifer, "Victim Compensation: Antisemitism and the Austrian Left."

147. William J. Kole, "New effort launched to fight anti-Semitism," *USA Today*, 10 Nov. 2008.

148. Michael Rendi, "Right of Reply: Don't judge Austria based on Haider," *Jerusalem Post*, 13 Nov. 2008.

149. Ibid.

150. Hans Winkler, "Winkler on Austria's chairmanship of the International Holocaust Task Force," Austrian Foreign Ministry, 2008.

151. Barbara Prammer, "Statement of Ms. Barbara Prammer President of the Austrian Parliament" (Paper presented on the occasion of the Opening of the Task Force for International Cooperation on Holocaust Education, Remembrance, and

Research Plenary Session, Vienna, 16 Dec. 2008).

152. Pfeifer, "Victim Compensation: Antisemitism and the Austrian Left."

153. Winkler, "Winkler on Austria's chairmanship of the International Holocaust Task Force."

154. Quoted in Tony Paterson, "Reich Mother on the March in Hitler's Homeland, "*Independent*, 24 Apr. 2010.

155. "Chancellor calls for 'murderous' Nazi crimes to remembered," *Austrian Times*, 27 Jan. 2010.

156. Ibid.

157. Agence France-Presse, "Far-right Austrian Party Ambivalent on Hitler Debate," 26 June 2011.

158. Ibid.

159. European Union Agency for Fundamental Rights (FRA), *Anti-Semitism: Summary overview of the situation in the European Union 2001–2010* (Vienna, 2011), 5.

160. Ibid., 31; European Union Agency for Fundamental Rights (FRA), *Annual Report* (Vienna, 2009), 26.

161. Quoted in Richard Mitten, "Jews and Other Victims: The 'Jewish Questions' and Discourses of Victimhood in Postwar Austria" in *Austria in the European Union*, edited by Günter Bischof, Anton Pelinka, and Michael Gehler (New Brunswick, N.J., 2002), 224.

162. Matti Bunzl, "Austrian Zionism and the Jews of the New Europe," *Jewish Social Studies* 9 no. 2 (2003): 162.

163. Ibid., 167.

164. Bleich, *Freedom to Be Racist?*, 57.

CHAPTER FIVE

Jews and the Ironies of Integration

For "Europe's" architects, economic integration offered an antidote to ethnic antagonisms, including antisemitism. If the economic antidote left poisonous remnants of discrimination, the Member States would have to resolve them. Scholars of European antisemitism therefore turned their sights on specific states with limited or no attention to EU politics while EU scholars otherwise attentive to discrimination ignored antisemitism. This work, in contrast, considered the circumstances that eventually obliged the EU to act against antisemitism and analyzed the effectiveness of the EU's efforts through two often-overlooked and ostensibly very different Member States—Sweden and Austria. In this final section, I offer a brief synopsis of my chief findings and consider the continued challenges faced by Europe's Jews.

In the 1990s, the European Commission went from unequivocally asserting that it lacked an explicit legal basis to intervene against antisemitism to insisting that the problem was one it should address, alongside other manifestations of discrimination. The left-leaning European Parliament had demanded transnational action a decade earlier, but its Joint 1986 Declaration against Racism and Xenophobia, related reports, and limited powers rendered antisemitism secondary and its efforts against it largely symbolic. Moreover, a careful sifting through that evidence suggests MEPs may have been less concerned with countering antisemitism than with curtailing the mounting power of their right-wing rivals. Even the Parliament's later resolution (of 2000) that condemned Haider's racism and xenophobia contained no express recognition of the rampant antisemitism that rendered his far right Austrian party successful and its populism distinctive. Still, Europe's parliamentarians were not alone in downplaying the specific threat to Jews posed by the extreme right's ascent in Austria and elsewhere.

Other EU actors behaved similarly, especially when antisemitism migrated from the right's outer edges into the mainstream of European politics. Recall, for instance, the European Union Monitoring Centre on Racism and Xenophobia (EUMC) and its reticence to acknowledge antisemitism among Muslims and leftists. Though one might criticize the EU for its inadequate approach to antisemitism, Europe's polity has never been particularly distinguished by a general commitment to anti-discrimination.[1] As noted earlier, this results not only from its principal emphasis on economics, but also from the very structure of its polity.

The EU's byzantine governance structure can inhibit anti-discrimination efforts; every sector passes on responsibility for redress so that relief is endlessly deferred. From the moment the 1997 Treaty of Amsterdam expanded the legal community's capacity to intervene against unlawful discrimination, assistance has been fragmented. The treaty's general non-discrimination clause now reads, "The Council, acting unanimously in accordance with a special legislative procedure and after obtaining the consent of the European Parliament, may take appropriate action to combat discrimination based on sex, racial or ethnic origin, religion or belief, disability, age or sexual orientation."[2] Requiring the Council to reach a unanimous position (via a potentially arduous process) before it "may take appropriate action," means the Council remains under no obligation to act. Yet, even if action was obligatory, the level of consensus that is required hamstrings remedy. In consequence, the Member States did not establish an effective provision but, instead, left it to the Community institutions to adopt "appropriate" measures. These same institutions, in turn, emphasize the powers of the (now 28) Member States to do the same. Each level of governance engages in buck passing with no effective results.

The limited redress for discrimination available to Jews through two of the Commission's later Directives shifts our attention from the challenges of multi-level governance to those of intersectionality. The 2000 Race Directive offers (secular) Jews redress when they are willing and able to demonstrate that the bias against them stems from being treated as if they are racially (or ethnically) distinct. At the same time, the 2000 Framework Directive provides recourse when (religiously observant) Jews can demonstrate that the discrimination against them is religious in character. The often-inextricable racial, ethnic, cultural, and religious threads of antisemitism render these policy silos futile as responses to the lived realities of Jews and antisemites in Europe. Moreover, without the significant commitment of Member States, the shortcomings of these Directives begin to resemble those of the Treaty. That is, they may increase expectations through rhetoric about equality and anti-discrimination, but substantive redress remains scattered and elusive and unsanctioned prejudice persists.

In the aftermath of 9/11, when global antisemitism reached a level not seen since the defeat of Nazism, press reports proved so alarming that the EUMC commissioned researchers to provide the Community's first general overview of the problem. The EUMC then shelved the report when it revealed that antisemitism was especially pronounced within Europe's Muslim communities. Infuriated, the researchers went public concerning the suppression of their work. In response, the EUMC denied that its primary objective was in protecting Muslims against charges of discrimination. Instead, the Centre claimed the research was flawed and never intended for publication, an explanation that strained the public's credulity.

As controversy escalated over the EU's first focused (draft) report on antisemitism, the EUMC's director acknowledged the debate was her agency's strongest challenge. Yet, with limited evidence to suggest that the controversy had been satisfactorily resolved, the Commission expanded the agency's remit. No longer charged with monitoring only "racism, xenophobia and related intolerance" (e.g., antisemitism), its responsibilities now include all of the "thematic areas" covered by the Charter of Fundamental Rights. The EUMC was thus rebranded the Fundamental Rights Agency (FRA) and, in 2007, given new obligations without being released from old ones it had never managed to fulfill. Indeed, the EUMC disregarded the Commission's earlier (2003) call for a comprehensive and cohesive approach to tackling racism and antisemitism when it *withdrew* references to antisemitism at its own 2006 conference entitled "Racism, Xenophobia and the Media." Nonetheless, the next month the Austrian President of the Council, whose offices had helped organize the conference, praised the Centre for encouraging "informed dialogue" between minority communities. In addition, he commended the EU agency for its "comparable data on racism, xenophobia, islamophobia [*sic*] and anti-Semitism."[3] These self-congratulatory tributes bore little resemblance to reality. Conference organizers had essentially discounted Jewish concerns and no comparable (EU-wide) data exists pertaining to the racism directed against Jews.

With none of its added responsibilities contingent on any demonstrable improvements and no new mechanism to encourage the Community's institutions and Member States to pay attention to its findings, the FRA is now under no pressure to revise its record so that it might have practical effect. The agency's abandonment of the EUMC's 2005 "working definition of antisemitism" exemplifies this weakness and underscores the importance of *official legal* remedies for discrimination. For this reason, recent efforts to reinstate the working definition on the FRA's website are likely to offer limited redress.

Years after the working definition of antisemitism was to have aided in the identification of incidents that authorities could then counter through legislation, an FRA official conceded that the definition required further comment before its effectiveness could be established—a Catch-22 given the FRA had never bothered to publicize it.[4] And, the FRA was under no obligation to do so because the definition was *never officially adopted* (e.g., as a decision or even a recommendation). Thus, by 2008, so few Jewish community leaders and NGOs throughout the EU knew of its existence that the American Jewish Committee's European Forum translated the working definition into several languages. However, its "informal adoption" (i.e., lack of legal standing) means that the working definition has limited utility for even those Jews now aware of it. In light of their failing to employ (much less circulate) a consistent working definition of antisemitism in its own agency reports, it is no surprise that most Member States had neither official nor unofficial records from which the FRA could then render thoughtful comparisons within the EU. Yet, by casting aspersions on the Member States for this, the agency absolved itself from its own responsibilities to promote best (knowledge) practices.

Despite these and various other shortcomings, the EU's other institutions persist in emphasizing the FRA's role in monitoring and condemning antisemitism—a position that also contradicts the Commission's 2003 call for "mainstreaming" anti-racism efforts throughout all Member States and EU institutions. When later met with questions from the European Parliament on the need for targeted actions against antisemitism[5] and efforts to allay violence against Jews in Sweden,[6] the Commission commended the FRA for its data collection[7] and later stressed the protection already available to Jews through the Framework Decision.[8] This exchange is characteristic of the circumvention that Jews and others meet in their struggles against discrimination.

Those seeking greater accountability are likely to find the Commission's oversight troubling for several reasons. First, in keeping with the disappointing legacy of its predecessor, the FRA has not yet produced comparable data on antisemitism worthy of the Commission's commendation. Second, the Commission provided no details on the implementation of the 2008 Framework Decision until 2014. It then recognized that although nineteen Member States fell short of compliance, the Commission's ability to intervene was rather limited.[9] With hate speech migrating to cyberspace at an alarming pace, the EU's call for a European-bound remedy may seem quaint. Physical territoriality, however transnational, has its limitations. Reflecting on the growing presence of Italian antisemitism in cyberspace, scholars Betti Guetta and Stefano Gatti show that this altered terrain facilitates "a cultural climate that seems to permit attitudes and statements that would have been inadmissible a few years ago."[10] Their insights apply no less to the European level.

Especially concerning is the Commission's failure to condemn the anti-semitism of its own officials. Consider, for example, the European Commissioner for Trade, Karel De Gucht, who depicted Jews as opinionated. In reference to debates on the Middle East, he told a radio program, "It is not easy even with a moderate Jew to have a conversation."[11] When the Commission's spokesman was pressed repeatedly on whether the body disavows these remarks, he prevaricated and said only that the European Commission considers them "personal comments."[12] The next day De Gucht issued a written statement. He reiterated that his comments were simply his "personal point of view" and that he "did not mean in any possible way to cause offense or stigmatize the Jewish Community". He concluded, "I want to make clear that anti-Semitism has no place in today's world and is fundamentally against our European values."[13] Far from placating his critics, the European Jewish Congress (EJC) rejected the statement as insufficient. It noted that the Commissioner persisted in offering no apology for his personal (and no less antisemitic) point of view.[14] In fact, the EJC's president, Moshe Kantor, observed: "Since the economy started spiralling downward in 2009, many prominent European officials have felt the freedom to express very troubling anti-Semitic views."[15]

Even the EU Parliament provides ambivalent and occasionally contradictory responses to antisemitism. Its early anti-racist initiatives that distinguished the institution as progressive were rarely attentive to antisemitism and may have even downplayed it. Such was the case when, in 1985, MEPs issued their first report on racism and fascism (the *Evrigenis* Report). They concluded that, despite an increase in organized fascism, antisemitism was a limited phenomenon in Europe that was restricted to a small minority.[16] Years later, the MEP and chair of that investigation noted that (by 1989) antisemitism had become more explicit than any time since World War II.[17] Yet it was not until 1995 that the Parliament issued its first explicit condemnation of antisemitism through a Resolution on Racism, Xenophobia and Anti-Semitism.

When, in 2013, the EP held its first official ceremony for International Holocaust Remembrance Day, its President (Martin Schulz) insisted that the Holocaust "always be fresh in our minds and souls, in the conscience of humanity, and should serve as an incontrovertible warning for all time. Never again!"[18] Yet, the year prior, the EP appears to have neglected this duty when its members provided an annual allowance (of approximately 465,333 euro) to the Alliance of European National Movements (AENM), a coalition of political parties that includes the neo-Nazi British National Party, France's National Front, and Hungary's Jobbik Party. Although the head of Jobbik demanded his government draw up a list of Jews who pose "a national security risk" in November of 2012, the EP again considered the allowance. This led the European Network Against Racism (ENAR) to issue a press release in which it publicly excoriated the EP for contradicting its professed values.[19] With the controversy serving as a source of some embarrassment, the Commission has proposed new rules for party funding. These would require that parties observe "European values," including minority rights as codified in EU law.[20] Yet whatever the EU's shortcomings and related reforms, its (2012) Nobel Peace Prize has enabled EU politicians, like Schulz, to claim that the polity "no doubt, can serve as an inspiration to other regions of the world."[21] This strains credulity to the breaking point.

By 2014, Jews throughout the EU and beyond were somewhat shocked when the EU's top foreign policy chief, Catherine Ashton, omitted mention of Jews in the statement she gave to commemorate International Holocaust Memorial Day. It read:

> Today we honour every one of those brutally murdered in the darkest period of European history. We also want to pay a special tribute to all those who acted with courage and sacrifice to protect their fellow citizens against persecution.

She continued,

> On Holocaust Remembrance Day, we must keep alive the memory of this tragedy. It is an occasion to remind us all of the need to continue fighting prejudice and racism in our own time. We must remain vigilant against the dangers of hate speech and redouble our commitment to prevent any form of intolerance. The respect of human rights and diversity lies at the heart of what the European Union stands for.[22]

By substituting these platitudinous references to racism, intolerance, and human rights for antisemitism's centrality to the Holocaust, Ashton appeases those whose sympathy for Nazis is barely disguised. Additionally, her failure to acknowledge the genocidal murder of six million Jews appeals to Europeans who resent reminders of their moral shortcomings and, in response, may wish to utilize the *Shoah* as a means to chastise Jews for Israel's "occupation."

Notwithstanding the EU's modest efforts and self-satisfied rhetoric regarding its struggles against antisemitism, the conditions I've outlined are among many that point to the persistence of a less than encouraging legacy for the EU. The myriad ways that the EU has been able to evade action against antisemitism while sometimes appearing to provide remedy against it (e.g., through its monitoring agencies, working definition of antisemitism,

Fundamental Rights Charter, and other legislation) begs a question. What, if any, are the effects of this within the Member States and might they similarly circumvent remedy?

Our investigation into Sweden and Austria commenced in 1995, as both entered into an EU that had begun mobilizing against myriad discriminations. With regard to antisemitism more specifically, Austria had three years earlier revamped its law prohibiting Holocaust denial—the first of its kind in Europe and one that later served as a model for the 2008 Framework Decision. Sweden, by contrast, was about to reel from a national study that found that nearly a third of its teenagers doubted the *Shoah* had occurred. These doubts emerged in 1997 alongside news stories of Sweden's energetic trade with the Nazis and its forced sterilization programs that continued well into the 1970s under Social Democratic governance. With its progressive bona fides in question, Sweden's Prime Minister announced educational efforts to reverse the ignorance of his country's teens. Many of these focused not on Sweden's own transgressions but, rather, on those grave cruelties perpetrated by Europe's other states.

Against this backdrop, each state nevertheless swiftly succumbed to type—Sweden's unsavory past receded from the news and Austria's robust implementation of its model law received scant attention. By January 2000, standard assumptions about Swedish humanitarianism and Austrian authoritarianism were reinforced when the Nordic state welcomed delegates from throughout the world to an international conference at which the country established itself as the consummate source of Holocaust educational initiatives. As delegates met in Stockholm to reflect on Europe's Nazi past, Austria's then Chancellor (Viktor Klima, a previous EU President) and President (Thomas Klestil) warned their colleagues of the dangers posed by a far right poised to join the ranks of a new government. Having served as ambassador to the United States during the Waldheim affair, President Klestil was especially sensitive to Austria's international standing, a sensitivity that Michael Gehler suggests may have led this leader to create an "alarmist atmosphere" at the Stockholm conference.[23] According to Gehler, Klestil's "hectic telephone diplomacy for assistance and understanding from abroad" helped prompt EU-level action.[24]

As the Stockholm conference closed with a chorus of "never again," Member States (most of which were headed by Social Democrats) were in a quandary about whether and how to make an example of a newly-elected Austrian government that included a notorious antisemite, one whose far-right party trivialized Nazism. This was no simple problem. Austria's government had been democratically elected and had infringed neither on any of its own laws nor those of the EU. For this reason, the "EU of 14" imposed "bi-lateral" sanctions (not EU ones), a distinction minimized by the EU's own institutions. For example, both the European Parliament and the Commission welcomed the sanctions, though the later avoided addressing the procedure (or lack thereof) taken to accomplish their passage.

As "European values" of fairness, transparency, and solidarity hung in the balance, the EU was itself vulnerable to allegations of anti-democratic behavior that threatened Member State sovereignty. Such concerns rendered Austria's isolation unsustainable. An exit strategy was needed and in their rush to enact the sanctions, the Member States had not thought to provide one.[25] It thus fell to the EU's President to resolve the matter. After all, he was the leading spokesperson for the "EU of 14."

In what marks an interesting irony, the EU President bypassed EU institutions and, instead, relied on the Council of Europe's highest court, the European Court of Human Rights (ECtHR), to render a verdict about Austria and the effectiveness of the sanctions against it. That Court's President then appointed "three wise men" whose final report provided concessions to all involved. For itself, the Council of Europe (COE) established its competence to adjudicate the Charter, an EU agreement the report's authors insisted no Member State could ignore.

As for the EU, its response to Austria's presumed infringement, however slight, appeared to offer Jews in Austria a rhetorical fillip against escalating prejudice—a point often overlooked and one not mentioned in the report. Perhaps this was intentional. If, as analysts note, Austria's isolation similarly enhanced its willingness to negotiate with and compensate Jewish survivors for the property that its Nazis confiscated from them,[26] the report's authors might have thought it prudent to omit an outcome that would further enrage antisemites. Indeed, the "three wise men" reasoned that continuing sanctions would prove "counter-productive"—furthering a nationalist fervor they sought to limit. Data suggests they were right to be concerned. The pro-EU position among Austrians plummeted, from 45% in the fall of 1999 to 34% the next spring—marking a drop of nearly 50% from 1994 when 66% of Austrians approved of EU membership.[27]

In the end, the COE's report established that Austria's new government was no less democratic than its EU counterparts, all of whom retain considerable independence to interpret the EU's fundamental rights and anti-discrimination policies. Thus, the report affirmed the sovereignty of the Member States, the Austrian government and the opponents of sanctions, while also supporting the proponents of those measures. After all, the report credited these sanctions with enhancing the commitment of all EU members to Europe's "common values." In appearing to resolve the Austrian conundrum in a manner that gives offense to no one, the report nowhere explains why safe-guarding European values necessitates the intervention of external arbiters. This political paradox is likely to persist. It is, in the end, almost impossible to expect others to place their faith in EU actors and institutions when the EU's own president reached beyond them to resolve the conflicts that accompany struggles for social justice.

Having placed considerations of antisemitism at the perimeters of their investigations into the EU-14's sanctions, scholars have often neglected Sweden's role in their adoption and, instead, remarked on its apparent reservation over Austria's subsequent isolation.[28] While it is the case that Sweden (like Denmark and the United Kingdom) was less eager than others (e.g., France and Belgium) to have Austria rebuked, its international conference on the Holocaust helped foster a political climate in which this tact seemed necessary.

Yet far from finding Sweden a trailblazer in actions against antisemitism, I note that after its 2000 conference, the country neglected countless opportunities to counter antisemitism through public statements (e.g., the Declaration against Genocide), legal precedent (e.g., the Radio Islam ruling of 1990) and EU remedies (e.g., attention to the EUMC's working definition). Thus, whether one focuses on Sweden's refusal to condemn "suicide bombing" as a crime against humanity or considers its reluctance to enforce hate crime legislation against those who publicly demand the murder of Jews, the state has earned the opprobrium of the Simon Wiesenthal Center (SWC) and the European Jewish Congress (EJC). These are hardly the laudable hallmarks of a progressive crusade against antisemitism.

By 2010, the Wiesenthal Center issued a travel advisory that warned Jews against visiting Sweden's southern city of Malmö. Two years later, the European Jewish Congress insisted the country had become "a center of anti-Semitism."[29] This characterization followed from the government's refusal to meet with the organization's president, Moshe Kantor.

As the only government to decline a meeting with the European Jewish Congress to address domestic antisemitism, Sweden is worth watching. If global hostility against Jews increases, other states may follow suit and similarly ignore the issue. Had Austria denied a meeting with EJC, commentators may have attributed the snub to the state's past. Sweden, by contrast, does not have the inescapable burden of either Auschwitz or Haider. This Scandinavian state regards itself and is often seen by others as the world's moral compass. For that reason alone, its distance from issues of import to Jews— as expressed by the both the EJC and SWC—is especially disconcerting.

In sum, whatever their differences, the case studies of Sweden and Austria illustrate how two Member States have rebuffed efforts to redress anti-semitism while simultaneously claiming to decry it, a position that holds for the European Union as well. For Jews, their allies, and others around the world interested in social justice—recognizing this rather than denying it is the first step toward remedying it.

NOTES

1. R. Amy Elman, *Sexual Equality in an Integrated Europe: Virtual Equality* (New York, 2007).

2. Treaty of Amsterdam amending the Treaty on European Union, the Treaties Establishing the European Communities and Certain Related Acts (OJ C 340 10.11.1997), Article 19 TFEU, ex Article TEC.

3. Austrian Presidency, "EU Statement on the Tolerance and Implementation Meeting on Promoting Inter-Cultural, Inter-Religious and Inter-Ethnic Under-standing" (Almaty, 2006), para 8.

4. Alexander Pollak (Programme Manager for Social Research, Fundamental Rights Agency), in discussion with author, Vienna, 28 May 2009.

5. See, e.g., Parliamentary Questions, 11 Mar. 2010.

6. See, e.g., Parliamentary Questions, 12 July 2011.

7. Parliamentary Questions, 12 Apr. 2010.

8. Parliamentary Questions, 25 Aug. 2011.

9. European Commission, "International Holocaust Remembrance Day: Commission calls on Member States to criminalise denail of crimes against humanity," Brussels, 27 Jan. 2014, http://europa. eu/rapid/press-release_IP-14-75_en.htm.

10. Betti Guetta and Stefano Gatti, "Anti-Semitism in Italy 2011," 15 Mar. 2012, online report avalable through the Foundazione Centro di Documentazione Ebraica Contemporanea (CDEC), www.observatorioantisemitismo.it, 2. Conditions in Italy are complicated by the ascendent of populist Beppe Grillo and his Five Star Movement, with its complete reliance on social media to communicate with its followers. A former comic, Grillo offered a spirited defense of the notorious antisemitic actor Mel Gibson (in 2006) and his followers coninue to indulge in antsemitic polemics. For example, one insists "The Shoah Must Go On" to eliminiate Jewish fiscal dictatorship. Quoted in Stefano Gatti, "Fenomenologia di un comico che non fa più ridere, anzi ci preoccupa," Blog/News, Jan. 2013 online www.romaebraica.it. Grillo's comedic past allows him to indulge in hateful banter while offering the prevarication that he is "only joking." The declining credibility of (Italian) politicians has led to the popularity of populists like him.

11. John Miller, "EU Official in Trouble for Remarks on Jews," *Wall Street Journal*, 3 Sept. 2010.

12. Stephen Castle, "European Trade Chief Accused of Anti-Semitism," *New York Times*, 3 Sept. 2010.

13. Miller, "EU Official in Trouble." This reference to "European values" has legal bearing. Article 2 of the Treaty on European Union affirms that, "The Union is founded on the values of respect for human dignity, freedom, democracy, equality, the rule of law and respect for human rights, including the rights of persons belonging to

minorities."

14. Castle, "European Trade Chief Accused of Anti-Semitism."

15. Moshe Kantor, "Dealing with Europe's Soul, Not Just Economies," *Jerusalem Post*, 6 Dec. 2011.

16. European Parliament, *Committee of Inquiry into the Rise of Fascism and Racism in Europe: Report on the findings of inquiry* (Luxembourg, 1985), 52, see also note 171.

17. Glyn Ford, *Fascist Europe: The Rise of Racism and Xenophobia* (London, 1992), xi.

18. "Martin Schulz: 'The Holocaust must always be fresh in our minds and souls,'" *European Jewish Press*, 19 Jan. 2013, http://www.ejpress.org/article/64533.

19. European Network Against Racism (ENAR), "European representatives must stand up against hatred" (press release ENAR) 25 Jan. 2013, http://www.icare.to /article.php?id=43718&lang=en.

20. European Commission, "Proposal for a regulation of the European Parliament and of the Council on the statute and fund of European political parties and European political foundations," COM (2012) 499 final, 12.9.2012, 6–7.

21. "Martin Schulz: 'We need unity in our efforts to fight anti-Semitism and racism in Europe,'" *European Jewish Press*, 17 Oct. 2012, http://ejpress.org /article/62446.

22. European Union External Action Statement, "EU High Representative Catherine Ashton on Holocaust Remembrance Day (Brussels)," 27 Jan. 2014, http://eeas.europa.eu/statements/docs/2014/140127_01_en.pdf.

23. Michael Gehler, "'Preventive Hammer Blow' or Boomerang: The EU 'Sanction' Measures against Austria 2000" in *Austria in the European Union*, edited by Günter Bischof, Anton Pelinka, and Michael Gehler (Brunswick, N.J., 2002), 195–96.

24. Ibid., 196.

25. Ibid., 187.

26. Ibid., 192.

27. Ibid., 210.

28. See, for instance, Michael Merlingen, Cas Mudde, and Ulrich Sedelmeier, "The Right and the Righteous? European Norms, Domestic Politics and the Sanctions Against Austria," *Journal of Common Market Studies* 39, no. 1 (2001): 67. There are, however, some notable exceptions. See Gehler, "'Preventive Hammer Blow,'" 197–207; See also Jenny Wüstenberg and David Art, "Using the Past in the Nazi Successor States from 1945 to the Present," *Annals of the American Academy* 617, no.1 (2008): 82–83.

29. Cnaan Lipshiz, "EJC President: Sweden Center of Anti-Semitism," *Jerusalem Post*, 25 Jan. 2012.

Epilogue

In late 2013, the European Union's Fundamental Rights Agency (FRA) released its most comprehensive survey report on antisemitism, *Discrimination and Hate Crimes against Jews in EU Member States*.[1] The FRA's online survey covered eight Member States (Belgium, France, Germany, Hungary, Italy, Latvia, Sweden, and the UK), where an estimated 90% of the EU's Jews now live. According to the head of that agency's Equality and Citizens' Rights Department, the objective of the survey was to gather "the type of robust evidence" that "will assist EU institutions and national governments in taking the necessary measures that will ensure that the rights of Jewish people are fully respected, protected and fulfilled across the EU."[2] The FRA's poll, which focused on the experiences and perceptions of antisemitism among 5,847 self-identified Jews (from September and October of 2012), is a catalogue of disturbing findings.

One in five (21%) survey respondents noted they had personally experienced at least one incident of antisemitic harassment and/or a physical attack in the twelve months preceding the survey. Hungary, Belgium, and Sweden had the highest incident rates (with 30%, 28%, and 22% respectively), but the problem of antisemitism extends well beyond these three. On average, three-fourths (76%) believe conditions for Jews have worsened over the past five years in the country where they live. Two-thirds of the respondents (66%) consider antisemitism an EU-wide problem.

Respondents from all eight Member States perceived the perpetrators of the most serious antisemitic incidents as those with "Muslim extremist views" (27%), "left-wing political views" (22%), or "right-wing views" (19%).[3] Because survey respondents attributed antisemitism to perpetrators from across the political spectrum, classifying these assailants as "extremist" is misleading. Ameliorating antisemitism privileges candor over politically calculated condemnations of Europe's "extremists."

Innovative mobilization across the ideological divide and throughout the Member States is a political necessity. The central question that drives this work is whether the European polity is up to this task. That is, can the EU deliver the measures needed to tackle antisemitism within its Member States? Because the FRA is expected to provide guidance to policy makers in Member States and EU institutions, this epilogue examines the report's additional findings as well as the agency's response to them. Although the FRA's decision to include Sweden and not Austria in its survey hampers the fine-grained comparative analysis of the two Member States at the core of this book, I nevertheless welcome another opportunity to reflect more broadly on the consequences of Europe's integration for Member State Jews.

When specifically asked about the forms of harassment that they encountered, 75% of the nearly 6,000 respondents identified online antisemitism as the most widespread manifestation of abuse. Writing from Britain, one respondent commented, "the amount of antisemitic material circulating is phenomenal. This is in some ways setting us backwards as now young people are circulating content like the *Protocols of the Elders of Zion* which had, prior to the internet, pretty much died out." Another, from France, remarked on the antisemitic and anti-Zionist character of many YouTube videos. A respondent in Britain lamented, "Since going on Facebook, I have experienced more antisemitic comments in a few years than. . . throughout my whole life. This is very dispiriting. The speed at which hostile comments and misinformation can be passed around is frightening and leads to a sense of deep unease."[4]

Contempt against Jews is so often expressed through Holocaust trivialization and denial online that, within the year prior to the survey, an unsurprising 57% of respondents witnessed someone claim the *Shoah* was either a myth or an exaggeration. A slightly smaller percentage (54%) were aware that Member States had laws against Holocaust denial and trivialization, prohibitions in keeping with the EU's 2008 Framework Decision to counter *intentional* racial incitement. Nonetheless, the FRA's report concedes that these laws may be ineffectual because the transnational character of online antisemitism requires joint action among states, rather than mere prohibitions within them. And, as noted in Chapter 3, the considerable latitude extended to Member States in implementing the Decision rendered it weak. If Austria proves a notable exception, it is because its ambitious interventions preceded those of the EU.

With antisemitism now viral, one third (33%) of those surveyed worried about being physically attacked for their Judaism in public and over one fifth (23%) occasionally avoided Jewish events or sites because of safety concerns. This worry increased significantly when respondents were queried about their family's well-being. For instance, 66% of parents or grandparents of school-aged children worried their children and grandchildren would be subjected to harassment at school. Such concern is warranted when one considers that the survey's youngest respondents (between 16–29) were more likely (at 34%) to have experienced verbal and physical abuse than their elders.

The survey also asked whether respondents refrained from wearing, displaying, or carrying objects in public that might identify them as Jewish. These items include, but are not limited to, kippot (i.e., skull caps), Jewish themed jewelry (e.g., Jewish stars), and mezuzahs affixed to (external) doorframes. On average, 68% of all respondents acknowledged some reluctance to live openly as Jews; the highest percentage of those who answered that they "always avoid" wearing or carrying such items live in Sweden (34%), followed by France (29%) and Belgium (25%). A woman in Germany explained that as long as one remains "private" about their Jewish identity, "there seems to be no problem. However, as soon as we, like Christians or Muslims, also want to attach importance to our religion and to openly live our religion, the situation changes dramatically."[5] For Moshe Kantor, President of the European Jewish Congress, the fact that so many "Jews are not able to express their Jewishness because of fear should be a watershed moment for the continent of Europe and the European Union."[6]

Conditions have become so threatening that one in ten respondents report that they have either moved or are considering moving from their neighborhoods. Although this response varies markedly across the Member States, roughly a third (29%) of those surveyed thought of emigrating. Respondents in Hungary (51%), Belgium (41%), and France (49%) contemplated emigration more than other respondents, while those in the UK, Italy, and Sweden were less likely to consider this option (with 19%, 21%, and 21% respectively) than Jews in Germany and Latvia. Nonetheless, it is evident that Jews throughout the EU avoid even visiting neighborhoods where they perceive that they are manifestly unwelcome.

Given these dispiriting data, one might overlook the seemingly more subtle forms of antisemitism that a quarter (23%) of all respondents registered in acknowledging that they had experienced some form of discrimination on the basis of their religion or ethnic background within the twelve months prior to the poll. Indeed, one respondent criticized the survey for not having inquired into "institutional racism." She specifically mentioned the difficulties faced by observant Jews who must leave work early on Fridays. Moreover, she objected to the common expectation that social events occur on Fridays. To address this, the FRA called on Member States to encourage trade unions and employers' associations to adopt more flexible arrangements for Jewish employees. Despite the potential importance of such accommodations, there is more to consider when tackling antisemitism at work. For instance, Jews might refuse to identify themselves out of fear of not even getting in the door. Once employed, conditions can prove so horrendous that one wishes to leave but is paralyzed and unable to do so. One university teacher in Britain reported being so "traumatised" by the antisemitism of his students and co-workers that he was incapable of even looking for another position.[7] In all Member States, antisemitic discrimination frequently occurred at work (11%), when looking for work (10%), or at school or in training (8%)—arenas where the EU is legally empowered to intervene against bias though few victims seek redress.

Chief among the survey's most disturbing findings was that 82% of respondents did not report the most serious incident of anti-Jewish discrimination to any authority or organization. When asked why not, 57% said that nothing would have changed by reporting; a finding that suggests that the respondents recognized the public's general acceptance of their abuse. With so many political leaders across the ideological spectrum and within every Member State either subscribing to or excusing antisemitism, it would be foolish to expect Jews to believe (and thus behave) otherwise. From Sweden, one respondent wrote that the antisemitic remarks of political leaders not only affected him personally, they aroused his concern for the future of Jews in Sweden more generally. In Hungary, another commented on the dangers to Jews posed by bigoted politicians and called for their prompt removal from public life. In response, the FRA insists that politicians and opinion makers have a special responsibility to refrain from antisemitism, and that "they should clearly denounce and condemn such statements *when* made by others *in public debates*."[8] This was one of several proposals made by the FRA to tackle antisemitism. Other suggestions included, but were not limited to, specialized police units to monitor online antisemitism, consciousness-raising activities within Member States to support victims and "third party reporting." The latter would empower civil society organizations to report antisemitic crimes on behalf of victims.

In concluding its report, the FRA warned that the best efforts of legislators cannot achieve their intended effect if people are unaware of the information, assistance, and protection afforded them by law. Thus, the agency underscored the importance of current legal remedies (e.g., the Race and Framework Directives) while attributing (however implicitly) the reluctance of respondents to use them to ignorance. Given the dearth of evidence showing that present measures are (or might be) effective antidotes to antisemitism, this emphasis seems empirically misplaced and suspect.

Ironically, in the months leading up to the report's release, the FRA buried the working definition of antisemitism. It was the one tool its predecessor (the EUMC) had initially claimed was essential to effectively monitor, analyze, and combat hate crimes and discrimination against Jews. In fact, in its 2003 final report on antisemitism, the EUMC insisted that without a consistent definition of the very abuse it sought to stem, systematic efforts against antisemitism would prove futile. Five years later, the EUMC posted the working definition of antisemitism onto its website. There, despite the efforts of Jewish organizations to publicize it, the (English only) definition languished. Thus, the American Jewish Committee translated it from English into over two dozen languages and promoted the working definition through its Forum website. Perhaps the definition then became a victim of its own success. The U.S. State Department and the Canadian Parliament found the definition an especially important instrument against contemporary antisemitism's demonization of, and double standards for, Israel. So too did the Australian Online Hate Prevention Institute, which was established in 2012 to combat cyber hate. Despite all of this, the working definition lacked legal legitimacy within Europe; it was neither a directive nor a decision. Technically, this helps explain why the FRA never bothered to translate, much less refer to the definition, in any of its reports. One hopes that this lesson in EU policy-making is not lost on the many individuals and myriad human rights organizations that labor on behalf Jews. That the working definition of antisemitism was never formally adopted also accounts for the Commission's ability to later deny the definition's existence when asked to account for its 2013 removal from the FRA's website.

When a representative of the Simon Wiesenthal Center (SWC) insisted that the working definition of antisemitism was an important instrument in the arsenal against antisemitism and that its withdrawal (after five years) would "only comfort and encourage antisemites," the Commission responded.[9] It maintained "at the outset, that neither the Commission, nor the Union have an established definition of antisemitism" and that "there is no policy to create one."[10] It is true the EU never subscribed to an "established definition." However, the Commission's contention that "the FRA applies the terms racism, xenophobia, antisemitism, and intolerance as developed and used by the Council of Europe"[11] implies that the expertise needed to address antisemitism lies with the COE, a questionable proposition.

The COE's understanding of antisemitism deserves scrutiny given the Commission's explicit endorsement of it. According to paragraph four of the COE's 2007 Parliamentary Resolution 1563, antisemitism is

> hostility towards the Jews, their religion, their culture or their collective identity. Such hostility, which may extend to overt hatred, is expressed through behaviour and actions of varying

types: desecration of religious sites, vandalism, publications, insults, threats, aggression or even murder.

This resolution, "Combatting Antisemitism in Europe," mentioned Israel once (in paragraph 5) to advance its, as yet, unsubstantiated claim: "The Assembly regrets that the Israeli-Palestinian conflict continues to fuel anti-Semitic violence in Europe." Unfettered by a need to explain Israel's centrality as the rhetorical linchpin of and excuse for resurgent antisemitism in Europe, the Council of Europe has not had to consider evidence to the contrary. Yet, even the FRA accepts that research indicates that Muslim antisemitism has developed a substantial presence separate from national conflicts.[12] Daniel Goldhagen notes,

> looking to Israel and its conduct to explain antisemitism, or even antisemitism's public expression, around the world is akin to looking to some of the horrors perpetrated by some African countries to explain racism against African Americans.[13]

The working definition of antisemitism was compelling, in part, because it helped to expose questionable claims like the one contained in the Council of Europe's resolution that the EU states it will follow.

Once again, the EU discounted the potential of its own institutions to establish innovative initiatives against antisemitism. Having denied the polity the power necessary to effectively protect Europe's Jews, it too is vulnerable to the scourge of hatred.

NOTES

1. European Union Agency for Fundamental Rights (FRA), *Discrimination and Hate Crimes against Jews in EU Member States: experiences and perceptions of antisemitism* (Vienna, 2013).

2. European Union Agency for Fundamental Rights (FRA), *Discrimination and Hate Crimes against Jews in EU Member States: experiences and perceptions of antisemitism. Survey methodology, sample and questionnaire* (Vienna, 2013), 74.

3. European Union Agency for Fundamental Rights (FRA), *Discrimination and Hate Crimes against Jews in EU Member States: experiences and perceptions of antisemitism*, 13.

4. Ibid., 20.

5. Ibid., 36.

6. Bethany Bell, "Antisemitism 'on the rise' says Europe's Jews," BBC News Europe, Accessed 8 Nov. 2013, http://www.bbc.co.uk/news/world-europe-24857207.

7. European Union Agency for Fundamental Rights (FRA), *Discrimination and Hate Crimes against Jews in EU Member States: experiences and perceptions of antisemitism*, 55.

8. Ibid., 39, emphasis added. One wonders whether the FRA's emphasis on condemning public pronouncements of antisemitism implicitly allows more private

statements to go unchallenged. Moreover, Jewish public officials (and others perceived to be Jewish) are themselves subject to harassment. In November 2013, Ireland's Minister of Justice (Alan Shatter), was targeted by a poster that read: "Shatter has learned from his homeland how to crucify the little people." Another contained his picture and exclaimed, "Ye will all be poor as Palestinians when we are finished and be glad to have €5 a day." Minister Shatter noted his displeasure at those "who use the Palestinian cause as a flag of convenience for antisemitism." Stephen Collins, "Shatter urges those behind antisemitic posters to 'come clean,'" *Irish Times*, 11 Nov. 2013.

9. Shimon Samuels, "EU disowns the 'EU working definition of anti-semitism,'" Times of Israel Blog, Accessed 4 Dec. 2013. http://blogs.timesof israel.com/e-u-denies-validity-of-eu-working-definition-of-antisemitism.

10. Ibid.

11. Ibid.

12. See European Union Agency for Fundamental Rights, *Anti-Semitism: Summary overview of the situation in the European Union 2001–2008,* 24. For instance, the steady rise in antisemitic attacks during the 1990s occurred when the prospects of a peace agreement between the Palestinians and Israelis were highest. Conversely, years later, scholars in Belgium found no systematic and lasting link between events in the Middle East and acts of antisemitism following the intensification of the Israeli-Palestinian conflict (during the Israeli military operation Cast Lead from December 2008–January 2009). See Dirk Jacobs, Yoann Venny, Louise Callier, Barbara Herman, and Aurélie Descamps, "The Impact of the Conflict in Gaza on Antisemitism in Belgium," *Patterns of Prejudice*, no. 4 (2011).

13. Daniel Goldhagen, *The Devil that Never Dies: The Rise and Threat of Global Antisemitism* (New York, 2013), 177.

Appendix

The purpose of this document is to provide a practical guide for identifying incidents, collecting data, and supporting the implementation and enforcement of legislation dealing with antisemitism.

Working definition: "**Antisemitism is a certain perception of Jews, which may be expressed as hatred toward Jews. Rhetorical and physical manifestations of antisemitism are directed toward Jewish or non-Jewish individuals and/or their property, toward Jewish community institutions and religious facilities.**"

In addition, such manifestations could also target the state of Israel, conceived as a Jewish collectivity. Antisemitism frequently charges Jews with conspiring to harm humanity, and it is often used to blame Jews for "why things go wrong." It is expressed in speech, writing, visual forms and action, and employs sinister stereotypes and negative character traits.

Contemporary examples of antisemitism in public life, the media, schools, the workplace, and in the religious sphere could, taking into account the overall context, include, but are not limited to:

- Calling for, aiding, or justifying the killing or harming of Jews in the name of a radical ideology or an extremist view of religion.
- Making mendacious, dehumanizing, demonizing, or stereotypical allegations about Jews as such or the power of Jews as collective—such as, especially but not exclusively, the myth about a world Jewish conspiracy or of Jews controlling the media, economy, government or other societal institutions.
- Accusing Jews as a people of being responsible for real or imagined wrongdoing committed by a single Jewish person or group, or even for acts committed by non-Jews.
- Denying the fact, scope, mechanisms (e.g. gas chambers) or intentionality of the genocide of the Jewish people at the hands of

National Socialist Germany and its supporters and accomplices during World War II (the Holocaust).
- Accusing the Jews as a people, or Israel as a state, of inventing or exaggerating the Holocaust.
- Accusing Jewish citizens of being more loyal to Israel, or to the alleged priorities of Jews worldwide, than to the interests of their own nations.

Examples of the ways in which antisemitism manifests itself with regard to the State of Israel taking into account the overall context could include:

- Denying the Jewish people their right to self-determination, e.g., by claiming that the existence of a State of Israel is a racist endeavor.
- Applying double standards by requiring of it a behavior not expected or demanded of any other democratic nation.
- Using the symbols and images associated with classic antisemitism (e.g., claims of Jews killing Jesus or blood libel) to characterize Israel or Israelis.
- Drawing comparisons of contemporary Israeli policy to that of the Nazis.
- Holding Jews collectively responsible for actions of the state of Israel.

However, criticism of Israel similar to that leveled against any other country cannot be regarded as antisemitic.

Antisemitic acts are criminal when they are so defined by law (for example, denial of the Holocaust or distribution of antisemitic materials in some countries).

Criminal acts are antisemitic when the targets of attacks, whether they are people or property—such as buildings, schools, places of worship and cemeteries—are selected because they are, or are perceived to be, Jewish or linked to Jews.

Antisemitic discrimination is the denial to Jews of opportunities or services available to others and is illegal in many countries.

Source: http://www.european-forum-on-antisemitism.org/working-definition-of-antisemitism/english/

Timeline

1957   The Treaty of Rome establishes the European Economic Community.

1960   The Sub-Commission on the Prevention of Discrimination and Protection of Minorities (the UN's forerunner to its Committee for the Elimination of Racial Discrimination) initially includes antisemitism in its purview.

1965   The United Nation's International Convention on the Elimination of Racial Discrimination is adopted and excludes reference to antisemitism.

1979   The European Parliament holds its first democratic elections and Simone Veil, a survivor of Auschwitz, serves as the body's first president until 1982.

1984   The Group of the European Right (a far right group) emerges within the European Parliament.

1985   The Committee of Inquiry into the rise of fascism and racism in Europe submits its first report to the European Parliament.

1986   The European Commission, Council, and Parliament sign a Joint Declaration against Racism and Xenophobia. It marks the Community's first high-level acknowledgment that it should address racism.

1991   The European Parliament issues a follow-up report on racism.

1992   Austria amends its 1945 National Socialist Prohibition law, a law that informs the EU's 2008 Framework Decision, prohibiting Holocaust denial.

1995   The European Parliament adopts a Resolution on Racism, Xenophobia and Anti-Semitism.

1997   The European Union Monitoring Centre on Racism and Xenophobia (EUMC) is founded in Vienna and the Commission establishes 1997 as a Year against Racism.

1997   The Treaty of Amsterdam's Article 13 affirms EU anti-discrimination policy.

1998   UN Resolution officially recognizes antisemitism as a form of racism.

1999   The European Commission submits a collective resignation following allegations of incompetence and corruption (January).

1999   Austrian national elections are held and Haider's far right party captures 27 percent of the vote (October).

2000   An Austrian government forms and includes Haider (January 25).

2000   The Stockholm International Forum on Education, Remembrance and Research International Conference on the Holocaust convenes (January 29).

2000   The EU-14 take bilateral sanctions against Austria (February).

2000   Haider resigns as party leader (April).

2000   Both the Race Directive and Framework Directive are adopted (June).

2000   The EU president requests assistance from the President of the Council of Europe's Court of Human Rights to address the effectiveness of the EU's sanctions against Austria (July).

2000   "Three wise men" from the Council of Europe present their report and days later the EU-14 lift their bi-lateral sanctions (September).

2000   The EU Charter of Fundamental Rights is proclaimed (in December) but is not legally binding.

2001   UN World Conference on Anti-Racism is held in Durban, South Africa. Within days of concluding, Islamic militants attack the United States on "9/11" (September).

2002   World Jewish Congress convenes an executive emergency session in Brussels to address antisemitism throughout the EU.

2003   The EUMC issues its first EU-wide report on antisemitism (February).

2003   Organization for Security and Cooperation in Europe (OSCE) meets in Vienna to address antisemitism (June).

2005   The EUMC adopts the "Working Definition of Anti-Semitism."

2006   The conference "Racism, Xenophobia and the Media: Towards Respect and Understanding of All Religions and Cultures" deletes reference to antisemitism from its initial program, generating controversy and the EU's regret.

2007   The EUMC is rebranded the Fundamental Rights Agency.

2008   The Framework Decision is adopted, prohibiting Holocaust denial.

2009   The EU Charter of Fundamental Rights gained legal force through the Lisbon Treaty.

2010   The FRA recognizes the need for a survey on anti-Jewish discrimination.

2013   The FRA removed the "Working Definition of Anti-Semitism" from its website (May)

2013   The FRA releases its report on the Framework Decision on Racism and Xenophobia (October).

2013   The FRA releases its survey *Discrimination and Hate Crimes against Jews in EU Member States: experiences and perceptions of antisemitism* (November).

Selected References

Adamson, Göran. "Selective Perceptions: The Stockholm International Forem on the Holocaust." *Patterns of Prejudice* 34, no. 3 (2000): 65–71.

Arendt, Hannah. *The Origins of Totalitarianism.* New York: Harvest/HBJ Book, 1979.

————, and Jerome Kohn. *Essays in Understanding, 1930–1954.* 1st ed. New York: Harcourt Brace & Co., 1994.

Art, David. "Reacting to the Radical Right. Lessons from Germany and Austria." *Party Politics* 13, no. 3 (2007): 331–49.

Bachner, Henrik. *Återkomsten: Antisemitism i Sverige Efter 1945* (Resurgence: Antisemitism in Sweden after 1945). Stockholm: Natur och Kultur, 2000.

————. "Political Cultures of Denial? Antisemitism in Sweden and Scandinavia." In *Politics and Resentment: Antisemitism and Counter-Cosmopolitansim in the European Union*, edited by Lars Rensmann and Julius H. Schoeps, 329–62. Leiden: Brill, 2010.

Banton, Michael. *International Action against Racial Discrimination.* Oxford: Clarendon Press, 1996.

Beker, Avi. "Restitution Issues Destroy National Myths." In *Europe's Crumbling Myths: The Post-Holocaust Origins of Today's Anti-Semitism*, edited by Manfred Gerstenfeld, 162–70. Jerusalem: Jerusalem Center for Public Affairs, 2003.

Bell, Mark. *Anti-Discrimination Law and the European Union.* Oxford: Oxford University Press, 2008.

Beller, Steven. "Is Europe Good for the Jews? Jews and the Pluralist tradition in Historical Perspective." *European Judaism* 42, no. 1 (2009): 134–55.

Berger, Stefan. "Remembering the Second World War in Western Europe: 1945–2005." In *A European Memory? Contested Histories and Politics of Remembrance*, edited by Malgorzata Pakier and Bo Stråth, 119–36. New York: Berghahn Books, 2010.

Berggren, Lena. *Nationell Upplysning: Drag i Den Svenska Antisemitismens Idéhistoria* (National enlightenment: The influence of Swedish antisemitism on the history of ideas). Stockholm: Carlssons, 1999.

Berman, Paul. *The Flight of the Intellectuals.* Brooklyn, N.Y.: Melville House, 2010.

Betz, Hans-Georg. "Haider's Revolution or the Future Has Just Begun." In *Austria in the European Union*, edited by Günter Bischof, Anton Pelinka, and Michael Gehler, 118–43. New Brunswick, N.J.: Transaction Publishers, 2002.

Bischof, Günter, Anton Pelinka, and Michael Gehler, eds. *Austria in the European Union*. Contemporary Austrian Studies, vol. 10. New Brunswick, N.J.: Transaction Publishers, 2002.

Bleich, Erik. *The Freedom to be Racist? How the United States and Europe Struggle to Preserve Freedom and Combat Racism*. New York: Oxford University Press, 2011.

Boëthius, Maria-Pia. *Heder Och Samvete: Sverige Och Andra Världskriget* (Honor and conscience: Sweden and World War II). Stockholm: PAN/Norstedt, 1992.

Boström, Donald. *Inshallah: Konflicten Mellan Israel Och Palestina* (Inshallah: The conflict between Israel and Palestine). Stockholm: Ordfront, 2001.

Bruchfeld, Stéphane, and Paul A. Levine. *Tell Ye Your Children: A Book about the Holocaust in Europe 1933–1945*. Stockholm: Regeringskansliet Levande Historia, 1998.

Bunzl, Matti. "Austrian Zionism and the Jews of the New Europe." *Jewish Social Studies* 9, no. 2 (2003): 154–73.

Búrca, Gráinne de. "The Drafting of the European Union Charter of Fundamental Rights." *European Law Review* 26 (Apr. 2001): 126–38.

Cohen, Naomi W. "*Shaare Tefila Congregation v. Cobb*: A New Departure in American Jewish Defense?." *Jewish History* 3, no. 1 (1988): 95–108.

Copel, Jason, and Aidan O'Neill. "The ECJ: Taking Rights Seriously." *Legal Studies* 12 (1992): 227–45.

Eiglad, Eirik. *The Anti-Jewish Riots in Oslo*. Porsgrunn: The Communalism Press, 2010.

Eley, Geoff. "The Trouble with 'Race': Migrancy, Cultural Difference, and the Remaking of Europe." In *After the Nazi Racial State: Difference and Democracy in Germany and Europe*, edited by Rita C. K. Chin, 137–81. Ann Arbor, Mich.: University of Michigan Press, 2009.

Elman, R. Amy. "The EU and Women: Virtual Equality." In *The State of the European Union: Deepening and Widening*, edited by Pierre-Henri Laurent and Marc Maresceau, 225–39. Boulder, Colo.: Lynne Rienner Publishers, Inc., 1998.

———. *Sexual Equality in an Integrated Europe: Virtual Equality*. New York: Palgrave Macmillan, 2007.

————. "Testing the Limits of European Citizenship: Ethnic Hatred and Male Violence." *National Women's Studies Association Journal* 13, no. 3 (2001): 49–69.

Ford, Glyn. *Fascist Europe: The Rise of Racism and Xenophobia.* London: Pluto Press, 1992.

Gehler, Michael. "'Preventive Hammer Blow' or Boomerang: The EU 'Sanction' Measures against Austria 2000." In *Austria in the European Union*, edited by Günter Bischof, Anton Pelinka, and Michael Gehler, 180–222. New Brunswick, N.J.: Transaction Publishers, 2002.

Gerstenfeld, Manfred, "An Interview with Zvi Mazel: Anti-Israelism and Anti-Semitism in Sweden." In *Behind the Humanitarian Mask: The Nordic Countries, Israel, and the Jews*, edited by Manfred Gerstenfeld, 81–88. Jerusalem: Jerusalem Center for Public Affairs, Friends of Simon Wiesenthal Center for Holocaust Studies, 2008.

————, ed., *Behind the Humanitarian Mask: The Nordic Countries, Israel, and the Jews.* Jerusalem: Jerusalem Center for Public Affairs, Friends of Simon Wiesenthal Center for Holocaust Studies, 2008.

————, ed. *Europe's Crumbling Myths: The Post-Holocaust Origins of Today's Anti-Semitism.* Jerusalem: Jerusalem Center for Public Affairs, Yad Vashem, World Jewish Congress, 2003.

Gilman, Sander. *The Jew's Body.* London: Routledge, 1991.

Glück, David, Aaron Neuman, and Jacqueline Stare. *Sveriges Judar, Deras Historia, Tro Och Traditioner* (Sweden's Jews, their history, faith and traditions). Stockholm: Jewish Museum, 1997.

Goldhagen, Daniel. *The Devil that Never Dies: The Rise and Threat of Global Antisemitism.* New York: Little Brown, 2013.

Hannett, Sarah. "Equality at the Intersections: The Legislative and Judicial Failure to Tackle Multiple Discrimination." *Oxford Journal of Legal Studies* 23, no. 1 (2003): 65–86.

Harrison, Bernard. "Anti-Zionism, Antisemitism, and the Rhetorical Manipulation of Reality." In *Resurgent Antisemitism: Global Perspectives*, edited by Alvin H. Rosenfeld. Bloomington, Ind.: Indiana University Press, 2013.

Heni, Clemens. *Antisemitism: A Specific Phenomenon.* Berlin: Edition Critic, 2013.

Herf, Jeffrey. *Nazi Propaganda for the Arab World.* New Haven, Conn.: Yale University Press, 2009.

Hertzberg, Arthur. *The Zionist Idea: A Historical analysis and Reader.* Philadelphia: Jewish Publication Society, 1997.

Hilberg, Raul. *The Destruction of the European Jews.* Chicago: Quadrangle books, 1961.

Howard, Erica. *The EU Race Directive: Developing the Protection against Racial Discrimination within the EU.* London: Routledge, 2010.

———. "The European Union Agency for Fundamental Rights." *European Human Rights Law Reporter*, no. 4 (2006): 445–55.

Howard, Marc Marjé. "Can Populism Be Suppressed in a Democracy? Austria, Germany, and the European Union." *East European Politics and Societies* 14, no. 2 (2000): 18–32.

Hugg, Patrick R. "Accession Aspirations Degenerate: A New Chapter for Turkey and the EU." *Washington University Global Studies Law Review* 9, no. 225 (2010): 225–81.

Jahn, D., and A.-S. Storsved. "Legitimacy through Referendum? The Nearly Successful Domino-Strategy of the EU-Referendums in Austria, Finland, Sweden and Norway." *West European Politics* 18, no. 4 (1995): 18–37.

Judt, Tony. "Tale from the Vienna Woods." *New York Review of Books,* 23 March 2000, 8–9.

Kaplan, Edward, and Charles Small. "Anti-Israel Sentiment Predicts Anti-Semitism in Europe." *Journal of Conflict Resolution* 50, no. 4 (2006): 548–61.

Knight, Robert, ed. *Ich Bin Dafür, Die Sache in Die Länge Zu Ziehen: Wortprotokolle Der Österreichischen Bundesregierung von 1945–1952 Über Die Entschädigung Der Juden* (I favor taking the matter slowly. Transcription of the Austrian Federal Republic's Assembly Meetings of 1945 regarding reparations to Jews). Frankfurt: Athenäem, 1988.

———. "'Neutrality,' Not Sympathy: Jews in Post-War Austria." In *Austrians and Jews in the Twentieth Century*, edited by Robert S. Wistrich, 220–29, New York: St. Martin's Press, 1992.

Koblick, Steven, David Mel Paul, and Margareta Paul. *The Stones Cry Out: Sweden's Response to the Persecution of the Jews, 1933–1945.* New York: Holocaust Library, 1988.

Küntzel, Matthias. *Jihad and Jew-Hatred: Islamism, Nazism and the Roots of 9/11.* New York: Telos Press, 2007.

Laqueur, Walter. *The Changing Face of Antisemitism: From Ancient Times to the Present Day.* New York: Oxford University Press, 2006.

Le Rider, Jacques. "Diary of a Trip to Vienna: Jörg Haider's Austria." In *Euro-Skepticism*, edited by Ronald Tiersky, 235–43. Lanham, Md.: Rowman & Littlefield, 2001.

Lenaerts, Koen. "Fundamental Rights in the European Union." *European Law Review* 25 (Dec. 2000): 575–600.

Lerner, Michael. *The Socialism of Fools: Anti-Semitism on the Left.* Oakland, Calif.: Tikkun, 1992.

Lewis, Bernard. *Semites and Anti-Semites: An Inquiry into Conflict and Prejudice.* New York: Norton, 1987.

Lindberg, Hans. *Svensk Flyktingpolitik under Internationellt Tryck 1936–1941* (Swedish refugee policy under international pressure 1936–1941). Stockholm: Allmänna förlag, 1973.

Lipstadt, Deborah E. *Denying the Holocaust: The Growing Assault on Truth and Memory.* New York: Free Press, 1993.

Litvak, Meir, and Ester Webman. *From Empathy to Denial: Arab Responses to the Holocaust.* New York: Columbia University Press, 2009.

Maier, Robert. "Does a Supranational Europe Stimulate and/or Combat Racism?." In *Europe's New Racism: Causes, Manifestations, and Solutions,* edited by the Evens Foundation, 85–102. New York: Berghahn Books, 2002.

Manoschek, Walter. "FPÖ, ÖVP, and Austria's Nazi Past." In *The Haider Phenomenon in Austria,* edited by Ruth Wodak and Anton Pelinka, 3–15. New Brunswick, N.J.: Transaction Publishers, 2002.

———. "The Freedom Party of Austria (FPÖ)—an Austrian and European Phenomenon?." In *Austria in the European Union,* edited by Günter Bischof, Anton Pelinka, and Michael Gehler, 145–60. New Brunswick, N.J.: Transaction Publishers, 2002.

Marcovich, Malka. *Les Nations désunies:Comment L'ONU enterre les droits de l'homme* (The disunited United Nations: How the UN obliterates human rights). Paris: Éditions Jacob-Duvernet, 2008.

Marcus, Kenneth L. *Jewish Identity and Civil Rights in America.* New York: Cambridge University Press, 2010.

Markovits, Andrei S. "Austrian Exceptionalism: Haider, the European Union, the Austrian Past and Present." In *The Haider Phenomenon in Austria,* edited by Ruth Wodak and Anton Pelinka, 95–119. New Brunswick, N.J.: Transaction Publishers, 2002.

———. *Uncouth Nation: Why Europe Dislikes America.* Princeton, N.J.; Princeton University Press, 2007.

——— and Anson Rabinbach. "Why Waldheim Won in Austria." *Dissent* 33 (Fall 1986): 409–11.

Merlingen, Michael, Cas Mudde, and Ulrich Sedelmeier. "The Right and the Righteous? European Norms, Domestic Politics and the Sanctions against Austria." *Journal of Common Market Studies* 39, no. 1 (2001): 59–77.

Minow, Martha. "The Supreme Court 1986 Term Forward: Justice Engendered." *Harvard Law Review* 101, no. 1 (1987): 7–370.

Mitten, Richard. "Austria All Black and Blue: Jörg Haider, the European Sanctions, and the Political Crisis in Austria." In *The Haider Phenomenon in Austria*, edited by Ruth Wodak and Anton Pelinka, 179–212. New Brunswick, N.J.: Transaction Publishers, 2002.

———. "Jews and Other Victims: the 'Jewish Questions' and Discourses of Victimhood in Postwar Austria." In *Austria and the European Union*, edited by Günter Bischof, Anton Pelinka, and Michael Gehler, 223–70. New Brunswick, N.J.: Transaction Publishers, 2002.

Morgan, Glyn. *The Idea of a European Superstate: Public Justification and European Integration*. Princeton, N.J.: Princeton University Press, 2005.

Nagorski, Andrew. "The Politics of Guilt: Austria's Bigot, Europe's Burden." *Foreign Affairs* 79, no. 3 (2000): 18–22.

Nordin, Dennis S. *A Swedish Dilemma: A Liberal European Nation's Struggle with Racism and Xenophobia, 1990–2000*. Lanham, Md.: University Press of America, 2005.

Ottolenghi, Emanuele. "Making Sense of European Anti-Semitism." *Human Rights Review* 8, no. 2 (2007): 104–26.

Pakier, Malgorzata, and Bo Stråth. "A European Memory?." In *A European Memory? Contested Histories and Politics of Remembrance*, edited by Malgorzata Pakier and Bo Stråth, 1–20. New York: Berghahn Books, 2010.

Pech, Laurent. "The Law of Holocaust Denial in Europe: Towards a (Qualified) EU-Wide Criminal Prohibition." In *Genocide Denials and the Law*, edited by Ludovic Hennebel and Thomas Hochmann. Oxford: Oxford University Press, 2011.

Pelinka, Anton. *Austria: Out of the Shadow of the Past.* Boulder, Colo.: Westview Press, 1998.

———. "The FPÖ in the European Context." In *The Haider Phenomenon in Austria*, edited by Anton Pelinka and Ruth Wodak, 213–29. New Brunswick, N.J.: Transaction Publishers, 2002.

Phillips, Melanie. "The New Anti-Semitism." In *Those Who Forget the Past: The Question of Anti-Semitism*, edited by Ron Rosenbaum, 251–57. New York: Random House, 2004.

Power Samantha. *A Problem from Hell: America and the Age of Genocide.* 1st Perennial ed. New York: Perennial, 2003.

Pred, Allan. *Even in Sweden: Racisms, Racialized Spaces and the Popular Geographical Imagination*. Berkeley, Calif.: University of California Press, 2000.

Rensmann, Lars, and Julius H. Schoeps. *Politics and Resentment: Antisemitism and Counter-Cosmopolitanism in the European Union.* Jewish Identities in a Changing World. Leiden: Brill, 2010.

————. "Politics and Resentment: Examining Antisemitism and Counter-Cosmopolitanism in the European Union and Beyond." In *Politics and Resentment: Antisemitism and Counter-Cosmopolitanism in the European Union,* edited by Lars Rensmann and Julius H. Schoeps, 3–79. Leiden: Brill, 2010.

Rosenfeld, Alvin H. *Resurgent Antisemitism: Global Perspectives.* Bloomington, Ind.: Indiana University Press, 2013.

Rosenthal, John. "Anti-Semitism and Ethnicity in Europe." *Policy Review* (Oct.–Nov. 2003): 17–38.

Ruzza, Carlo. "Anti-Racism and EU Institutions." *Journal of European Integration* 22, no. 2 (2000): 145–71.

Saltiel, David H. "Austria: Crossroads or Roadblock in a New Europe." *Mediterranean Quarterly* (Spring 2000): 41–58.

Sassen, Saskia. *Guests and Aliens.* New York: New Press, 1999.

Segev, Tom. *Simon Wiesenthal: The Life and Legends.* 1st ed. New York: Doubleday, 2010.

Melanie A. *The Haider Phenomenon.* East European Monographs, no. 484. Boulder, Colo. and New York: East European Monographs, distributed by Columbia University Press, 1997.

Svanberg, Ingvar, and Mattias Tydén. *Sverige Och Förintelsen: Debatt Och Dokument Om Europas Juddar 1933–1945* (Sweden and the Holocaust: Debates and documents concerning Europe's Jews 1933–1945). Stockholm: Arena, 1997.

————. *Tusen År Av Invandring* (A thousand years of immigration). Stockholm: Gidlunds Bokförlag, 1992.

Taguieff, Pierre-André. *Rising from the Muck: The New Anti-Semitism in Europe.* Chicago: Ivan R. Dee, 2004.

Thornton, Bruce S. *Decline and Fall: Europe's Slow-Motion Suicide.* 1st ed. New York: Encounter Books, 2007.

Tossavainen, Mikael. "The Aftonbladet Organ-Trafficking Affair: A Case Study." *Jewish Political Studies Review* 95, no. 1 (2010).

————. "Arab and Muslim Anti-Semitism in Sweden." *Jewish Political Studies Review* 17, no. 3–4 (2005): 109–18.

Turner, Jenia Iontcheva. "The Expressive Dimension of EU Criminal Law." *American Journal of Comparative Law* 60, no. 2 (2012): 555–84.

Weiler, Joseph. *The Constitution of Europe: "Do the New Clothes Have an Emperor?" And Other Essays on European Integration.* Cambridge, U.K.: Cambridge University Press, 1999.

Whine, Michael. "Expanding Holocaust Denial and Legislation against It." In *Extreme Speech and Democracy*, edited by Ivan Hare and James Weinstein, 538–56. Oxford: Oxford University Press, 2009.

Williams, Andrew. *EU Human Rights Policies: A Study in Irony.* Oxford: Oxford University Press, 2004.

Wistrich, Robert S. *Anti-Zionism and Antisemitism: The Case of Bruno Kreisky.* ACTA Series no. 30. Jerusalem: SICSA, The Hebrew University of Jerusalem, 2007.

———. "European Anti-Semitism Reinvents Itself." New York: American Jewish Committee, 2005.

———. "Fighting Antisemitism." *Midstream* 50, no. 2 (2004): 21–23.

———. *From Ambivalence to Betrayal: The Left, the Jews, and Israel.* Lincoln, Neb.: University of Nebraska Press, 2012.

———. "Haider and His Critics." *Commentary* 109, no. 4 (2000): 30–35.

———. *A Lethal Obsession: Anti-Semitism from Antiquity to the Global Jihad.* 1st ed. New York: Random House, 2010.

———. "Something is Rotten in the State of Europe: Antisemitism as a Civilizational Pathology." In *Israel and Europe: An Expanding Abyss?*, edited by Manfred Gerstenfeld, 95–109. Jerusalem: Jerusalem Center for Public Affairs, 2005.

Wodak, Ruth. "Discourse and Politics: The Rhetoric of Exclusion." In *The Haider Phenomenon in Austria*, edited by Ruth Wodak and Anton Pelinka, 33–60. New Brunswick, N.J.: Transaction Publishers, 2002.

———. "The Waldheim Affair and Anti-Semitic Prejudice in Austrian Public Discourse." *Patterns of Prejudice* 24, no. 2–4 (1990): 18–33.

———, and Anton Pelinka. *The Haider Phenomenon in Austria.* New Brunswick, N.J.: Transaction Publishers, 2002.

Wüstenberg, Jenny, and David Art. "Using the Past in the Nazi Successor States from 1945 to the Present." *Annals of the American Academy* 617, no. 1 (2008): 72–87.

Index

R. **Amy Elman** is the Weber Professor in Social Science at Kalamazoo College, Michigan. She is author of *Sexual Equality in an Integrated Europe* (2007), *Sexual Subordination and State Intervention: Comparing Sweden and the United States* (1996), and editor of *Sexual Politics and the European Union: The New Feminist Challenge* (1996).